CPAC
12/08

W9-AXV-289

BATMAN
Jekyll & Hyde

BATMAN
Jekyll & Hyde

Paul Jenkins Writer

Jae Lee (Chapters 1-3) / **Sean Phillips (Chapters 4-6)** Artists

June Chung Colorist

Rob Leigh Letterer

Sean Phillips Original series covers

Batman created by Bob Kane

DAN DIDIO Senior VP-Executive Editor / **MIKE CARLIN** Editor-original series / **MICHAEL SIGLAIN** Assistant Editor-original series
ANTON KAWASAKI SEAN MACKIEWICZ Editors-collected edition / **ROBBIN BROSTERMAN** Senior Art Director / **PAUL LEVITZ** President & Publisher
GEORG BREWER VP-Design & DC Direct Creative / **RICHARD BRUNING** Senior VP-Creative Director / **PATRICK CALDON** Executive VP-Finance & Operations
CHRIS CARAMALIS VP-Finance / **JOHN CUNNINGHAM** VP-Marketing / **TERRI CUNNINGHAM** VP-Managing Editor / **ALISON GILL** VP-Manufacturing
DAVID HYDE VP-Publicity / **HANK KANALZ** VP-General Manager, WildStorm / **JIM LEE** Editorial Director-WildStorm
PAULA LOWITT Senior VP-Business & Legal Affairs / **MARYELLEN McLAUGHLIN** VP-Advertising & Custom Publishing
JOHN NEE Senior VP-Business Development / **GREGORY NOVECK** Senior VP-Creative Affairs / **SUE POHJA** VP-Book Trade Sales
STEVE ROTTERDAM Senior VP-Sales & Marketing / **CHERYL RUBIN** Senior VP-Brand Management
JEFF TROJAN VP-Business Development, DC Direct / **BOB WAYNE** VP-Sales

Cover by Sean Phillips.

BATMAN: JEKYLL & HYDE

Published by DC Comics. Cover and compilation Copyright © 2008 DC Comics. All Rights Reserved.

Originally published in single magazine form in BATMAN: JEKYLL & HYDE 1-6. Copyright © 2005 DC Comics. All Rights Reserved. All characters, their distinctive likenesses and related elements featured in this publication are trademarks of DC Comics. The stories, characters and incidents featured in this publication are entirely fictional. DC Comics does not read or accept unsolicited submissions of ideas, stories or artwork.

DC Comics, 1700 Broadway, New York, NY 10019
A Warner Bros. Entertainment Company
Printed in Canada. First Printing.
ISBN: 978-1-4012-1821-8

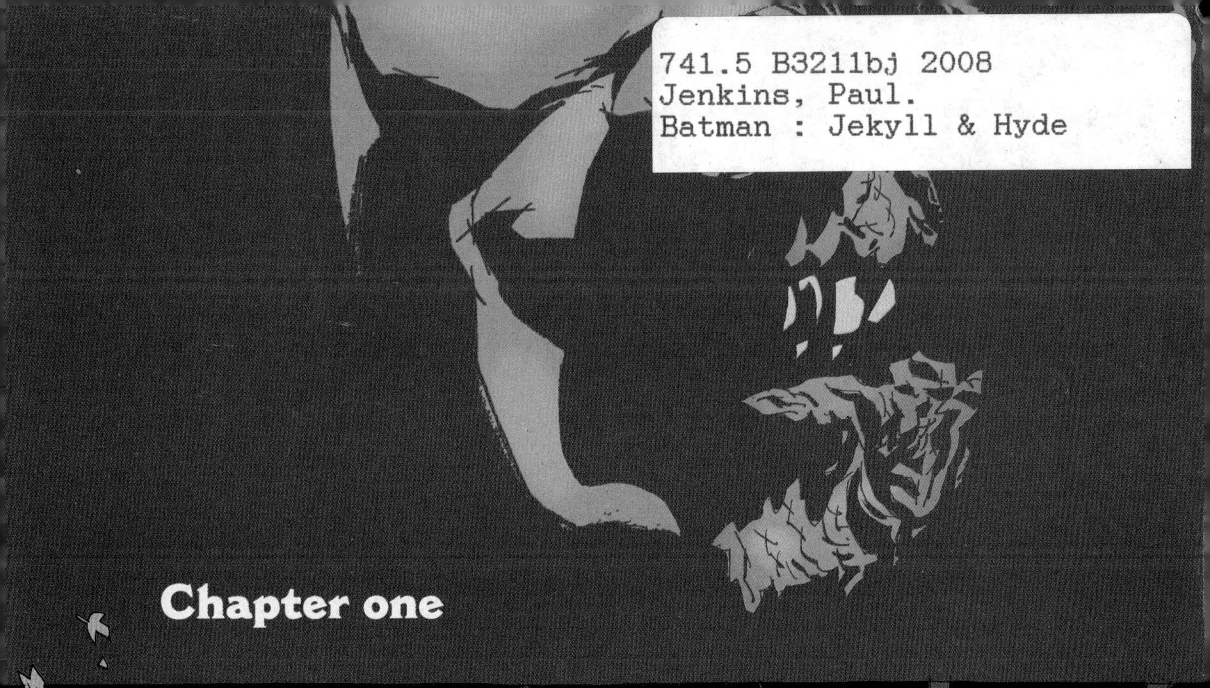

Chapter one

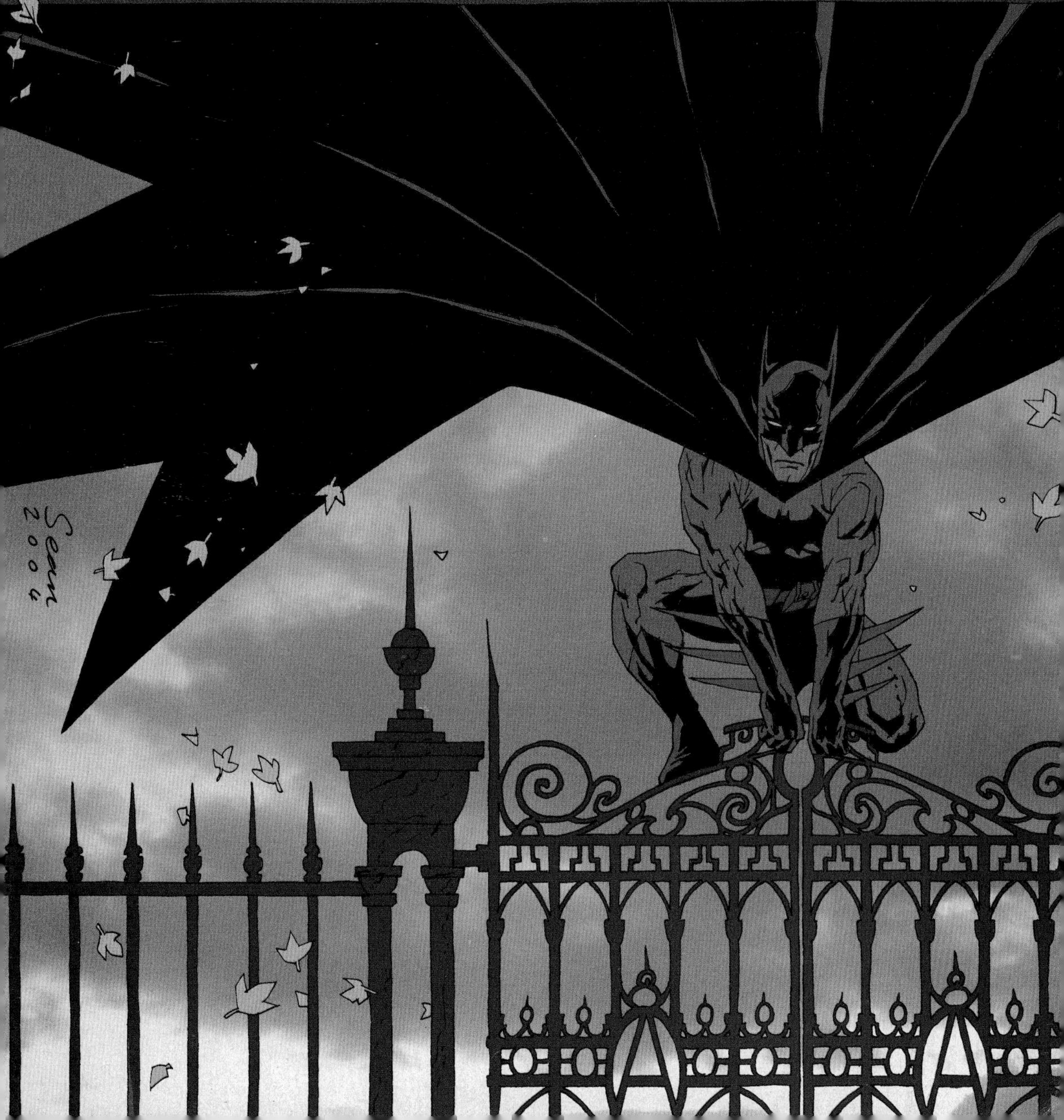
Sean
2004

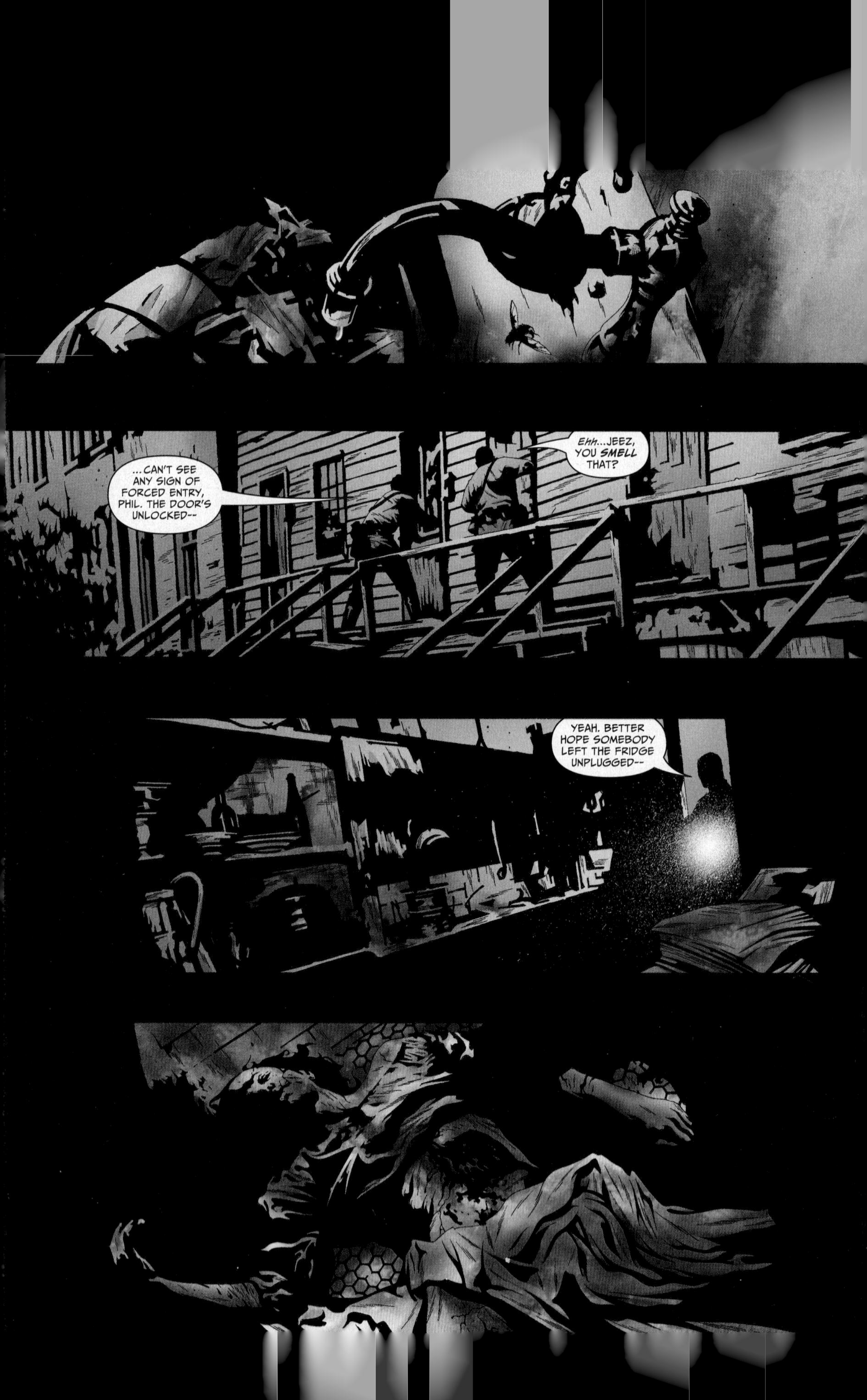
...CAN'T SEE ANY SIGN OF FORCED ENTRY, PHIL. THE DOOR'S UNLOCKED--
Ehh...JEEZ, YOU **SMELL** THAT?
YEAH. BETTER HOPE SOMEBODY LEFT THE FRIDGE UNPLUGGED--

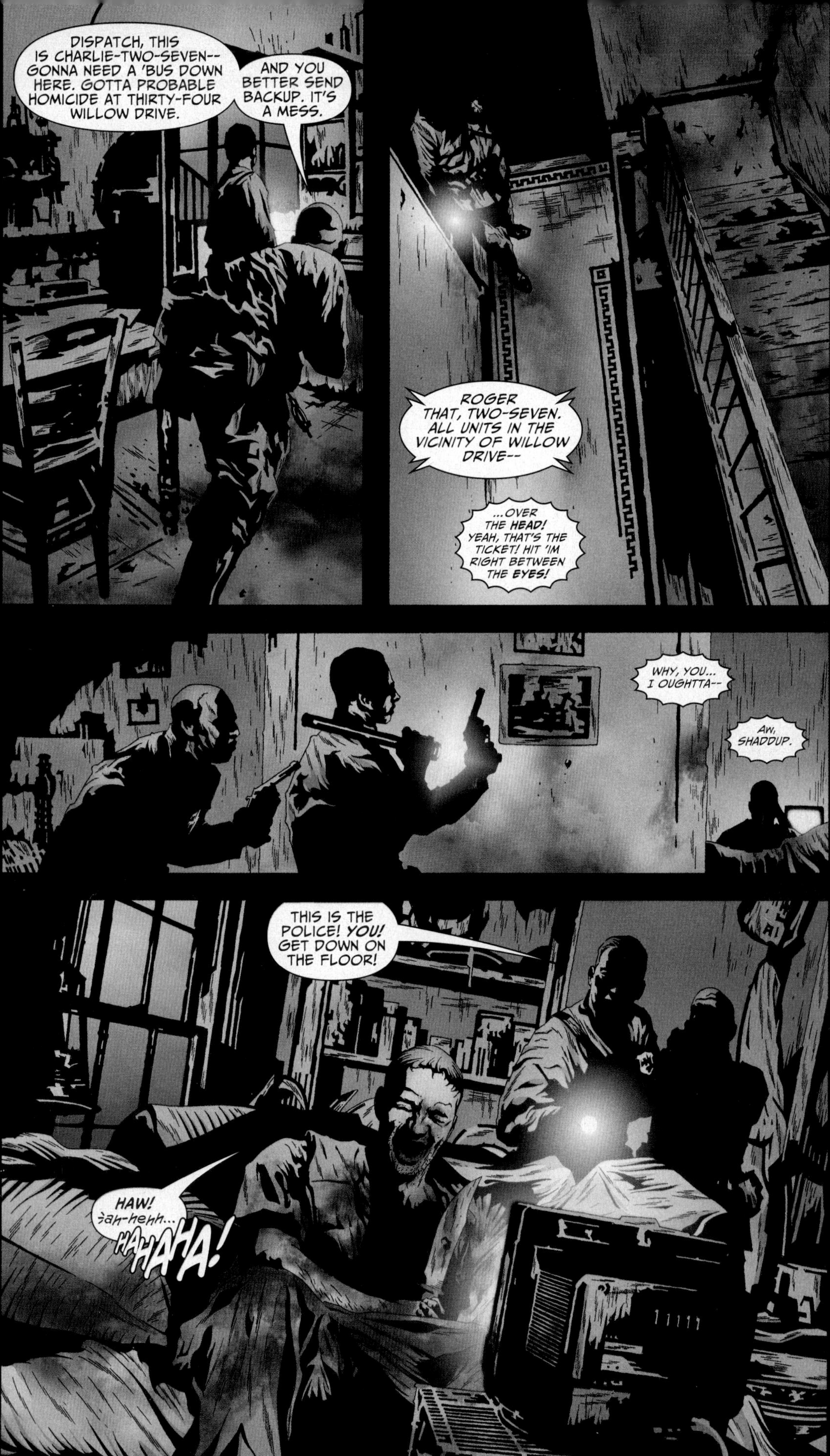
DISPATCH, THIS IS CHARLIE-TWO-SEVEN-- GONNA NEED A 'BUS DOWN HERE. GOTTA PROBABLE HOMICIDE AT THIRTY-FOUR WILLOW DRIVE.
AND YOU BETTER SEND BACKUP. IT'S A MESS.
ROGER THAT, TWO-SEVEN. ALL UNITS IN THE VICINITY OF WILLOW DRIVE--
...OVER THE HEAD! YEAH, THAT'S THE TICKET! HIT 'IM RIGHT BETWEEN THE EYES!
WHY, YOU... I OUGHTTA--
AW, SHADDUP.
THIS IS THE POLICE! YOU! GET DOWN ON THE FLOOR!
HAW! ah-hehh... HAHAHA!

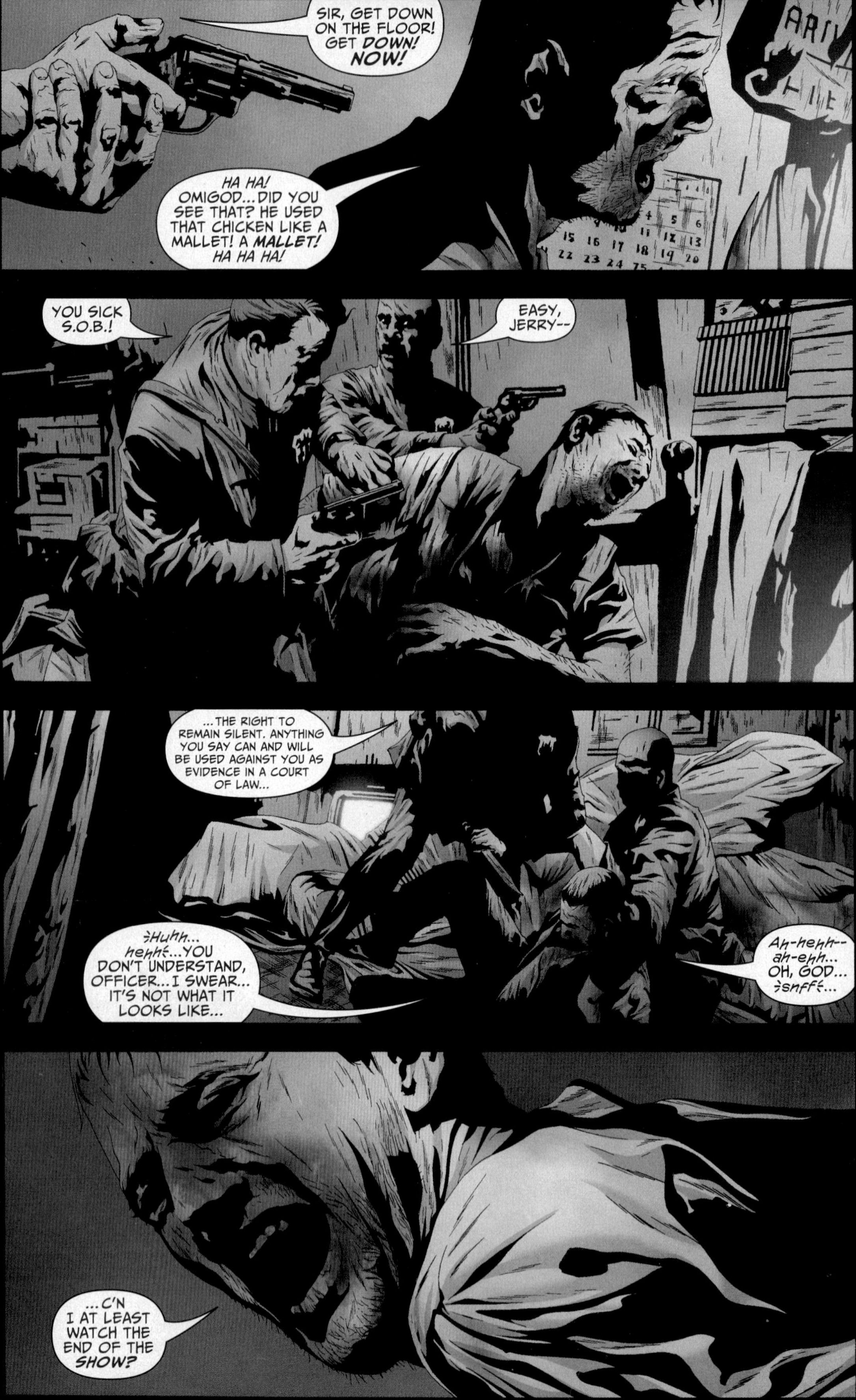
SIR, GET DOWN ON THE FLOOR! GET DOWN! NOW!
HA HA! OMIGOD... DID YOU SEE THAT? HE USED THAT CHICKEN LIKE A MALLET! A MALLET! HA HA HA!
YOU SICK S.O.B.!
EASY, JERRY--
...THE RIGHT TO REMAIN SILENT. ANYTHING YOU SAY CAN AND WILL BE USED AGAINST YOU AS EVIDENCE IN A COURT OF LAW...
Huhh... hehh...YOU DON'T UNDERSTAND, OFFICER... I SWEAR... IT'S NOT WHAT IT LOOKS LIKE...
Ah-hehh-ah-ehh... OH, GOD... snff...
...C'N I AT LEAST WATCH THE END OF THE SHOW?

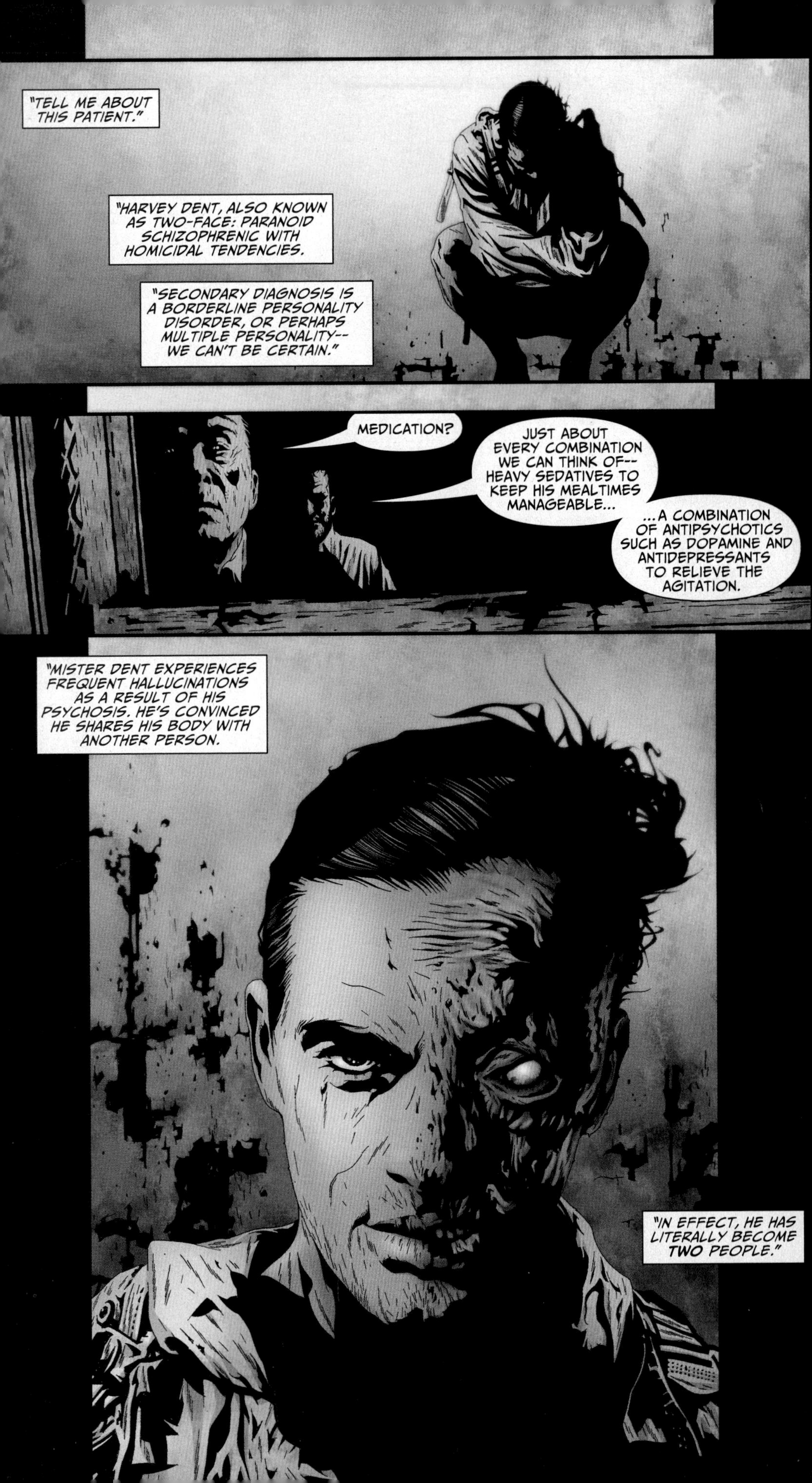
"TELL ME ABOUT THIS PATIENT."
"HARVEY DENT, ALSO KNOWN AS TWO-FACE: PARANOID SCHIZOPHRENIC WITH HOMICIDAL TENDENCIES.
"SECONDARY DIAGNOSIS IS A BORDERLINE PERSONALITY DISORDER, OR PERHAPS MULTIPLE PERSONALITY-- WE CAN'T BE CERTAIN."
MEDICATION?
JUST ABOUT EVERY COMBINATION WE CAN THINK OF-- HEAVY SEDATIVES TO KEEP HIS MEALTIMES MANAGEABLE...
...A COMBINATION OF ANTIPSYCHOTICS SUCH AS DOPAMINE AND ANTIDEPRESSANTS TO RELIEVE THE AGITATION.
"MISTER DENT EXPERIENCES FREQUENT HALLUCINATIONS AS A RESULT OF HIS PSYCHOSIS. HE'S CONVINCED HE SHARES HIS BODY WITH ANOTHER PERSON.
"IN EFFECT, HE HAS LITERALLY BECOME TWO PEOPLE."

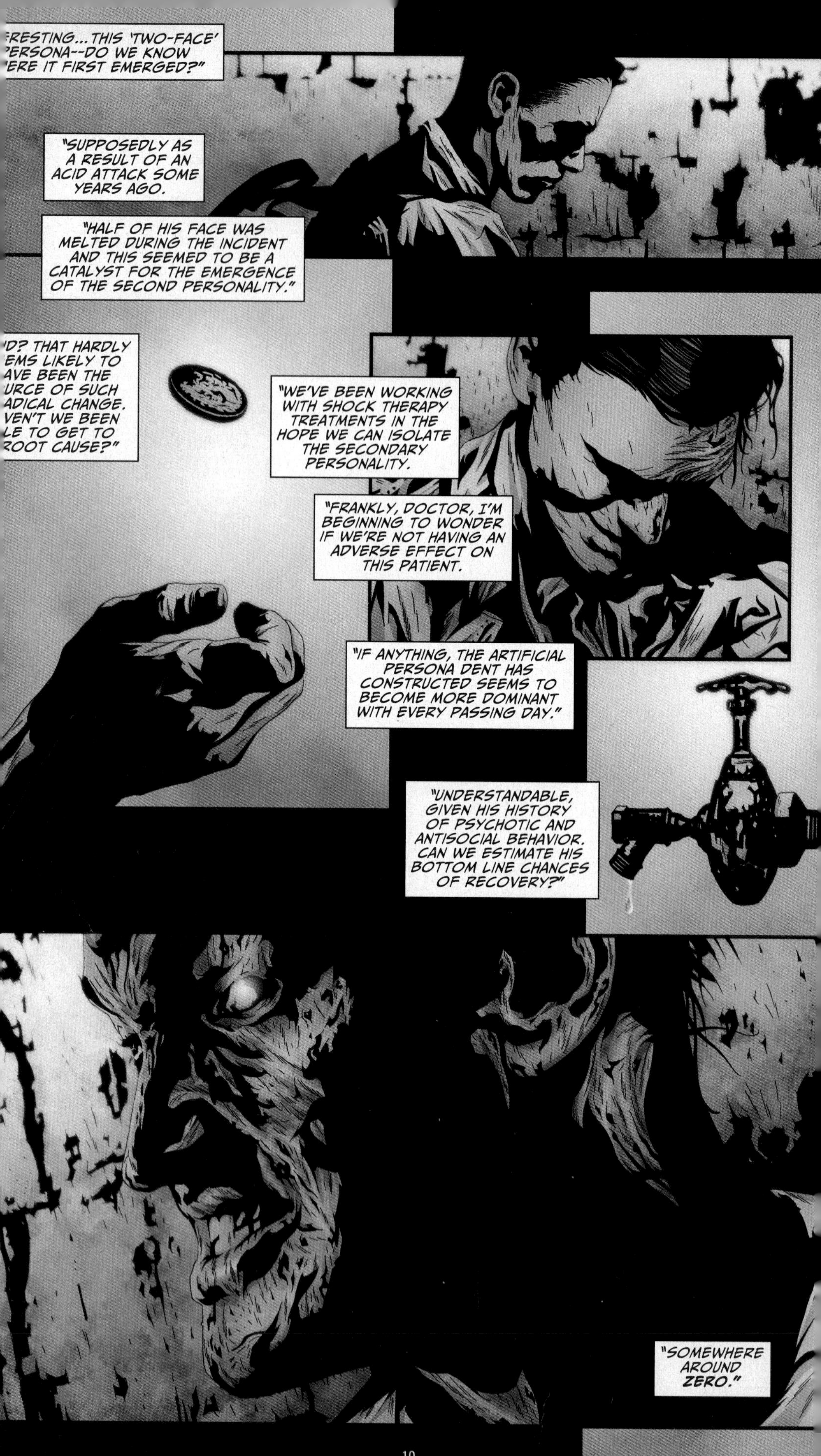

-ERESTING...THIS 'TWO-FACE' PERSONA--DO WE KNOW -ERE IT FIRST EMERGED?"
"SUPPOSEDLY AS A RESULT OF AN ACID ATTACK SOME YEARS AGO.
"HALF OF HIS FACE WAS MELTED DURING THE INCIDENT AND THIS SEEMED TO BE A CATALYST FOR THE EMERGENCE OF THE SECOND PERSONALITY."
-D? THAT HARDLY -EMS LIKELY TO -AVE BEEN THE -URCE OF SUCH -ADICAL CHANGE. -VEN'T WE BEEN -LE TO GET TO -ROOT CAUSE?"
"WE'VE BEEN WORKING WITH SHOCK THERAPY TREATMENTS IN THE HOPE WE CAN ISOLATE THE SECONDARY PERSONALITY.
"FRANKLY, DOCTOR, I'M BEGINNING TO WONDER IF WE'RE NOT HAVING AN ADVERSE EFFECT ON THIS PATIENT.
"IF ANYTHING, THE ARTIFICIAL PERSONA DENT HAS CONSTRUCTED SEEMS TO BECOME MORE DOMINANT WITH EVERY PASSING DAY."
"UNDERSTANDABLE, GIVEN HIS HISTORY OF PSYCHOTIC AND ANTISOCIAL BEHAVIOR. CAN WE ESTIMATE HIS BOTTOM LINE CHANCES OF RECOVERY?"
"SOMEWHERE AROUND ZERO."

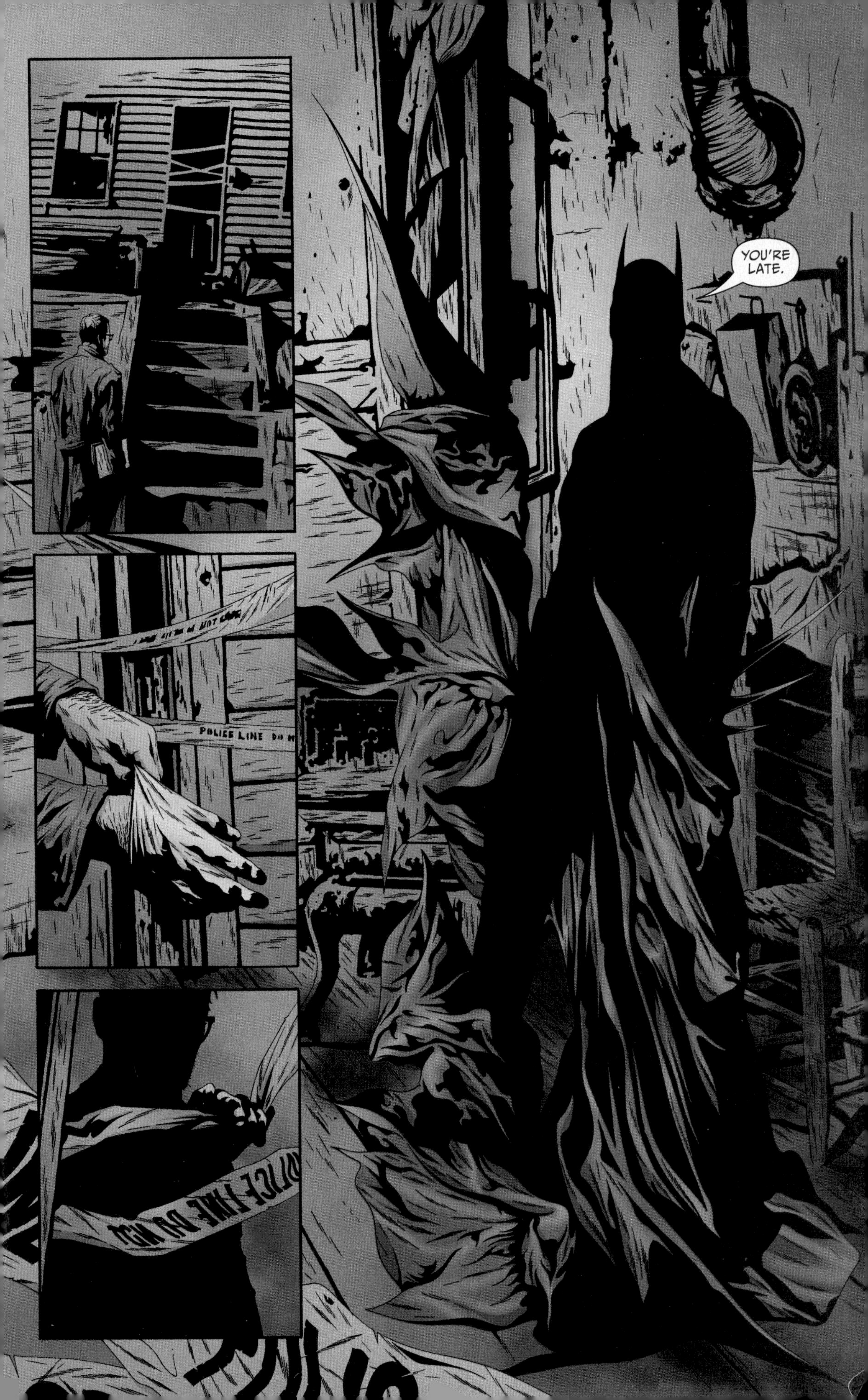
YOU'RE LATE.

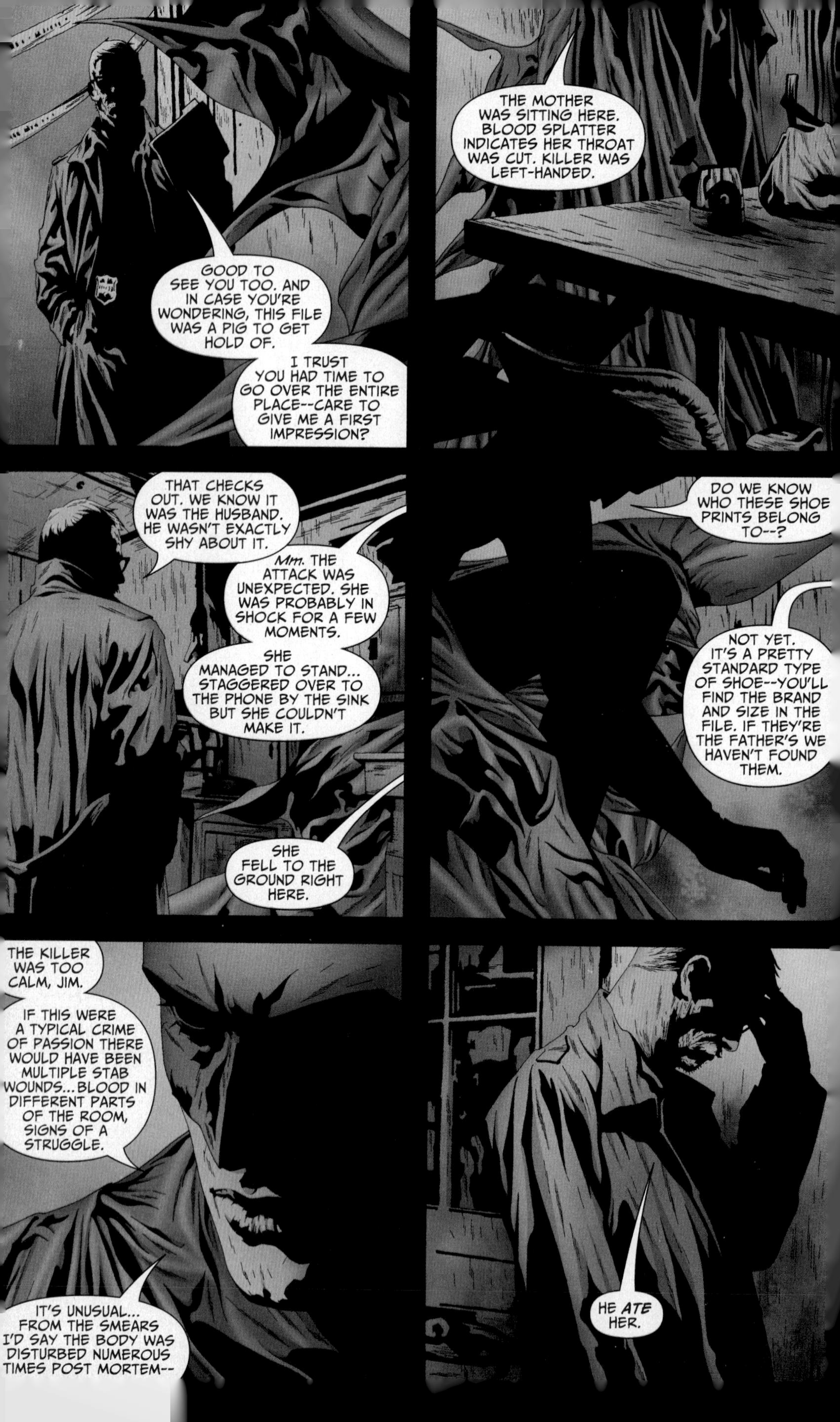
GOOD TO SEE YOU TOO. AND IN CASE YOU'RE WONDERING, THIS FILE WAS A PIG TO GET HOLD OF.
I TRUST YOU HAD TIME TO GO OVER THE ENTIRE PLACE--CARE TO GIVE ME A FIRST IMPRESSION?
THE MOTHER WAS SITTING HERE. BLOOD SPLATTER INDICATES HER THROAT WAS CUT. KILLER WAS LEFT-HANDED.
THAT CHECKS OUT. WE KNOW IT WAS THE HUSBAND. HE WASN'T EXACTLY SHY ABOUT IT.
Mm. THE ATTACK WAS UNEXPECTED. SHE WAS PROBABLY IN SHOCK FOR A FEW MOMENTS.
SHE MANAGED TO STAND... STAGGERED OVER TO THE PHONE BY THE SINK BUT SHE COULDN'T MAKE IT.
SHE FELL TO THE GROUND RIGHT HERE.
DO WE KNOW WHO THESE SHOE PRINTS BELONG TO--?
NOT YET. IT'S A PRETTY STANDARD TYPE OF SHOE--YOU'LL FIND THE BRAND AND SIZE IN THE FILE. IF THEY'RE THE FATHER'S WE HAVEN'T FOUND THEM.
THE KILLER WAS TOO CALM, JIM.
IF THIS WERE A TYPICAL CRIME OF PASSION THERE WOULD HAVE BEEN MULTIPLE STAB WOUNDS...BLOOD IN DIFFERENT PARTS OF THE ROOM, SIGNS OF A STRUGGLE.
IT'S UNUSUAL... FROM THE SMEARS I'D SAY THE BODY WAS DISTURBED NUMEROUS TIMES POST MORTEM--
HE *ATE* HER.

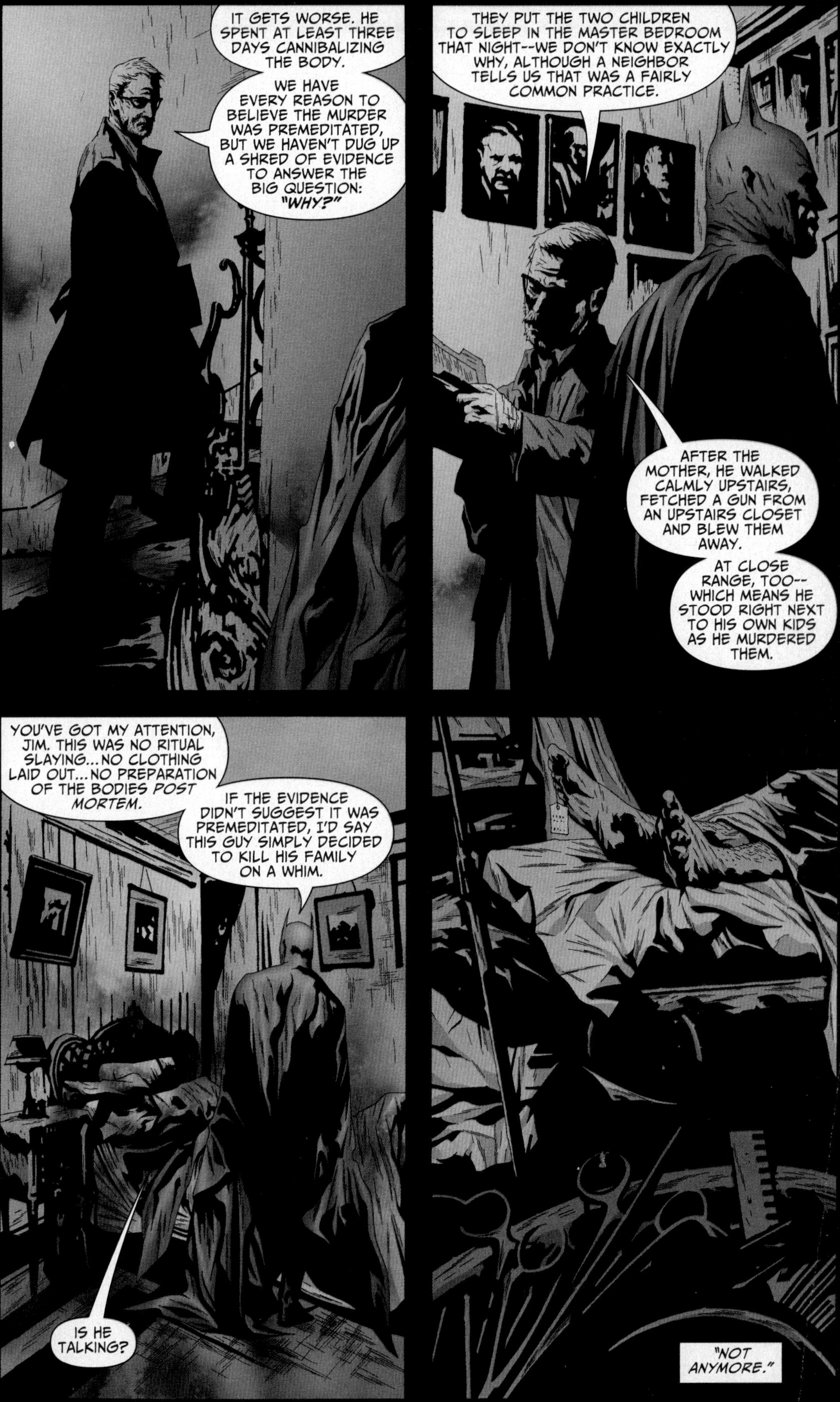
IT GETS WORSE. HE SPENT AT LEAST THREE DAYS CANNIBALIZING THE BODY.
WE HAVE EVERY REASON TO BELIEVE THE MURDER WAS PREMEDITATED, BUT WE HAVEN'T DUG UP A SHRED OF EVIDENCE TO ANSWER THE BIG QUESTION: "WHY?"
THEY PUT THE TWO CHILDREN TO SLEEP IN THE MASTER BEDROOM THAT NIGHT--WE DON'T KNOW EXACTLY WHY, ALTHOUGH A NEIGHBOR TELLS US THAT WAS A FAIRLY COMMON PRACTICE.
AFTER THE MOTHER, HE WALKED CALMLY UPSTAIRS, FETCHED A GUN FROM AN UPSTAIRS CLOSET AND BLEW THEM AWAY.
AT CLOSE RANGE, TOO--WHICH MEANS HE STOOD RIGHT NEXT TO HIS OWN KIDS AS HE MURDERED THEM.
YOU'VE GOT MY ATTENTION, JIM. THIS WAS NO RITUAL SLAYING...NO CLOTHING LAID OUT...NO PREPARATION OF THE BODIES POST MORTEM.
IF THE EVIDENCE DIDN'T SUGGEST IT WAS PREMEDITATED, I'D SAY THIS GUY SIMPLY DECIDED TO KILL HIS FAMILY ON A WHIM.
IS HE TALKING?
"NOT ANYMORE."

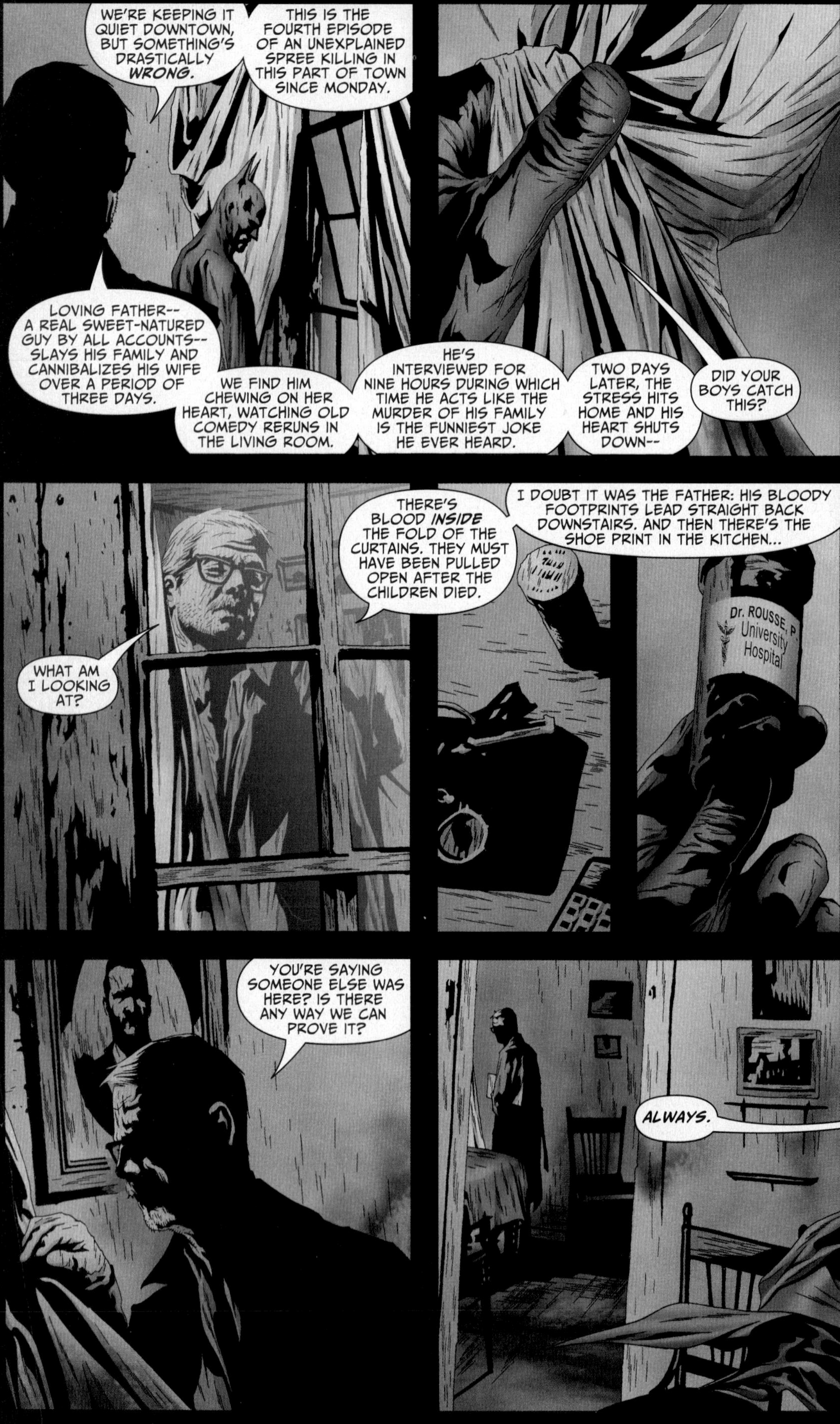
WE'RE KEEPING IT QUIET DOWNTOWN, BUT SOMETHING'S DRASTICALLY WRONG.
THIS IS THE FOURTH EPISODE OF AN UNEXPLAINED SPREE KILLING IN THIS PART OF TOWN SINCE MONDAY.
LOVING FATHER-- A REAL SWEET-NATURED GUY BY ALL ACCOUNTS-- SLAYS HIS FAMILY AND CANNIBALIZES HIS WIFE OVER A PERIOD OF THREE DAYS.
WE FIND HIM CHEWING ON HER HEART, WATCHING OLD COMEDY RERUNS IN THE LIVING ROOM.
HE'S INTERVIEWED FOR NINE HOURS DURING WHICH TIME HE ACTS LIKE THE MURDER OF HIS FAMILY IS THE FUNNIEST JOKE HE EVER HEARD.
TWO DAYS LATER, THE STRESS HITS HOME AND HIS HEART SHUTS DOWN--
DID YOUR BOYS CATCH THIS?
WHAT AM I LOOKING AT?
THERE'S BLOOD INSIDE THE FOLD OF THE CURTAINS. THEY MUST HAVE BEEN PULLED OPEN AFTER THE CHILDREN DIED.
I DOUBT IT WAS THE FATHER: HIS BLOODY FOOTPRINTS LEAD STRAIGHT BACK DOWNSTAIRS. AND THEN THERE'S THE SHOE PRINT IN THE KITCHEN...
Dr. ROUSSE, P.
University Hospital
YOU'RE SAYING SOMEONE ELSE WAS HERE? IS THERE ANY WAY WE CAN PROVE IT?
ALWAYS.

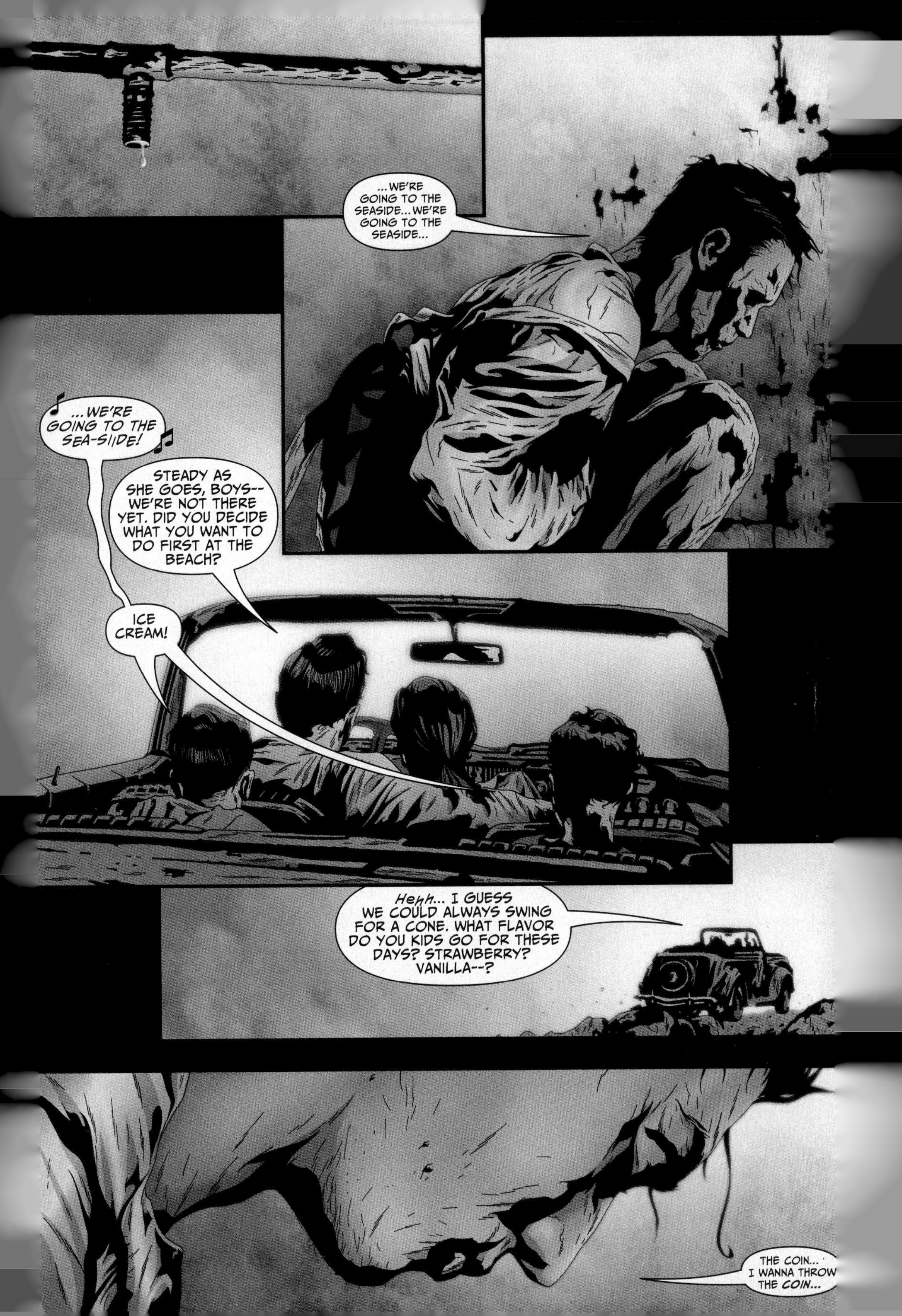
...WE'RE GOING TO THE SEASIDE...WE'RE GOING TO THE SEASIDE...
...WE'RE GOING TO THE SEA-SIIDE!
STEADY AS SHE GOES, BOYS--WE'RE NOT THERE YET. DID YOU DECIDE WHAT YOU WANT TO DO FIRST AT THE BEACH?
ICE CREAM!
Hehh... I GUESS WE COULD ALWAYS SWING FOR A CONE. WHAT FLAVOR DO YOU KIDS GO FOR THESE DAYS? STRAWBERRY? VANILLA--?
THE COIN... I WANNA THROW THE COIN...

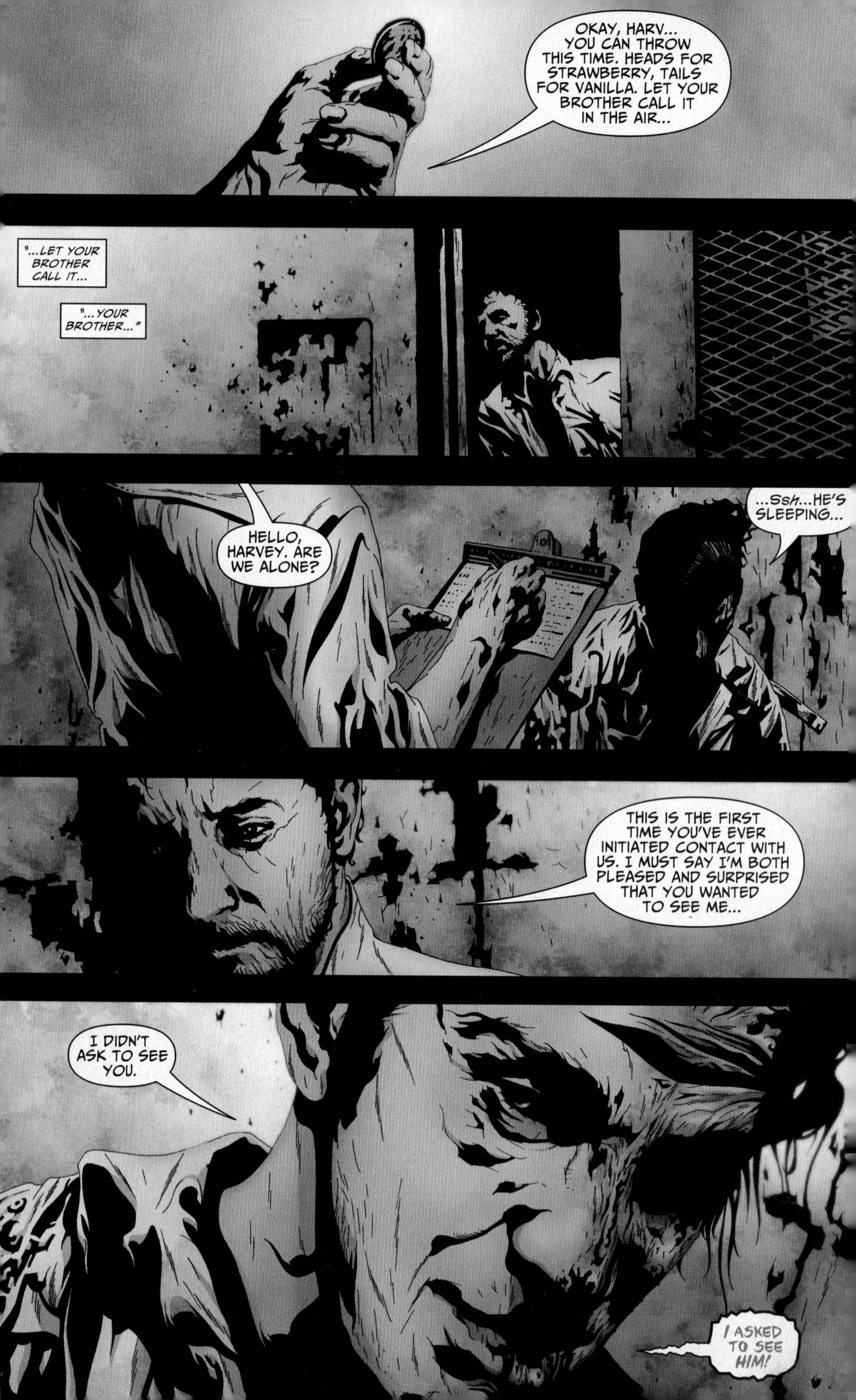
OKAY, HARV... YOU CAN THROW THIS TIME. HEADS FOR STRAWBERRY, TAILS FOR VANILLA. LET YOUR BROTHER CALL IT IN THE AIR...
"...LET YOUR BROTHER CALL IT...
"...YOUR BROTHER..."
HELLO, HARVEY. ARE WE ALONE?
...Ssh...HE'S SLEEPING...
THIS IS THE FIRST TIME YOU'VE EVER INITIATED CONTACT WITH US. I MUST SAY I'M BOTH PLEASED AND SURPRISED THAT YOU WANTED TO SEE ME...
I DIDN'T ASK TO SEE YOU.
I ASKED TO SEE HIM!

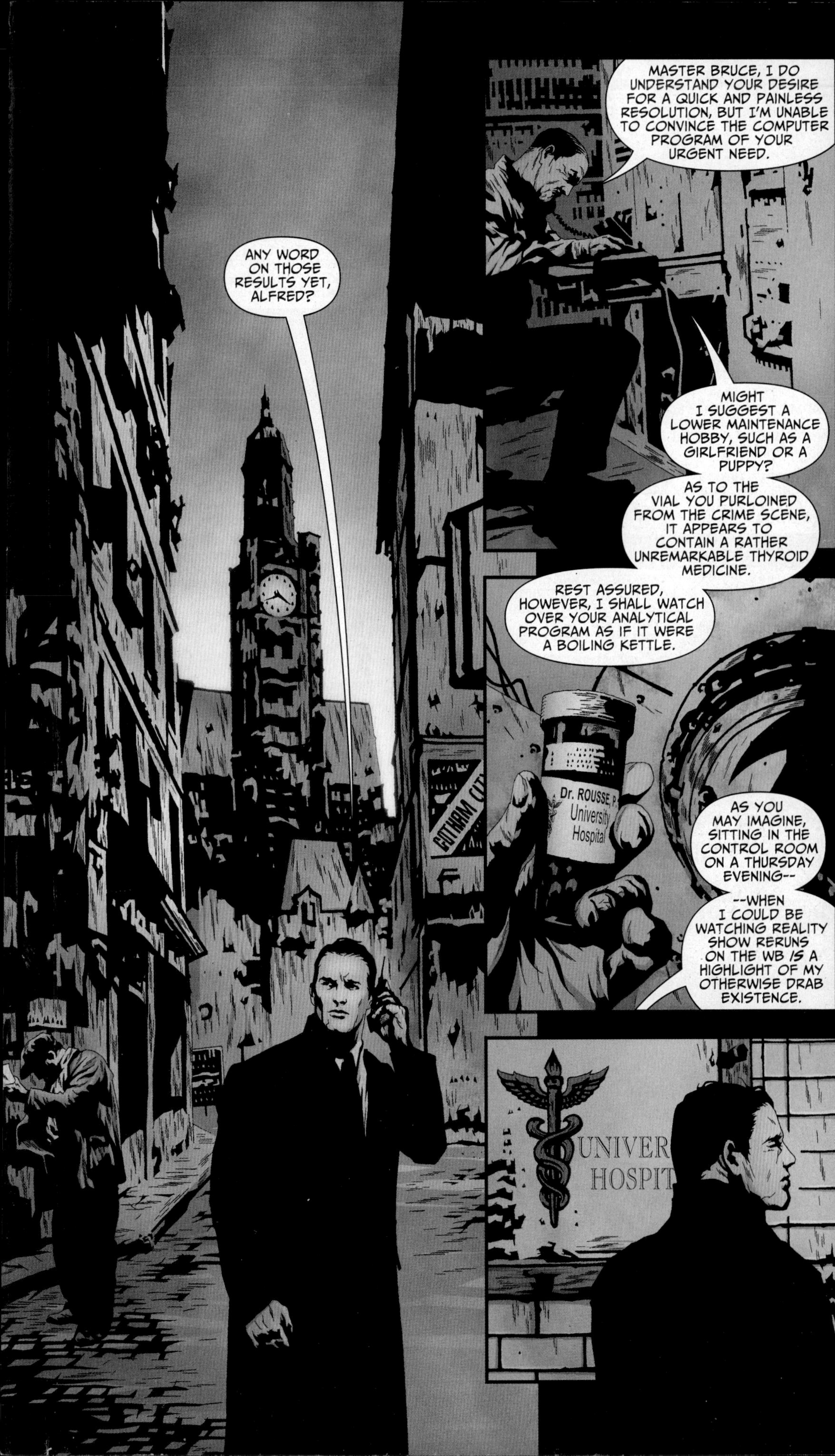
ANY WORD ON THOSE RESULTS YET, ALFRED?
MASTER BRUCE, I DO UNDERSTAND YOUR DESIRE FOR A QUICK AND PAINLESS RESOLUTION, BUT I'M UNABLE TO CONVINCE THE COMPUTER PROGRAM OF YOUR URGENT NEED.
MIGHT I SUGGEST A LOWER MAINTENANCE HOBBY, SUCH AS A GIRLFRIEND OR A PUPPY?
AS TO THE VIAL YOU PURLOINED FROM THE CRIME SCENE, IT APPEARS TO CONTAIN A RATHER UNREMARKABLE THYROID MEDICINE.
GOTHAM CITY
REST ASSURED, HOWEVER, I SHALL WATCH OVER YOUR ANALYTICAL PROGRAM AS IF IT WERE A BOILING KETTLE.
Dr. ROUSSE, P.
University Hospital
AS YOU MAY IMAGINE, SITTING IN THE CONTROL ROOM ON A THURSDAY EVENING--
--WHEN I COULD BE WATCHING REALITY SHOW RERUNS ON THE WB *IS* A HIGHLIGHT OF MY OTHERWISE DRAB EXISTENCE.
UNIVER
HOSPIT

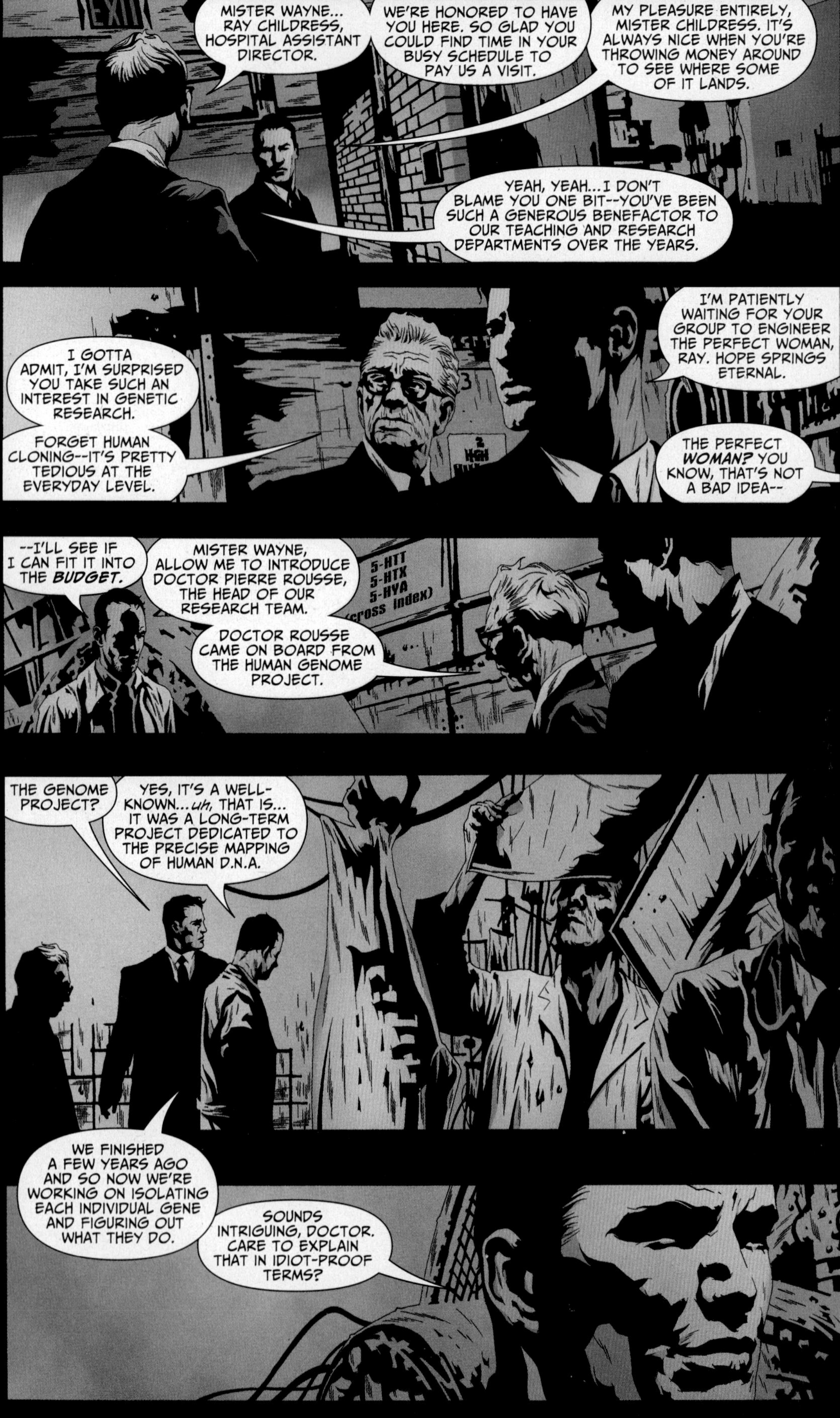
EXIT
MISTER WAYNE... RAY CHILDRESS, HOSPITAL ASSISTANT DIRECTOR.
WE'RE HONORED TO HAVE YOU HERE. SO GLAD YOU COULD FIND TIME IN YOUR BUSY SCHEDULE TO PAY US A VISIT.
MY PLEASURE ENTIRELY, MISTER CHILDRESS. IT'S ALWAYS NICE WHEN YOU'RE THROWING MONEY AROUND TO SEE WHERE SOME OF IT LANDS.
YEAH, YEAH...I DON'T BLAME YOU ONE BIT--YOU'VE BEEN SUCH A GENEROUS BENEFACTOR TO OUR TEACHING AND RESEARCH DEPARTMENTS OVER THE YEARS.
I GOTTA ADMIT, I'M SURPRISED YOU TAKE SUCH AN INTEREST IN GENETIC RESEARCH.
FORGET HUMAN CLONING--IT'S PRETTY TEDIOUS AT THE EVERYDAY LEVEL.
I'M PATIENTLY WAITING FOR YOUR GROUP TO ENGINEER THE PERFECT WOMAN, RAY. HOPE SPRINGS ETERNAL.
THE PERFECT *WOMAN?* YOU KNOW, THAT'S NOT A BAD IDEA--
--I'LL SEE IF I CAN FIT IT INTO THE *BUDGET.*
MISTER WAYNE, ALLOW ME TO INTRODUCE DOCTOR PIERRE ROUSSE, THE HEAD OF OUR RESEARCH TEAM.
DOCTOR ROUSSE CAME ON BOARD FROM THE HUMAN GENOME PROJECT.
5-HTT
5-HTX
5-HYA
(cross index)
THE GENOME PROJECT?
YES, IT'S A WELL-KNOWN...*uh*, THAT IS... IT WAS A LONG-TERM PROJECT DEDICATED TO THE PRECISE MAPPING OF HUMAN D.N.A.
WE FINISHED A FEW YEARS AGO AND SO NOW WE'RE WORKING ON ISOLATING EACH INDIVIDUAL GENE AND FIGURING OUT WHAT THEY DO.
SOUNDS INTRIGUING, DOCTOR. CARE TO EXPLAIN THAT IN IDIOT-PROOF TERMS?

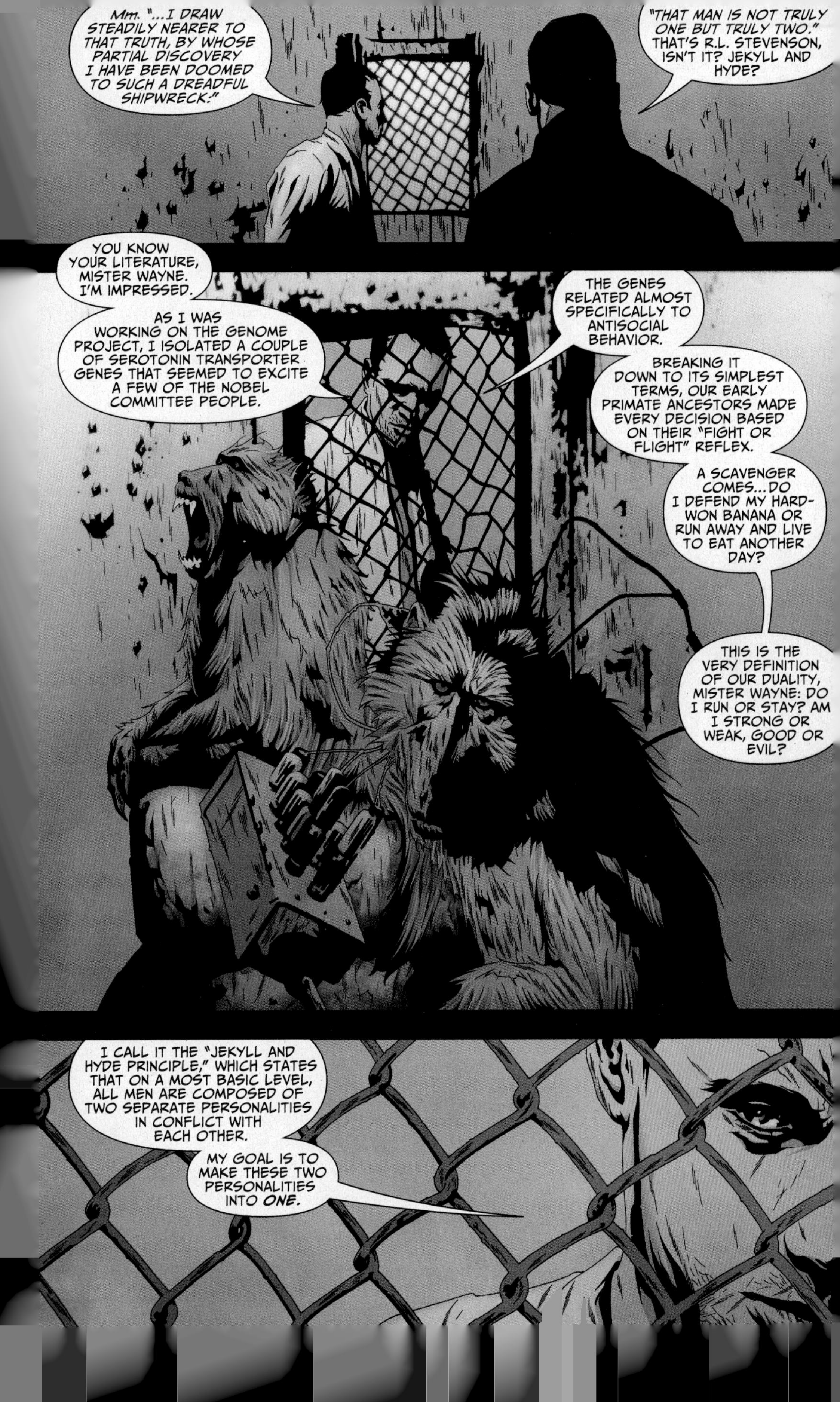
Mm. "...I DRAW STEADILY NEARER TO THAT TRUTH, BY WHOSE PARTIAL DISCOVERY I HAVE BEEN DOOMED TO SUCH A DREADFUL SHIPWRECK."
"THAT MAN IS NOT TRULY ONE BUT TRULY TWO." THAT'S R.L. STEVENSON, ISN'T IT? JEKYLL AND HYDE?
YOU KNOW YOUR LITERATURE, MISTER WAYNE. I'M IMPRESSED.
AS I WAS WORKING ON THE GENOME PROJECT, I ISOLATED A COUPLE OF SEROTONIN TRANSPORTER GENES THAT SEEMED TO EXCITE A FEW OF THE NOBEL COMMITTEE PEOPLE.
THE GENES RELATED ALMOST SPECIFICALLY TO ANTISOCIAL BEHAVIOR.
BREAKING IT DOWN TO ITS SIMPLEST TERMS, OUR EARLY PRIMATE ANCESTORS MADE EVERY DECISION BASED ON THEIR "FIGHT OR FLIGHT" REFLEX.
A SCAVENGER COMES...DO I DEFEND MY HARD-WON BANANA OR RUN AWAY AND LIVE TO EAT ANOTHER DAY?
THIS IS THE VERY DEFINITION OF OUR DUALITY, MISTER WAYNE: DO I RUN OR STAY? AM I STRONG OR WEAK, GOOD OR EVIL?
I CALL IT THE "JEKYLL AND HYDE PRINCIPLE," WHICH STATES THAT ON A MOST BASIC LEVEL, ALL MEN ARE COMPOSED OF TWO SEPARATE PERSONALITIES IN CONFLICT WITH EACH OTHER.
MY GOAL IS TO MAKE THESE TWO PERSONALITIES INTO *ONE*.

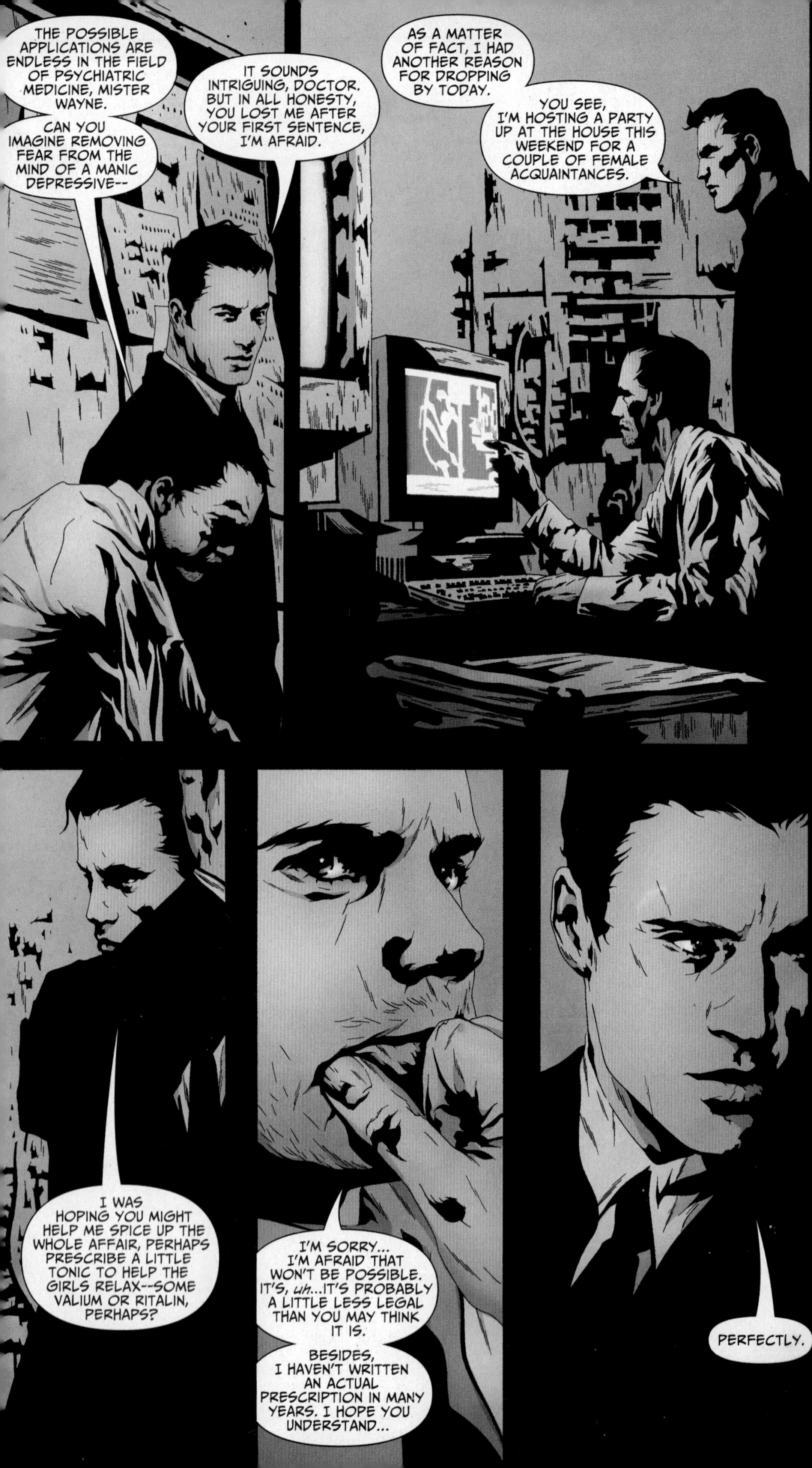
THE POSSIBLE APPLICATIONS ARE ENDLESS IN THE FIELD OF PSYCHIATRIC MEDICINE, MISTER WAYNE.
CAN YOU IMAGINE REMOVING FEAR FROM THE MIND OF A MANIC DEPRESSIVE--
IT SOUNDS INTRIGUING, DOCTOR. BUT IN ALL HONESTY, YOU LOST ME AFTER YOUR FIRST SENTENCE, I'M AFRAID.
AS A MATTER OF FACT, I HAD ANOTHER REASON FOR DROPPING BY TODAY.
YOU SEE, I'M HOSTING A PARTY UP AT THE HOUSE THIS WEEKEND FOR A COUPLE OF FEMALE ACQUAINTANCES.
I WAS HOPING YOU MIGHT HELP ME SPICE UP THE WHOLE AFFAIR, PERHAPS PRESCRIBE A LITTLE TONIC TO HELP THE GIRLS RELAX--SOME VALIUM OR RITALIN, PERHAPS?
I'M SORRY... I'M AFRAID THAT WON'T BE POSSIBLE. IT'S, *uh*...IT'S PROBABLY A LITTLE LESS LEGAL THAN YOU MAY THINK IT IS.
BESIDES, I HAVEN'T WRITTEN AN ACTUAL PRESCRIPTION IN MANY YEARS. I HOPE YOU UNDERSTAND...
PERFECTLY.

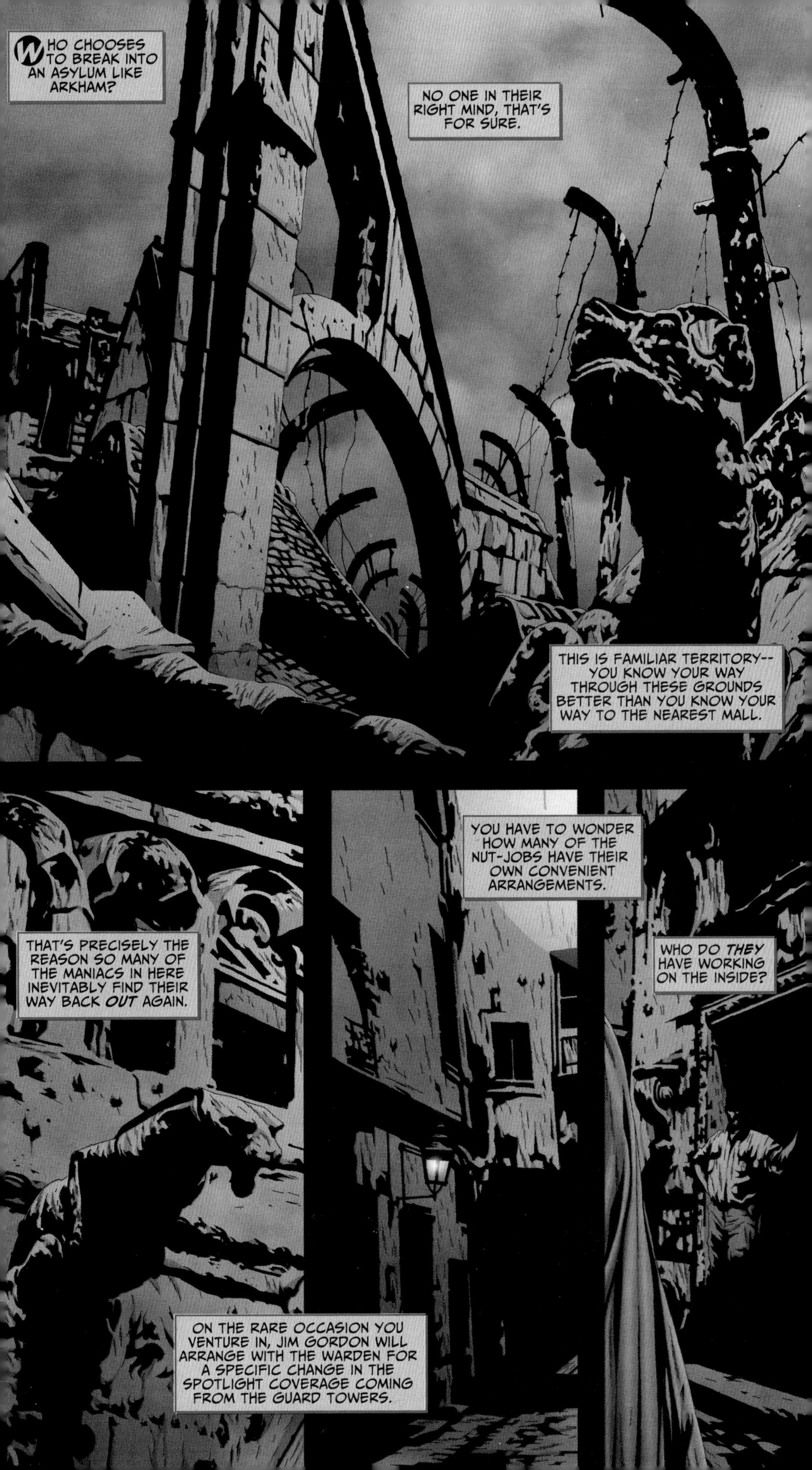
WHO CHOOSES TO BREAK INTO AN ASYLUM LIKE ARKHAM?
NO ONE IN THEIR RIGHT MIND, THAT'S FOR SURE.
THIS IS FAMILIAR TERRITORY-- YOU KNOW YOUR WAY THROUGH THESE GROUNDS BETTER THAN YOU KNOW YOUR WAY TO THE NEAREST MALL.
THAT'S PRECISELY THE REASON SO MANY OF THE MANIACS IN HERE INEVITABLY FIND THEIR WAY BACK OUT AGAIN.
ON THE RARE OCCASION YOU VENTURE IN, JIM GORDON WILL ARRANGE WITH THE WARDEN FOR A SPECIFIC CHANGE IN THE SPOTLIGHT COVERAGE COMING FROM THE GUARD TOWERS.
YOU HAVE TO WONDER HOW MANY OF THE NUT-JOBS HAVE THEIR OWN CONVENIENT ARRANGEMENTS.
WHO DO THEY HAVE WORKING ON THE INSIDE?

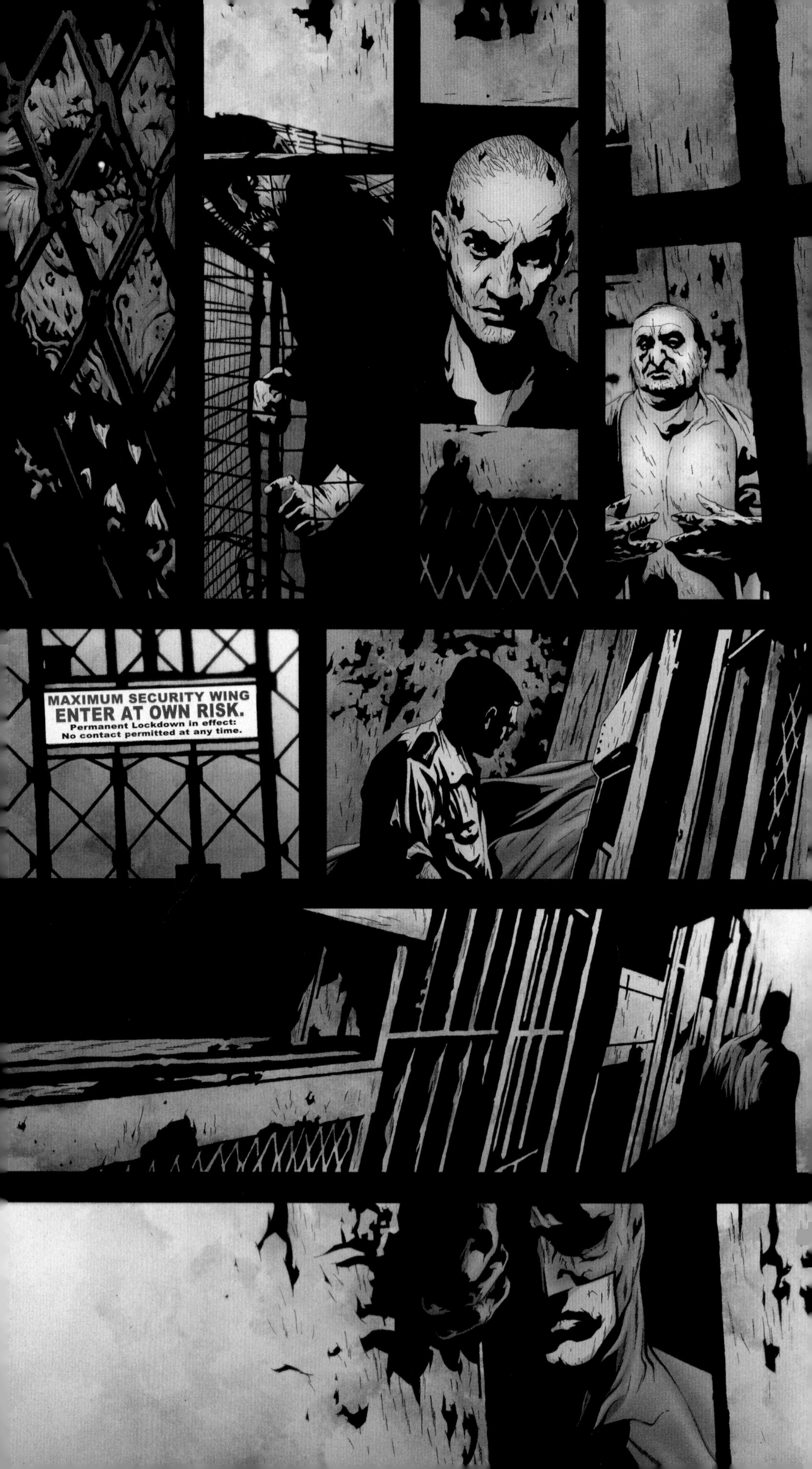
MAXIMUM SECURITY WING
ENTER AT OWN RISK.
Permanent Lockdown in effect:
No contact permitted at any time.

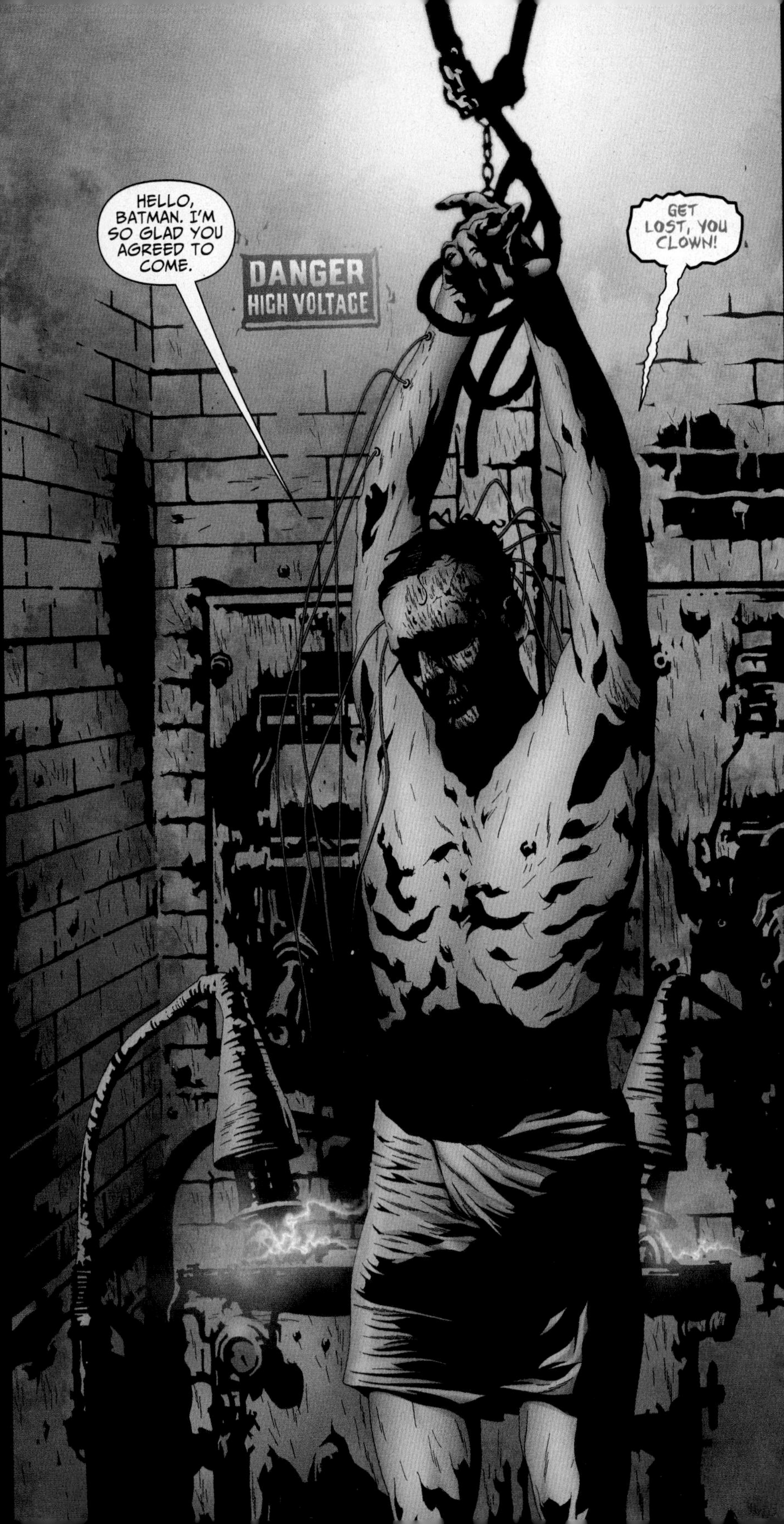
HELLO, BATMAN. I'M SO GLAD YOU AGREED TO COME.
DANGER
HIGH VOLTAGE
GET LOST, YOU CLOWN!

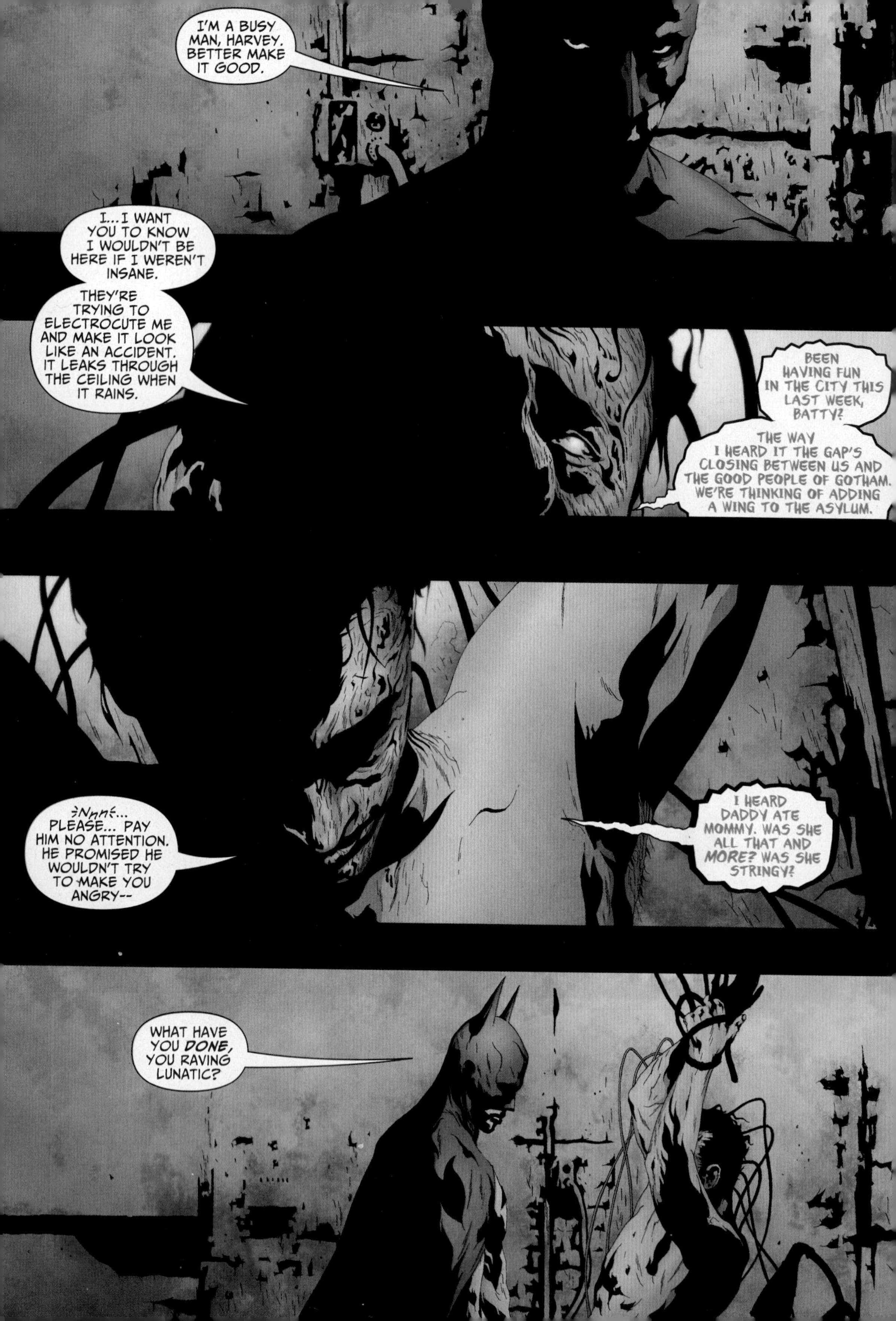

I'M A BUSY MAN, HARVEY. BETTER MAKE IT GOOD.
I...I WANT YOU TO KNOW I WOULDN'T BE HERE IF I WEREN'T INSANE.
THEY'RE TRYING TO ELECTROCUTE ME AND MAKE IT LOOK LIKE AN ACCIDENT. IT LEAKS THROUGH THE CEILING WHEN IT RAINS.
BEEN HAVING FUN IN THE CITY THIS LAST WEEK, BATTY?
THE WAY I HEARD IT THE GAP'S CLOSING BETWEEN US AND THE GOOD PEOPLE OF GOTHAM. WE'RE THINKING OF ADDING A WING TO THE ASYLUM.
NNN... PLEASE... PAY HIM NO ATTENTION. HE PROMISED HE WOULDN'T TRY TO MAKE YOU ANGRY--
I HEARD DADDY ATE MOMMY. WAS SHE ALL THAT AND *MORE?* WAS SHE STRINGY?
WHAT HAVE YOU *DONE,* YOU RAVING LUNATIC?

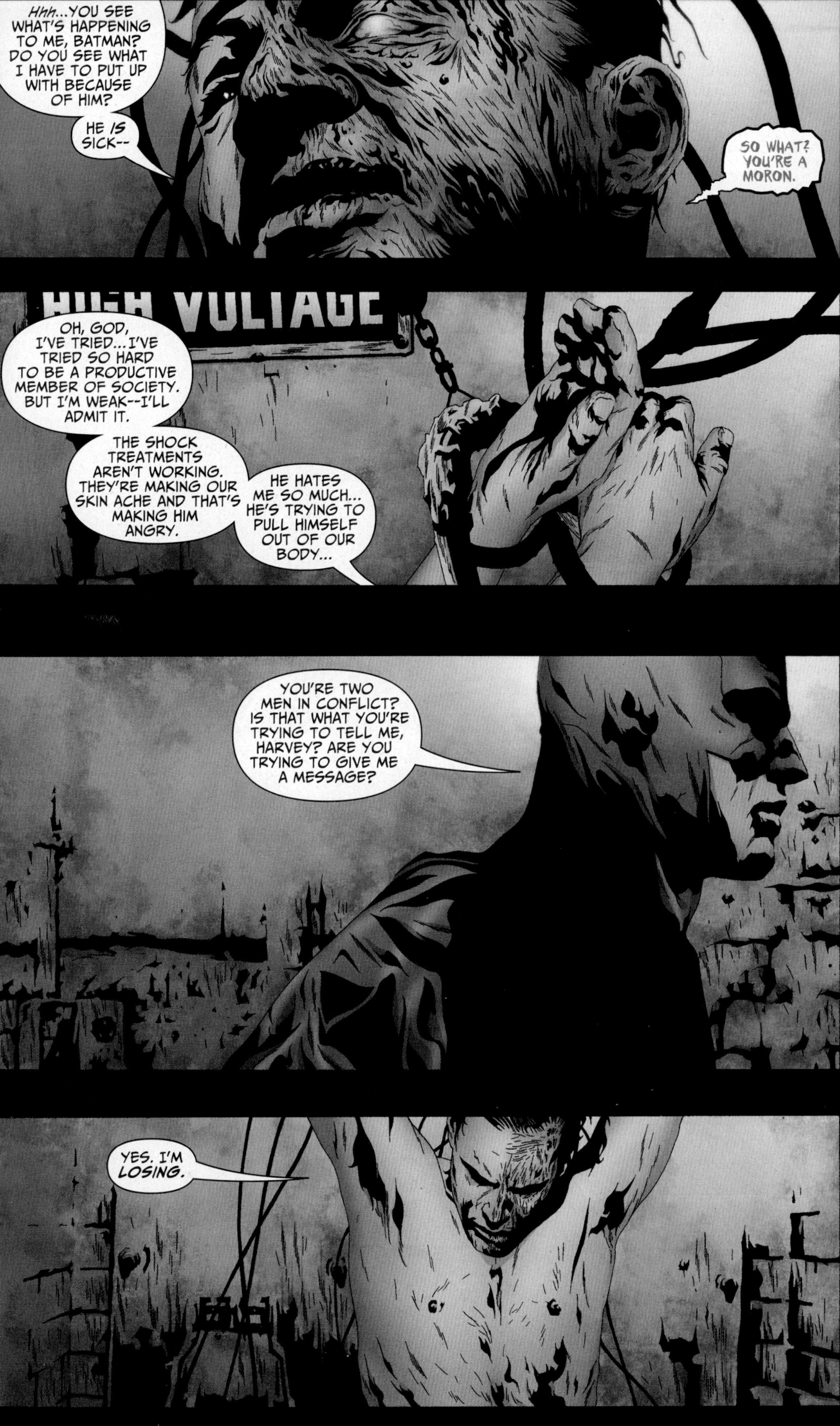
Hhh...YOU SEE WHAT'S HAPPENING TO ME, BATMAN? DO YOU SEE WHAT I HAVE TO PUT UP WITH BECAUSE OF HIM?
HE IS SICK--
SO WHAT? YOU'RE A MORON.
HIGH VOLTAGE
OH, GOD, I'VE TRIED...I'VE TRIED SO HARD TO BE A PRODUCTIVE MEMBER OF SOCIETY. BUT I'M WEAK--I'LL ADMIT IT.
THE SHOCK TREATMENTS AREN'T WORKING. THEY'RE MAKING OUR SKIN ACHE AND THAT'S MAKING HIM ANGRY.
HE HATES ME SO MUCH... HE'S TRYING TO PULL HIMSELF OUT OF OUR BODY...
YOU'RE TWO MEN IN CONFLICT? IS THAT WHAT YOU'RE TRYING TO TELL ME, HARVEY? ARE YOU TRYING TO GIVE ME A MESSAGE?
YES. I'M LOSING.

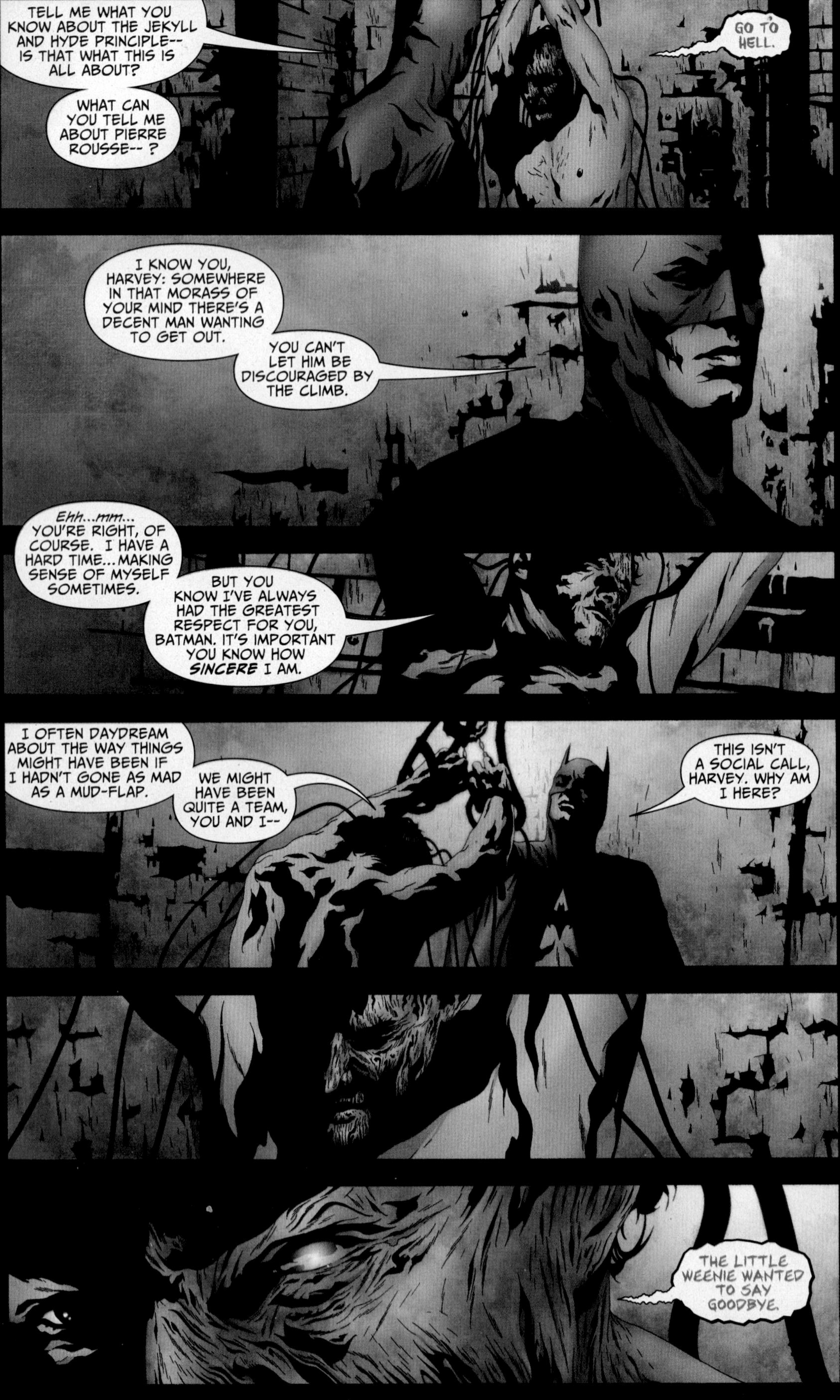
TELL ME WHAT YOU KNOW ABOUT THE JEKYLL AND HYDE PRINCIPLE-- IS THAT WHAT THIS IS ALL ABOUT?
WHAT CAN YOU TELL ME ABOUT PIERRE ROUSSE-- ?
GO TO HELL.
I KNOW YOU, HARVEY: SOMEWHERE IN THAT MORASS OF YOUR MIND THERE'S A DECENT MAN WANTING TO GET OUT.
YOU CAN'T LET HIM BE DISCOURAGED BY THE CLIMB.
Ehh...mm... YOU'RE RIGHT, OF COURSE. I HAVE A HARD TIME...MAKING SENSE OF MYSELF SOMETIMES.
BUT YOU KNOW I'VE ALWAYS HAD THE GREATEST RESPECT FOR YOU, BATMAN. IT'S IMPORTANT YOU KNOW HOW ***SINCERE*** I AM.
I OFTEN DAYDREAM ABOUT THE WAY THINGS MIGHT HAVE BEEN IF I HADN'T GONE AS MAD AS A MUD-FLAP.
WE MIGHT HAVE BEEN QUITE A TEAM, YOU AND I--
THIS ISN'T A SOCIAL CALL, HARVEY. WHY AM I HERE?
THE LITTLE WEENIE WANTED TO SAY GOODBYE.

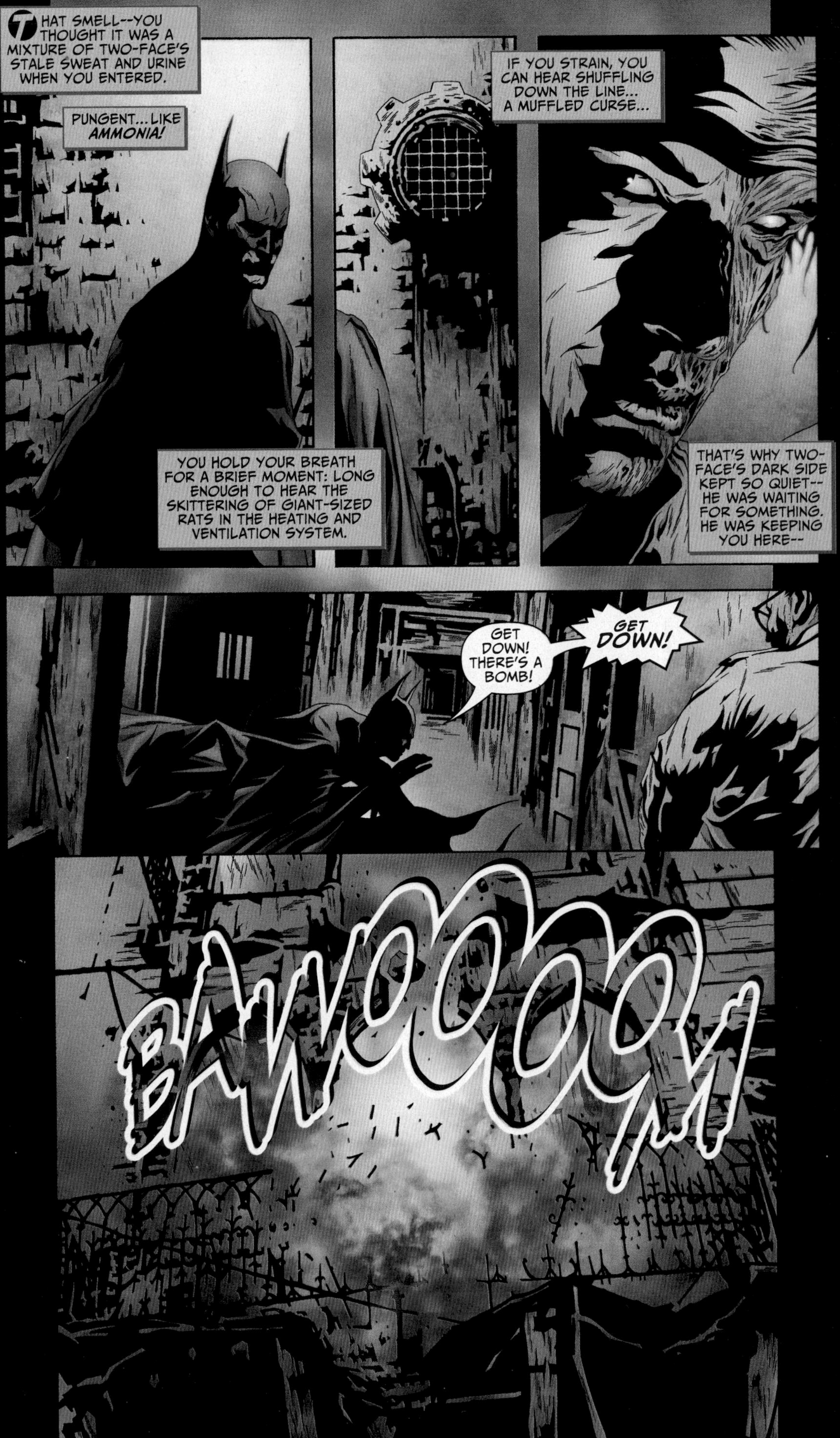
THAT SMELL--YOU THOUGHT IT WAS A MIXTURE OF TWO-FACE'S STALE SWEAT AND URINE WHEN YOU ENTERED.
PUNGENT...LIKE *AMMONIA!*
YOU HOLD YOUR BREATH FOR A BRIEF MOMENT: LONG ENOUGH TO HEAR THE SKITTERING OF GIANT-SIZED RATS IN THE HEATING AND VENTILATION SYSTEM.
IF YOU STRAIN, YOU CAN HEAR SHUFFLING DOWN THE LINE... A MUFFLED CURSE...
THAT'S WHY TWO-FACE'S DARK SIDE KEPT SO QUIET-- HE WAS WAITING FOR SOMETHING. HE WAS KEEPING YOU HERE--
GET DOWN! THERE'S A BOMB!
GET *DOWN!*
BAWOOOOM

Chapter two

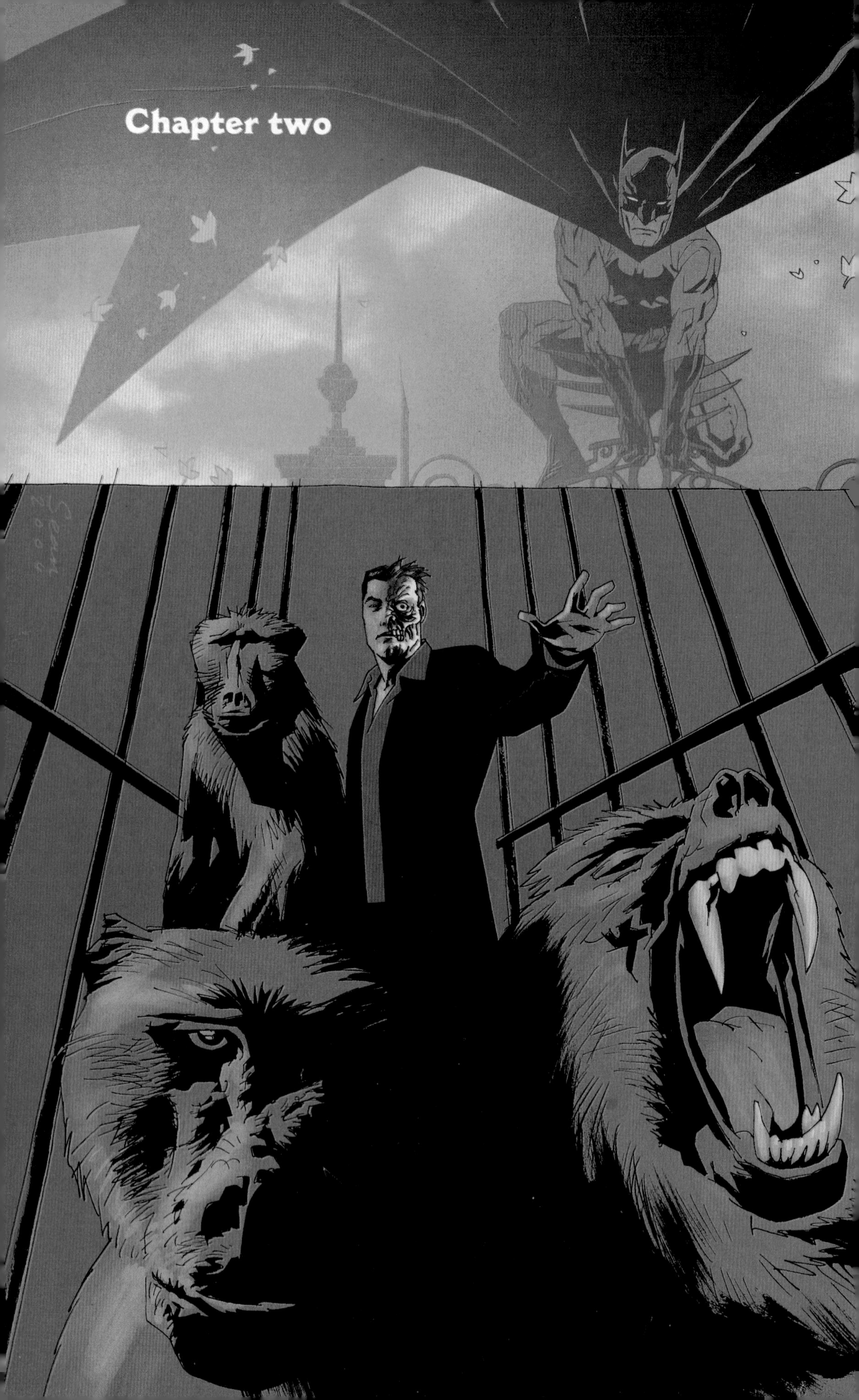

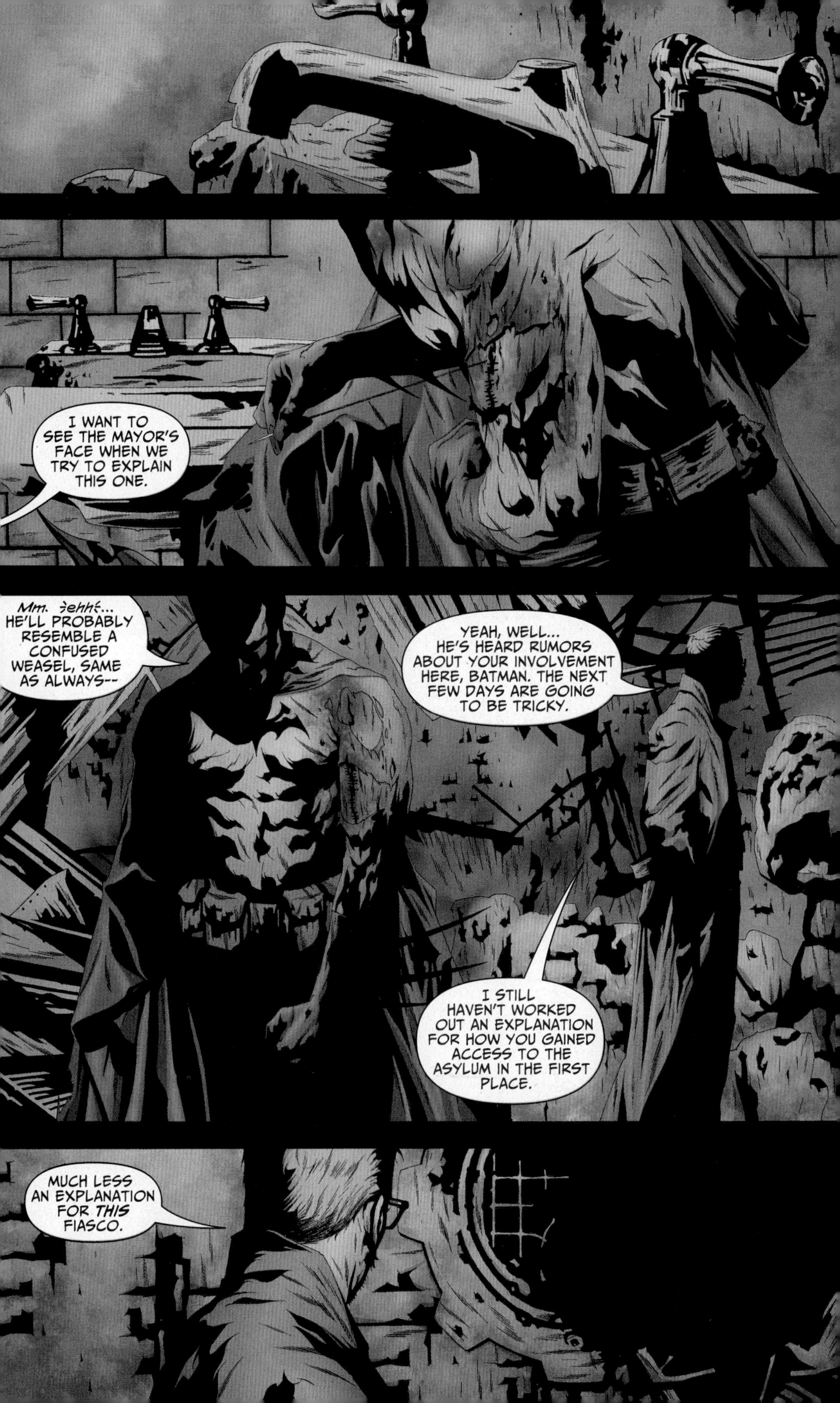

I WANT TO SEE THE MAYOR'S FACE WHEN WE TRY TO EXPLAIN THIS ONE.
Mm. Hehh... HE'LL PROBABLY RESEMBLE A CONFUSED WEASEL, SAME AS ALWAYS--
YEAH, WELL... HE'S HEARD RUMORS ABOUT YOUR INVOLVEMENT HERE, BATMAN. THE NEXT FEW DAYS ARE GOING TO BE TRICKY.
I STILL HAVEN'T WORKED OUT AN EXPLANATION FOR HOW YOU GAINED ACCESS TO THE ASYLUM IN THE FIRST PLACE.
MUCH LESS AN EXPLANATION FOR THIS FIASCO.

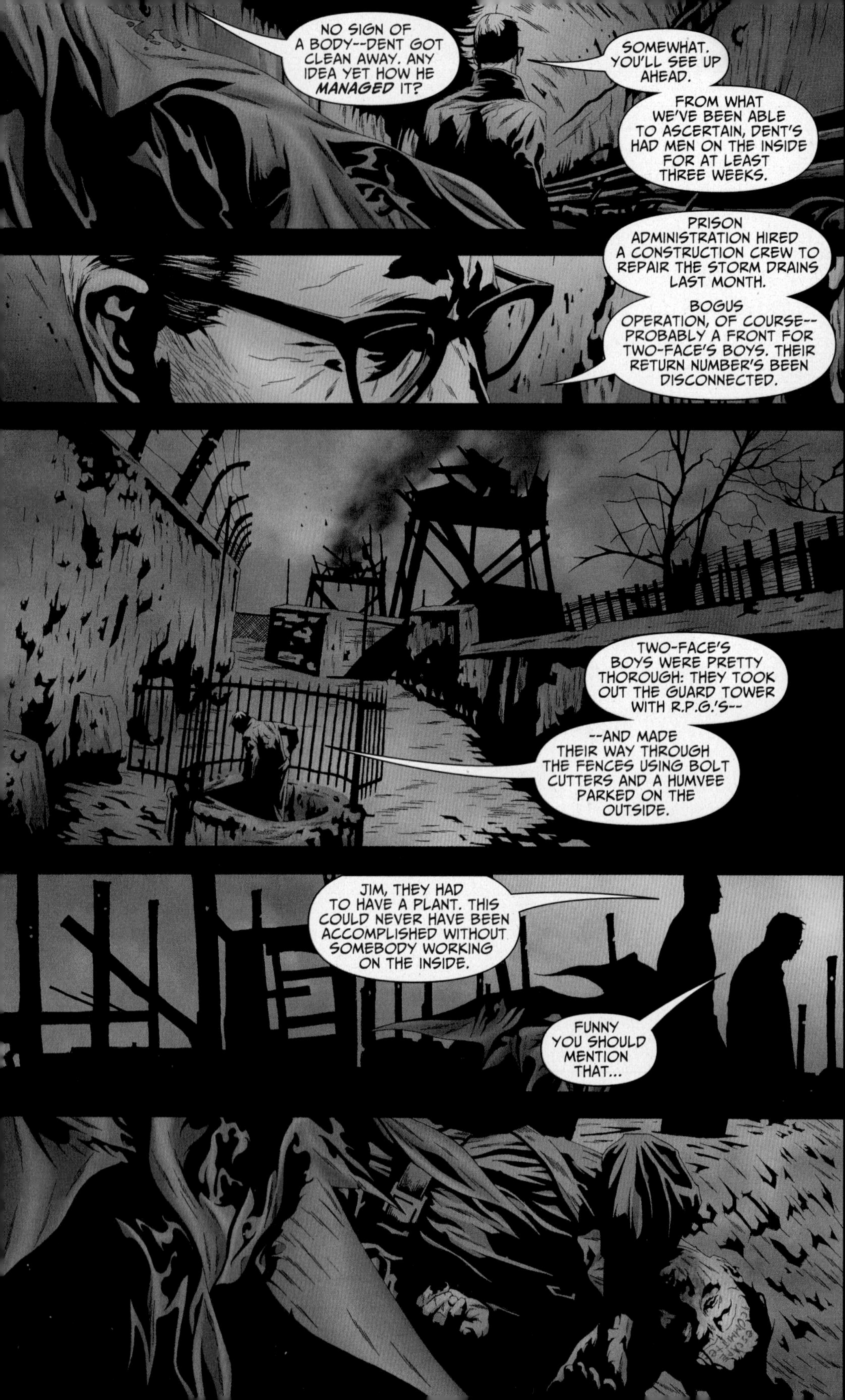
NO SIGN OF A BODY--DENT GOT CLEAN AWAY. ANY IDEA YET HOW HE *MANAGED* IT?
SOMEWHAT. YOU'LL SEE UP AHEAD.
FROM WHAT WE'VE BEEN ABLE TO ASCERTAIN, DENT'S HAD MEN ON THE INSIDE FOR AT LEAST THREE WEEKS.
PRISON ADMINISTRATION HIRED A CONSTRUCTION CREW TO REPAIR THE STORM DRAINS LAST MONTH.
BOGUS OPERATION, OF COURSE--PROBABLY A FRONT FOR TWO-FACE'S BOYS. THEIR RETURN NUMBER'S BEEN DISCONNECTED.
TWO-FACE'S BOYS WERE PRETTY THOROUGH: THEY TOOK OUT THE GUARD TOWER WITH R.P.G.'S--
--AND MADE THEIR WAY THROUGH THE FENCES USING BOLT CUTTERS AND A HUMVEE PARKED ON THE OUTSIDE.
JIM, THEY HAD TO HAVE A PLANT. THIS COULD NEVER HAVE BEEN ACCOMPLISHED WITHOUT SOMEBODY WORKING ON THE INSIDE.
FUNNY YOU SHOULD MENTION THAT...

DECEASED'S NAME IS MIKE MEISINGER-- HE'S BEEN HERE FOR EIGHT YEARS WITH NO PRIOR INCIDENT.

A LOT OF OUR GUYS GET DEATH THREATS...MAYBE THAT HAD SOMETHING TO DO WITH IT.

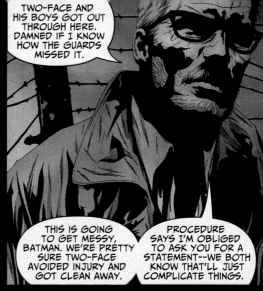

TWO-FACE AND HIS BOYS GOT OUT THROUGH HERE. DAMNED IF I KNOW HOW THE GUARDS MISSED IT.

THIS IS GOING TO GET MESSY, BATMAN. WE'RE PRETTY SURE TWO-FACE AVOIDED INJURY AND GOT CLEAN AWAY.

PROCEDURE SAYS I'M OBLIGED TO ASK YOU FOR A STATEMENT--WE BOTH KNOW THAT'LL JUST COMPLICATE THINGS.

I DON'T KNOW WHICH IS BIGGER: THE HOLE IN THE WALL OR THE HOLE IN THE POLICE WORK--

JIM, TWO-FACE SAID SOMETHING IMPORTANT BEFORE HE FLEW THE COOP-- I THOUGHT HE WAS JUST BEING DRAMATIC, BUT NOW I'M NOT SO SURE.

SOMETHING ABOUT THE TONE OF HIS VOICE... I'VE NEVER HEARD HIM SPEAK WITH SUCH CLARITY OF PURPOSE.

HE SAID HE WANTED TO SAY GOODBYE. I THINK HE WAS BEING SINCERE.

GOODBYE? WHAT THE HELL IS THAT SUPPOSED TO MEAN--?

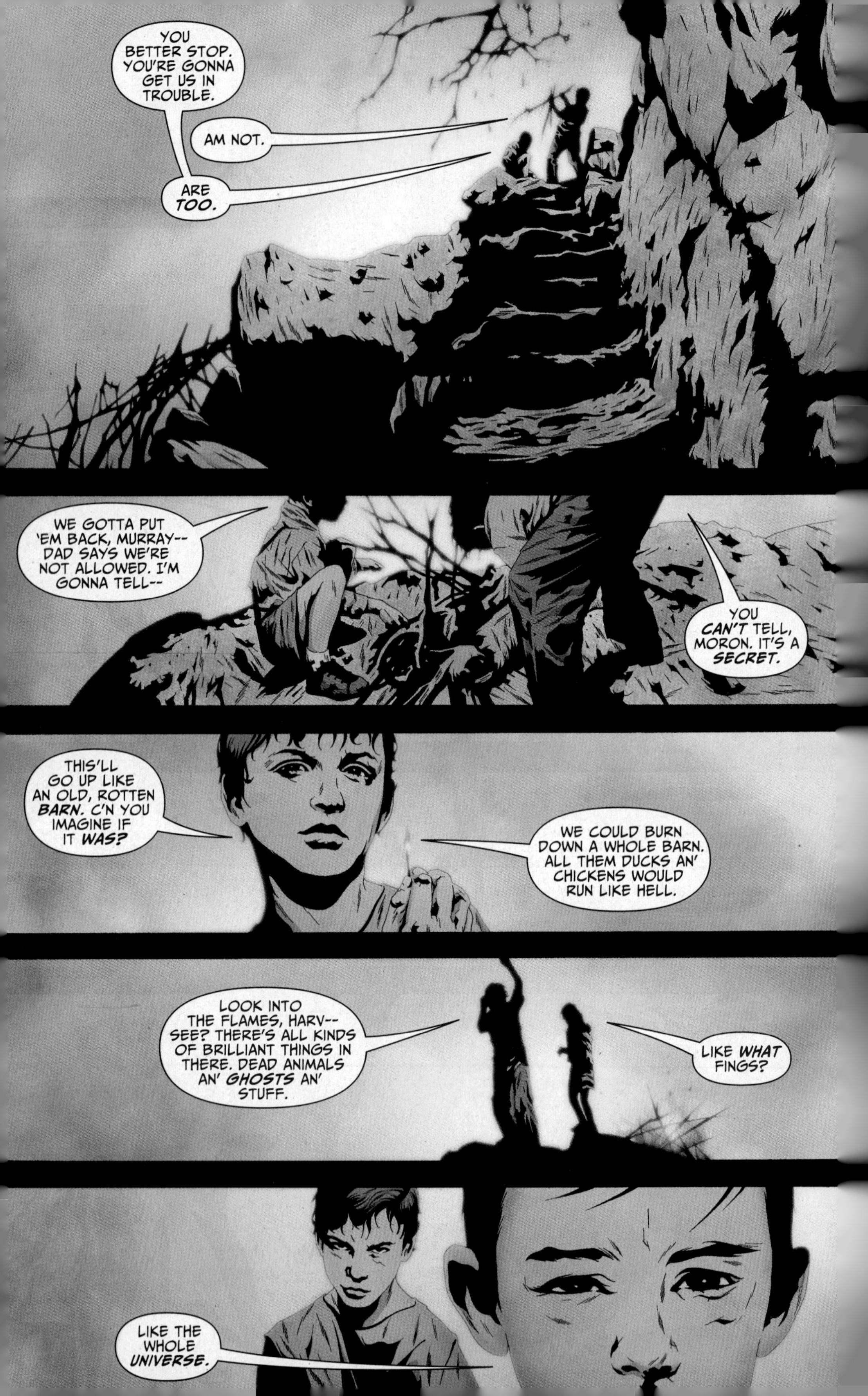
YOU BETTER STOP. YOU'RE GONNA GET US IN TROUBLE.
AM NOT.
ARE *TOO.*
WE GOTTA PUT 'EM BACK, MURRAY-- DAD SAYS WE'RE NOT ALLOWED. I'M GONNA TELL--
YOU *CAN'T* TELL, MORON. IT'S A *SECRET.*
THIS'LL GO UP LIKE AN OLD, ROTTEN *BARN.* C'N YOU IMAGINE IF IT *WAS?*
WE COULD BURN DOWN A WHOLE BARN. ALL THEM DUCKS AN' CHICKENS WOULD RUN LIKE HELL.
LOOK INTO THE FLAMES, HARV-- SEE? THERE'S ALL KINDS OF BRILLIANT THINGS IN THERE. DEAD ANIMALS AN' *GHOSTS* AN' STUFF.
LIKE *WHAT* FINGS?
LIKE THE WHOLE *UNIVERSE.*

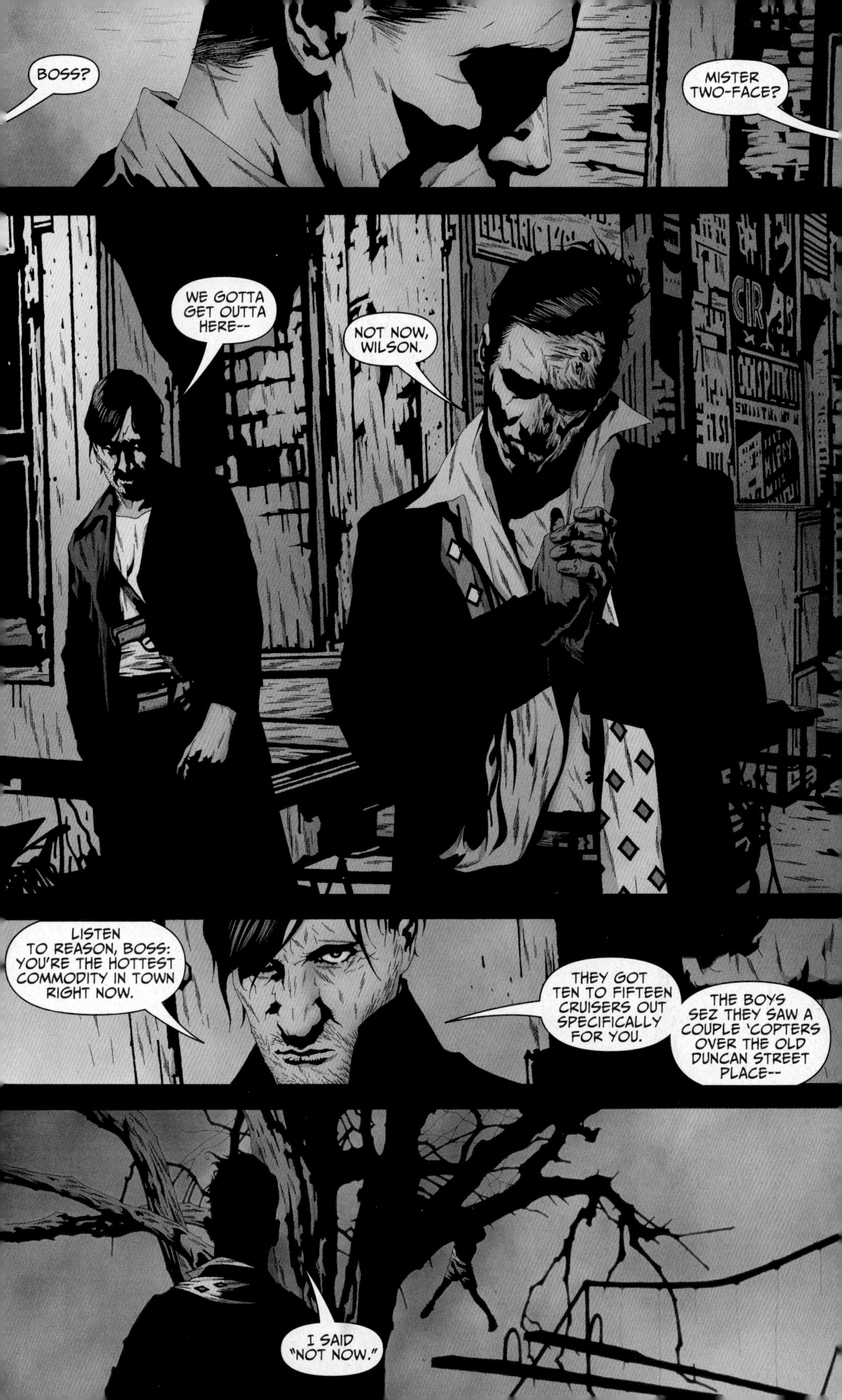
BOSS?
MISTER TWO-FACE?
WE GOTTA GET OUTTA HERE--
NOT NOW, WILSON.
LISTEN TO REASON, BOSS: YOU'RE THE HOTTEST COMMODITY IN TOWN RIGHT NOW.
THEY GOT TEN TO FIFTEEN CRUISERS OUT SPECIFICALLY FOR YOU.
THE BOYS SEZ THEY SAW A COUPLE 'COPTERS OVER THE OLD DUNCAN STREET PLACE--
I SAID "NOT NOW."

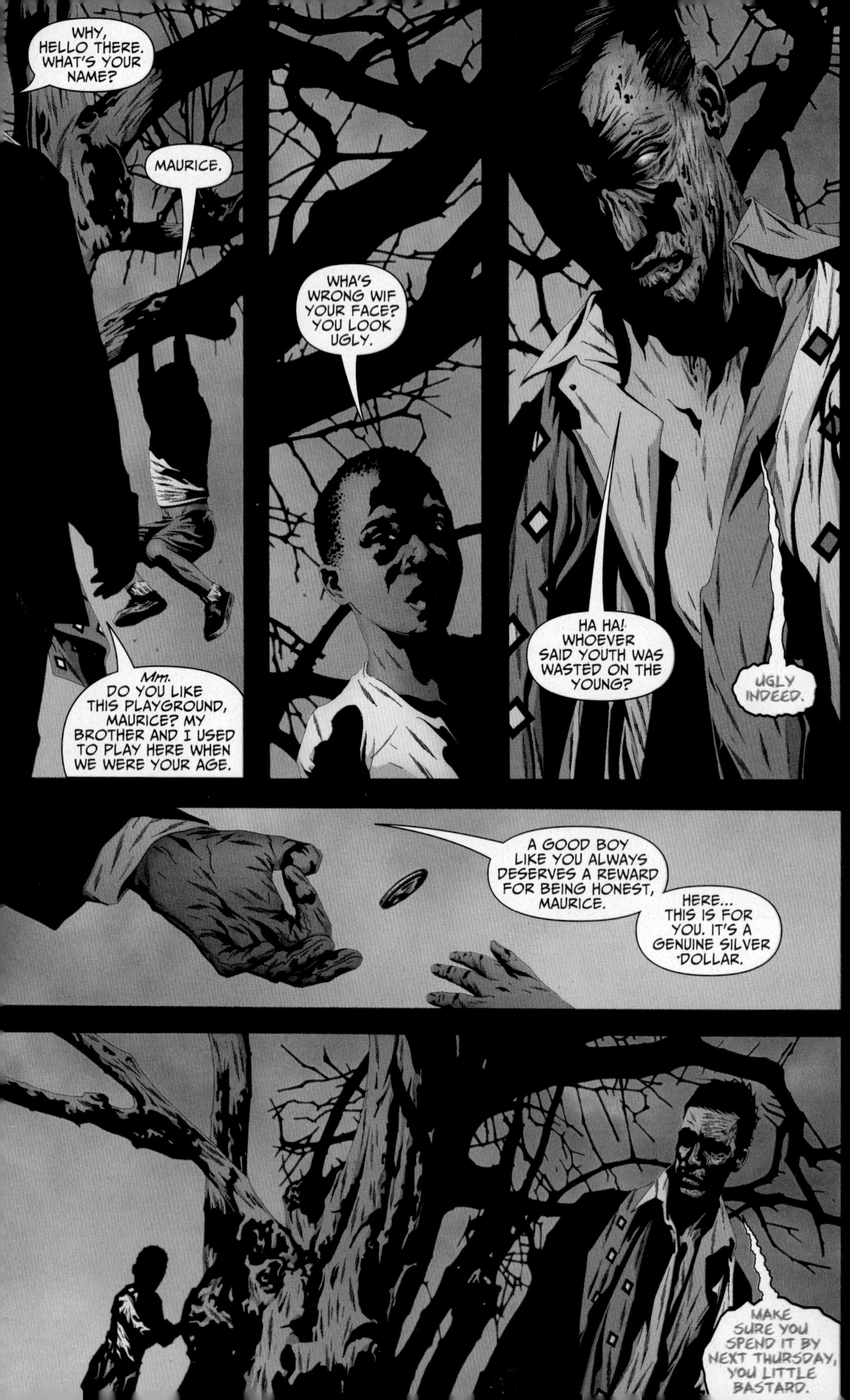
WHY, HELLO THERE. WHAT'S YOUR NAME?
MAURICE.
Mm. DO YOU LIKE THIS PLAYGROUND, MAURICE? MY BROTHER AND I USED TO PLAY HERE WHEN WE WERE YOUR AGE.
WHA'S WRONG WIF YOUR FACE? YOU LOOK UGLY.
HA HA! WHOEVER SAID YOUTH WAS WASTED ON THE YOUNG?
UGLY INDEED.
A GOOD BOY LIKE YOU ALWAYS DESERVES A REWARD FOR BEING HONEST, MAURICE.
HERE... THIS IS FOR YOU. IT'S A GENUINE SILVER DOLLAR.
MAKE SURE YOU SPEND IT BY NEXT THURSDAY, YOU LITTLE BASTARD.

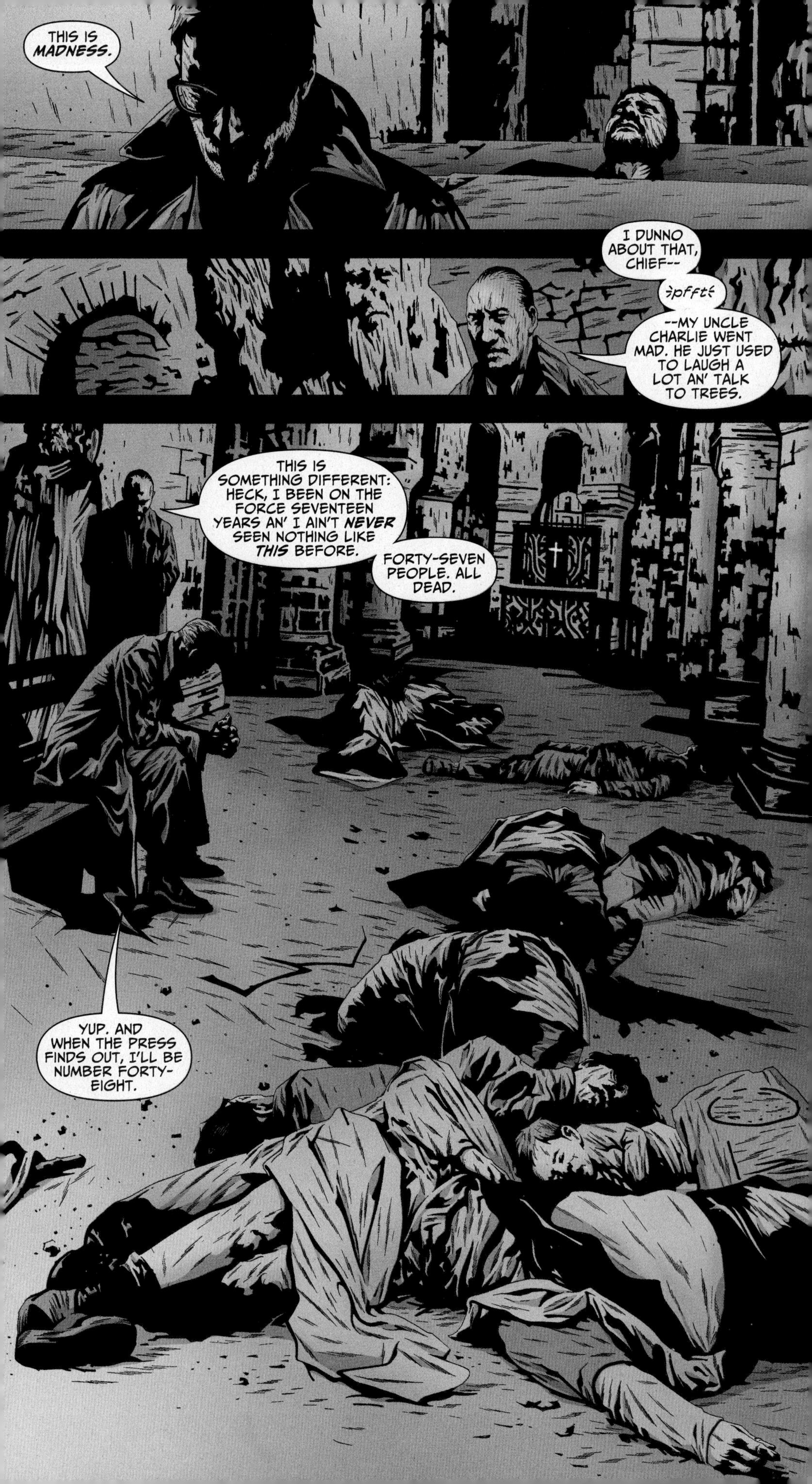
THIS IS MADNESS.
I DUNNO ABOUT THAT, CHIEF--
pfft
--MY UNCLE CHARLIE WENT MAD. HE JUST USED TO LAUGH A LOT AN' TALK TO TREES.
THIS IS SOMETHING DIFFERENT: HECK, I BEEN ON THE FORCE SEVENTEEN YEARS AN' I AIN'T NEVER SEEN NOTHING LIKE THIS BEFORE.
FORTY-SEVEN PEOPLE. ALL DEAD.
YUP. AND WHEN THE PRESS FINDS OUT, I'LL BE NUMBER FORTY-EIGHT.

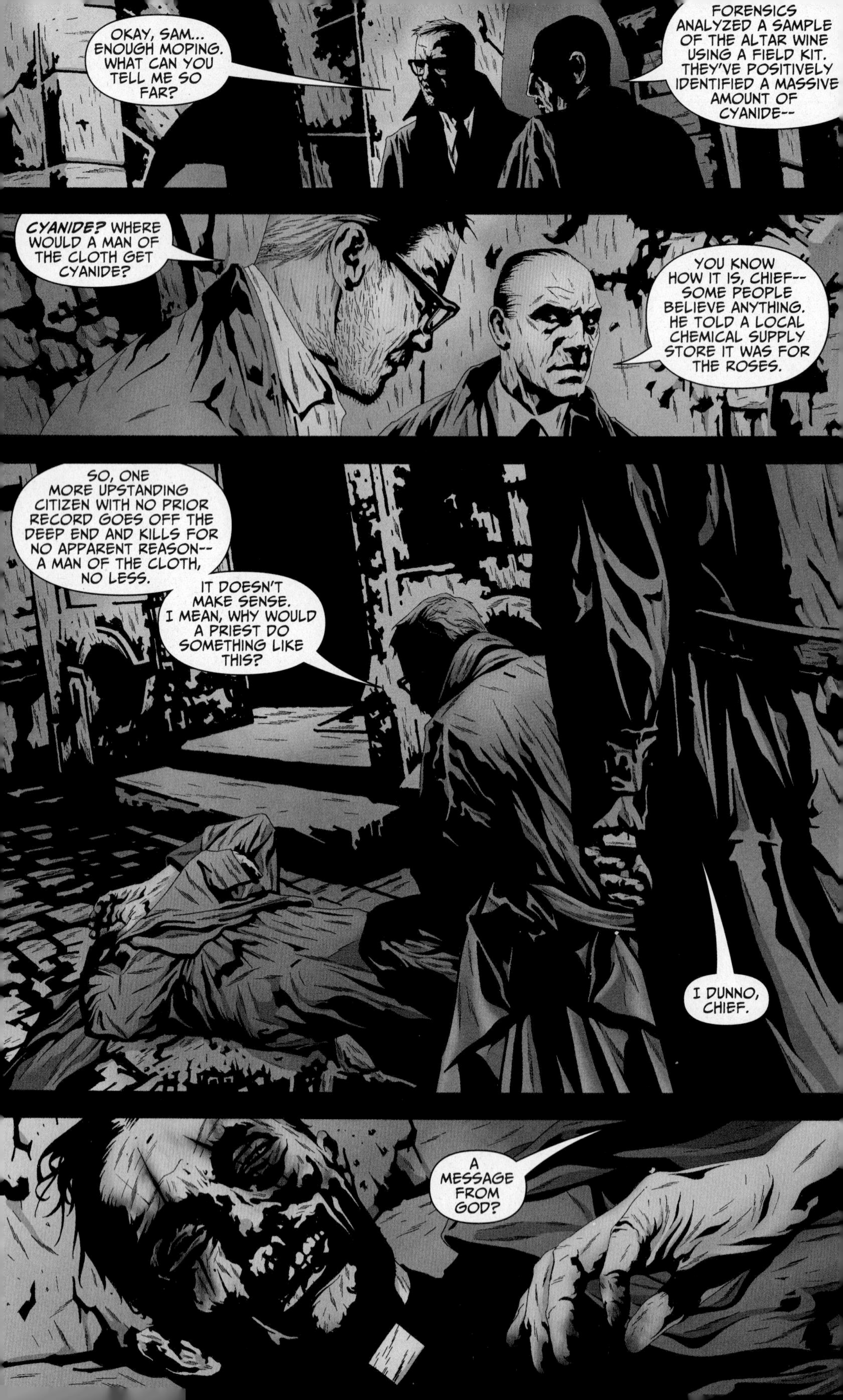
OKAY, SAM... ENOUGH MOPING. WHAT CAN YOU TELL ME SO FAR?
FORENSICS ANALYZED A SAMPLE OF THE ALTAR WINE USING A FIELD KIT. THEY'VE POSITIVELY IDENTIFIED A MASSIVE AMOUNT OF CYANIDE--
CYANIDE? WHERE WOULD A MAN OF THE CLOTH GET CYANIDE?
YOU KNOW HOW IT IS, CHIEF-- SOME PEOPLE BELIEVE ANYTHING. HE TOLD A LOCAL CHEMICAL SUPPLY STORE IT WAS FOR THE ROSES.
SO, ONE MORE UPSTANDING CITIZEN WITH NO PRIOR RECORD GOES OFF THE DEEP END AND KILLS FOR NO APPARENT REASON-- A MAN OF THE CLOTH, NO LESS.
IT DOESN'T MAKE SENSE. I MEAN, WHY WOULD A PRIEST DO SOMETHING LIKE THIS?
I DUNNO, CHIEF.
A MESSAGE FROM GOD?

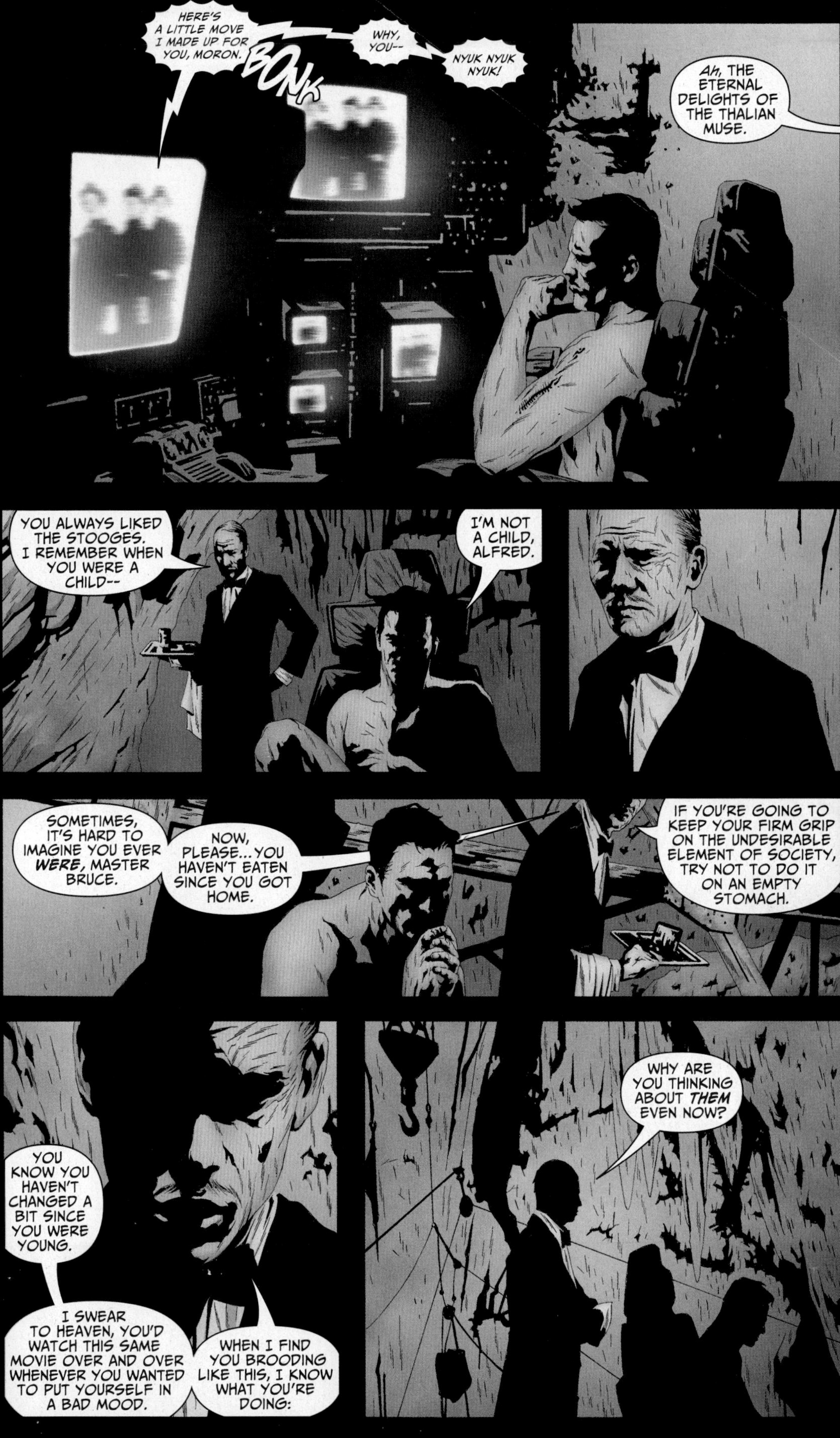
HERE'S A LITTLE MOVE I MADE UP FOR YOU, MORON.
BONK
WHY, YOU--
NYUK NYUK NYUK!
Ah, THE ETERNAL DELIGHTS OF THE THALIAN MUSE.
YOU ALWAYS LIKED THE STOOGES. I REMEMBER WHEN YOU WERE A CHILD--
I'M NOT A CHILD, ALFRED.
SOMETIMES, IT'S HARD TO IMAGINE YOU EVER WERE, MASTER BRUCE.
NOW, PLEASE... YOU HAVEN'T EATEN SINCE YOU GOT HOME.
IF YOU'RE GOING TO KEEP YOUR FIRM GRIP ON THE UNDESIRABLE ELEMENT OF SOCIETY, TRY NOT TO DO IT ON AN EMPTY STOMACH.
YOU KNOW YOU HAVEN'T CHANGED A BIT SINCE YOU WERE YOUNG.
I SWEAR TO HEAVEN, YOU'D WATCH THIS SAME MOVIE OVER AND OVER WHENEVER YOU WANTED TO PUT YOURSELF IN A BAD MOOD.
WHEN I FIND YOU BROODING LIKE THIS, I KNOW WHAT YOU'RE DOING:
WHY ARE YOU THINKING ABOUT THEM EVEN NOW?

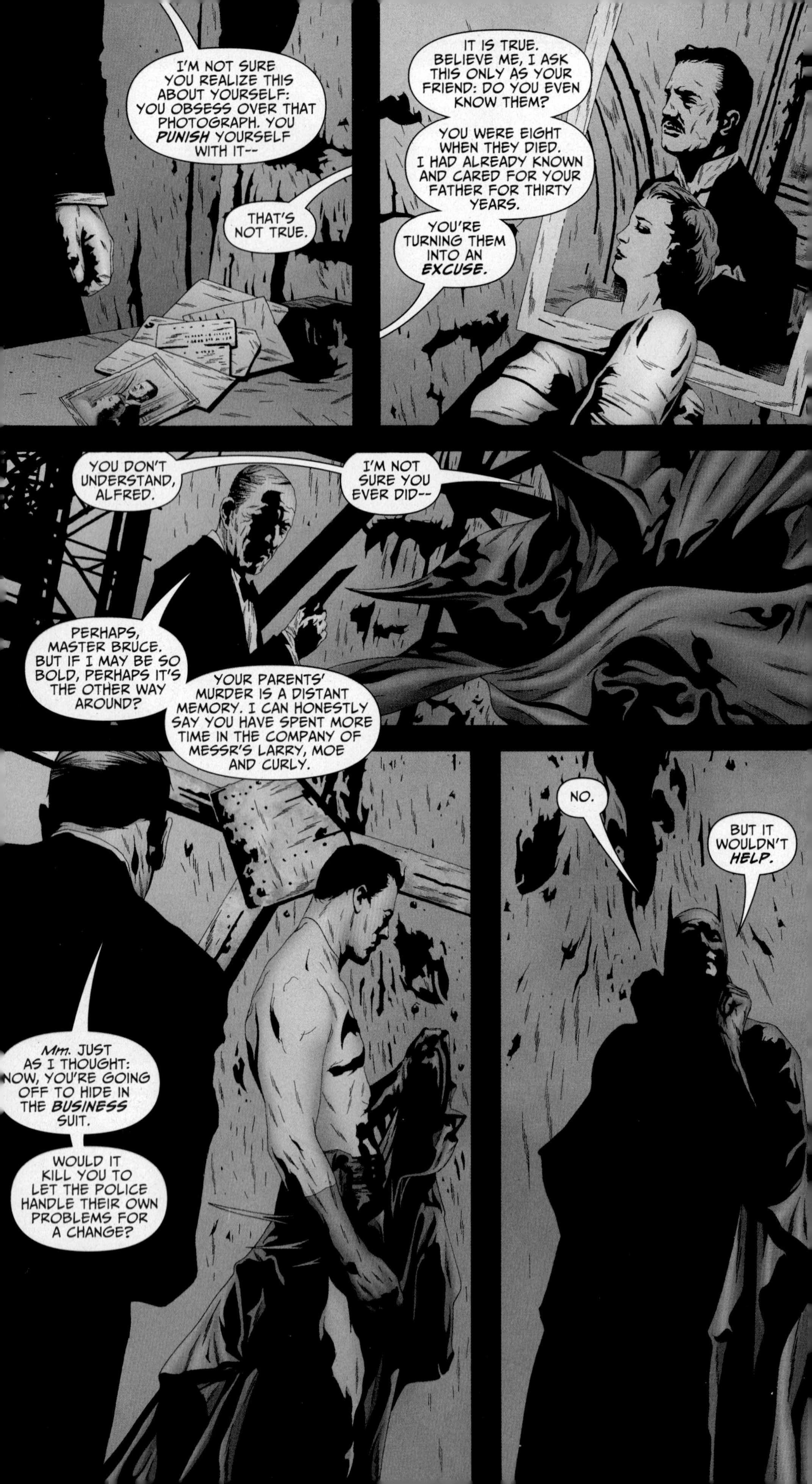
I'M NOT SURE YOU REALIZE THIS ABOUT YOURSELF: YOU OBSESS OVER THAT PHOTOGRAPH. YOU *PUNISH* YOURSELF WITH IT--
THAT'S NOT TRUE.
IT IS TRUE. BELIEVE ME, I ASK THIS ONLY AS YOUR FRIEND: DO YOU EVEN KNOW THEM?
YOU WERE EIGHT WHEN THEY DIED. I HAD ALREADY KNOWN AND CARED FOR YOUR FATHER FOR THIRTY YEARS.
YOU'RE TURNING THEM INTO AN *EXCUSE.*
YOU DON'T UNDERSTAND, ALFRED.
I'M NOT SURE YOU EVER DID--
PERHAPS, MASTER BRUCE. BUT IF I MAY BE SO BOLD, PERHAPS IT'S THE OTHER WAY AROUND?
YOUR PARENTS' MURDER IS A DISTANT MEMORY. I CAN HONESTLY SAY YOU HAVE SPENT MORE TIME IN THE COMPANY OF MESSR'S LARRY, MOE AND CURLY.
Mm. JUST AS I THOUGHT: NOW, YOU'RE GOING OFF TO HIDE IN THE *BUSINESS* SUIT.
WOULD IT KILL YOU TO LET THE POLICE HANDLE THEIR OWN PROBLEMS FOR A CHANGE?
NO.
BUT IT WOULDN'T *HELP.*

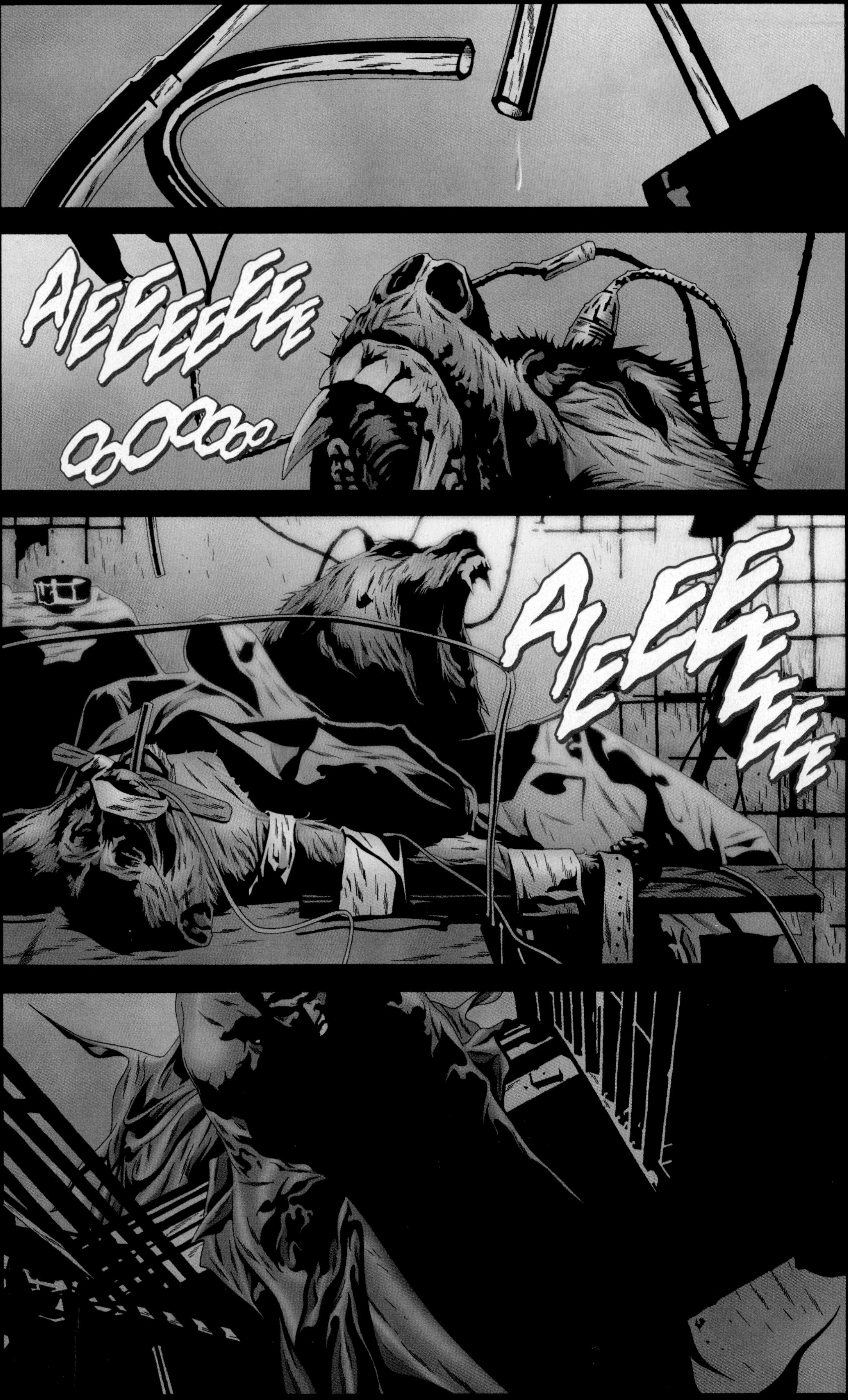
AIEEEEEEE
OoOOooo
AIEEEEEEEE

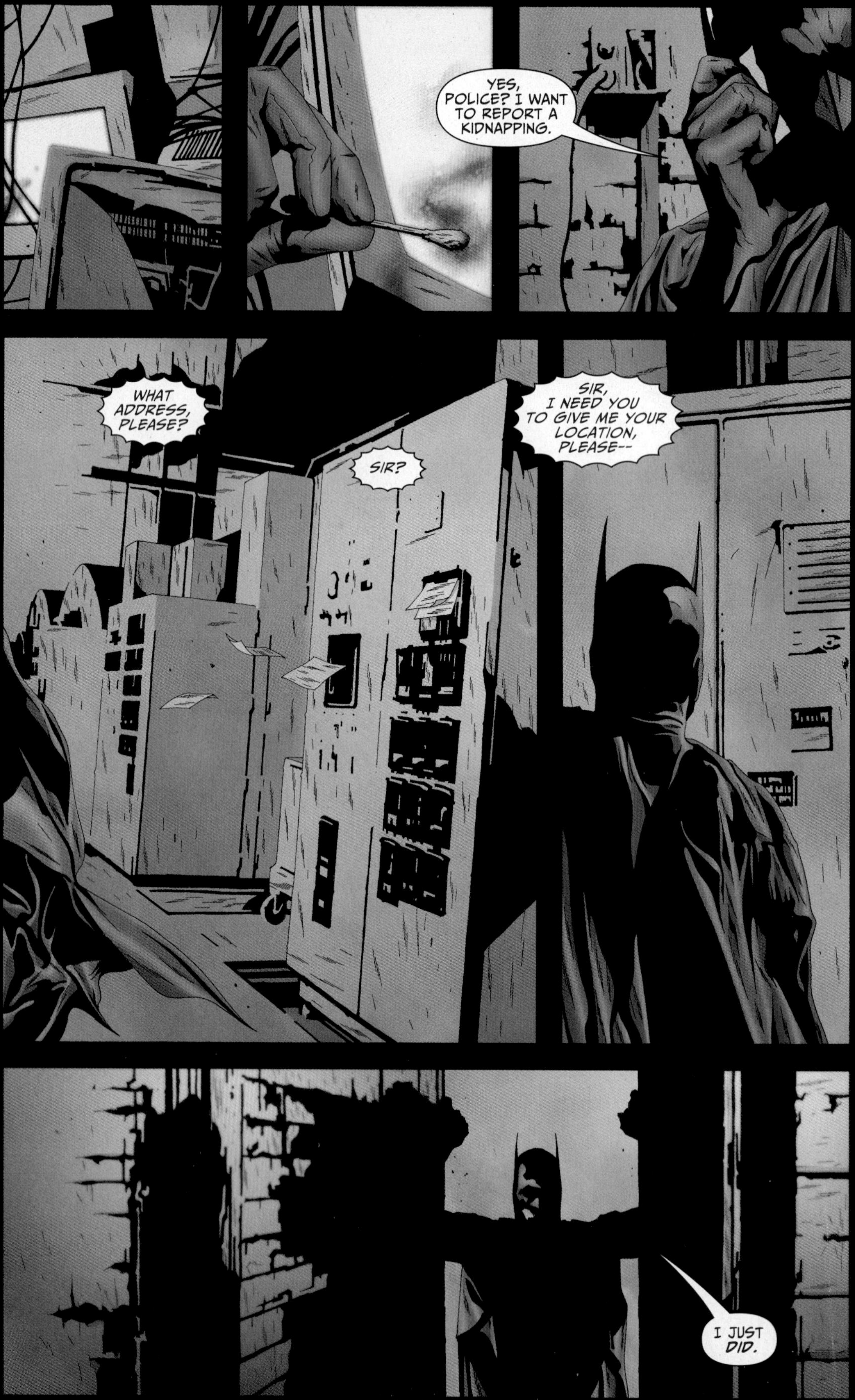
YES, POLICE? I WANT TO REPORT A KIDNAPPING.
WHAT ADDRESS, PLEASE?
SIR?
SIR, I NEED YOU TO GIVE ME YOUR LOCATION, PLEASE--
I JUST DID.

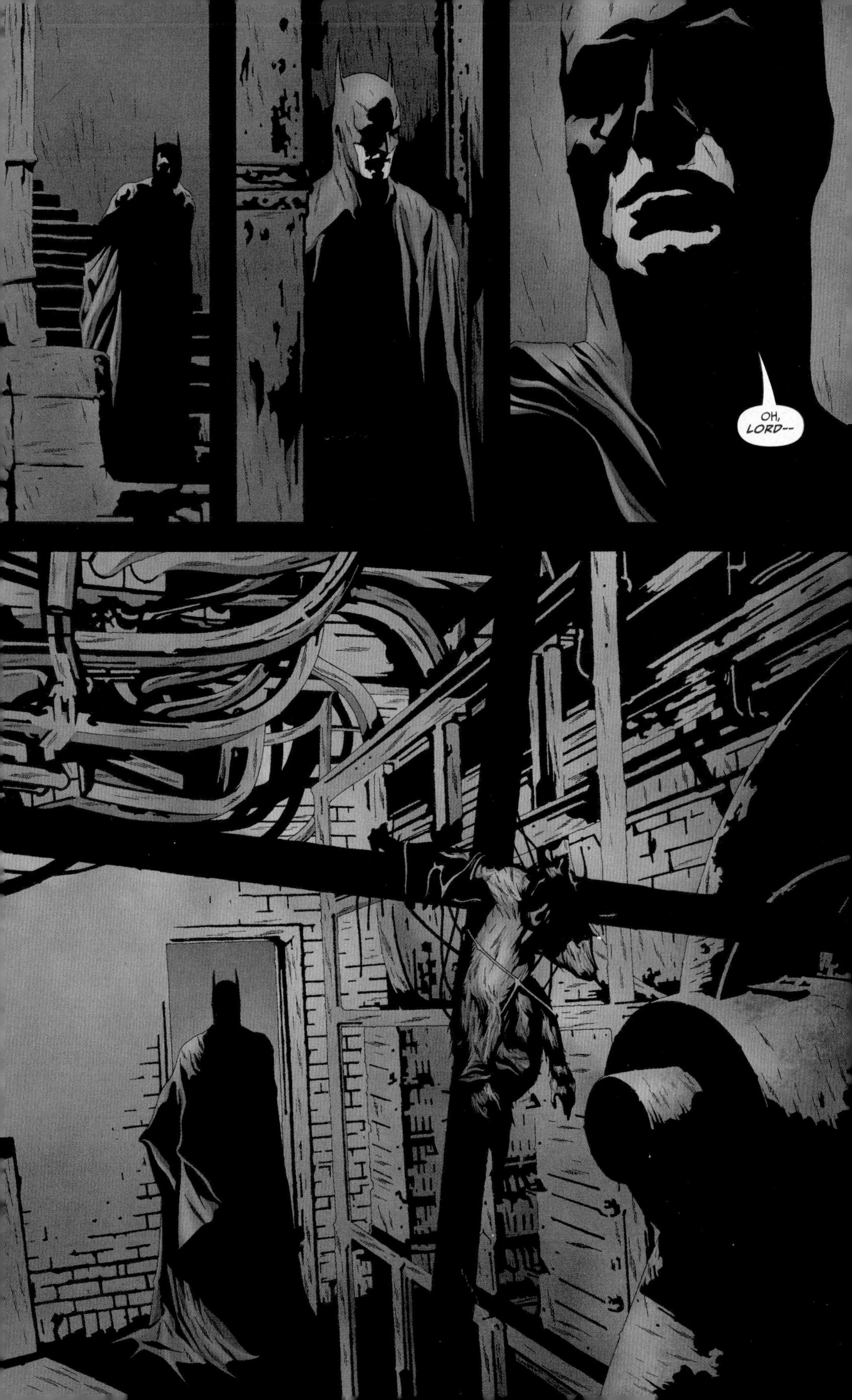
OH, LORD--

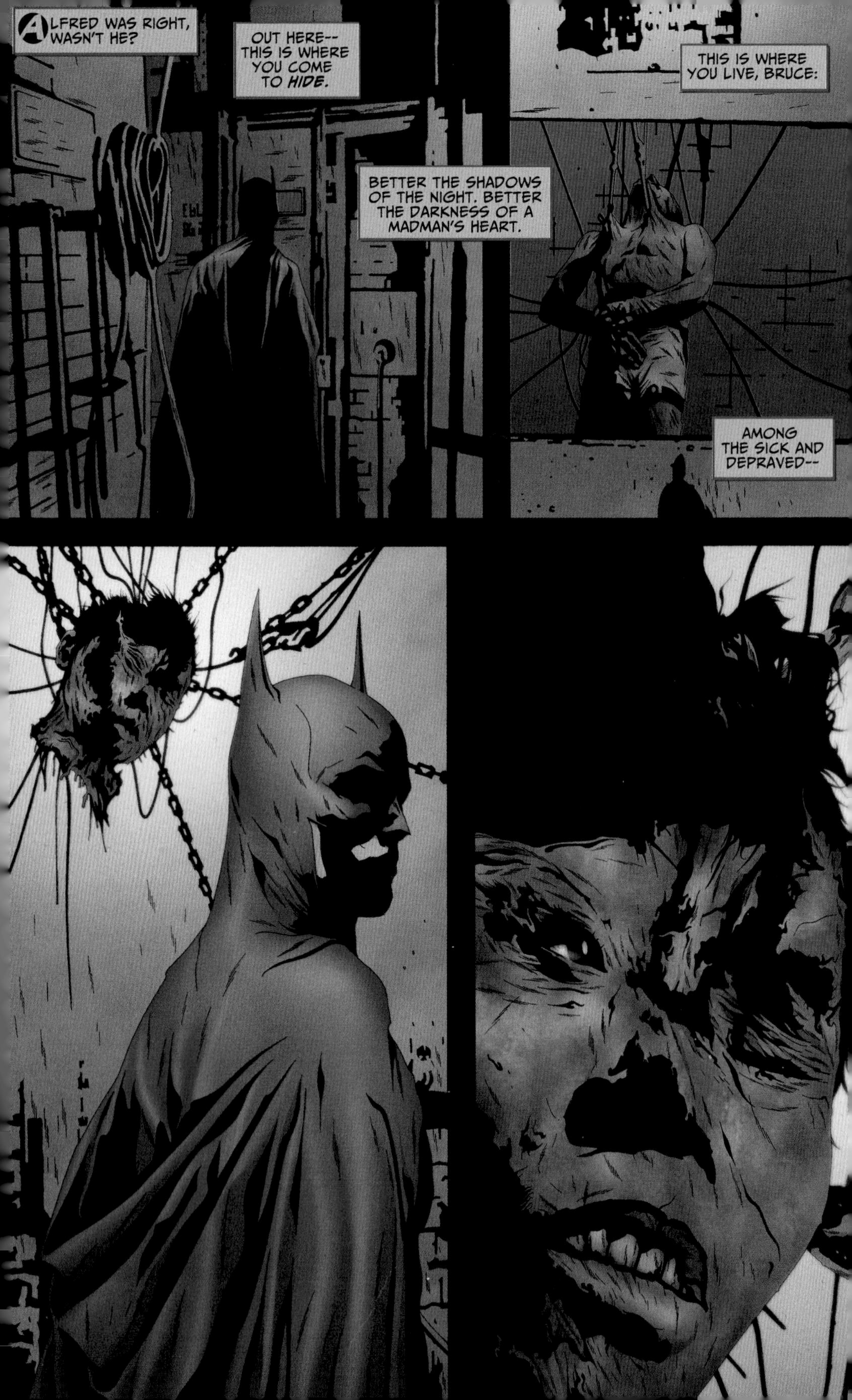
ALFRED WAS RIGHT, WASN'T HE?
OUT HERE-- THIS IS WHERE YOU COME TO *HIDE*.
BETTER THE SHADOWS OF THE NIGHT. BETTER THE DARKNESS OF A MADMAN'S HEART.
THIS IS WHERE YOU LIVE, BRUCE:
AMONG THE SICK AND DEPRAVED--

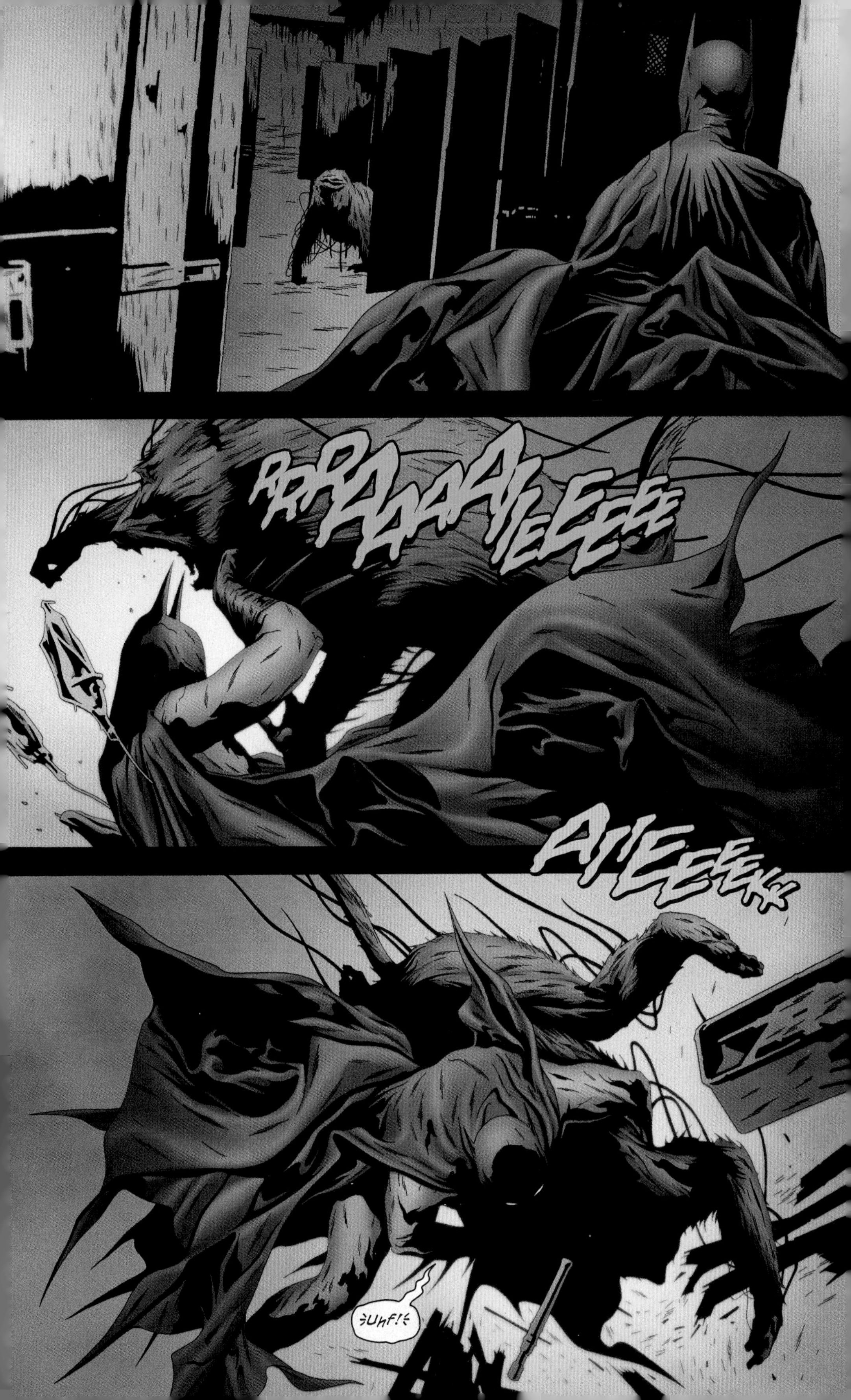
RRRAAAAIEEEEEE
AIEEEEK!!
UNF!

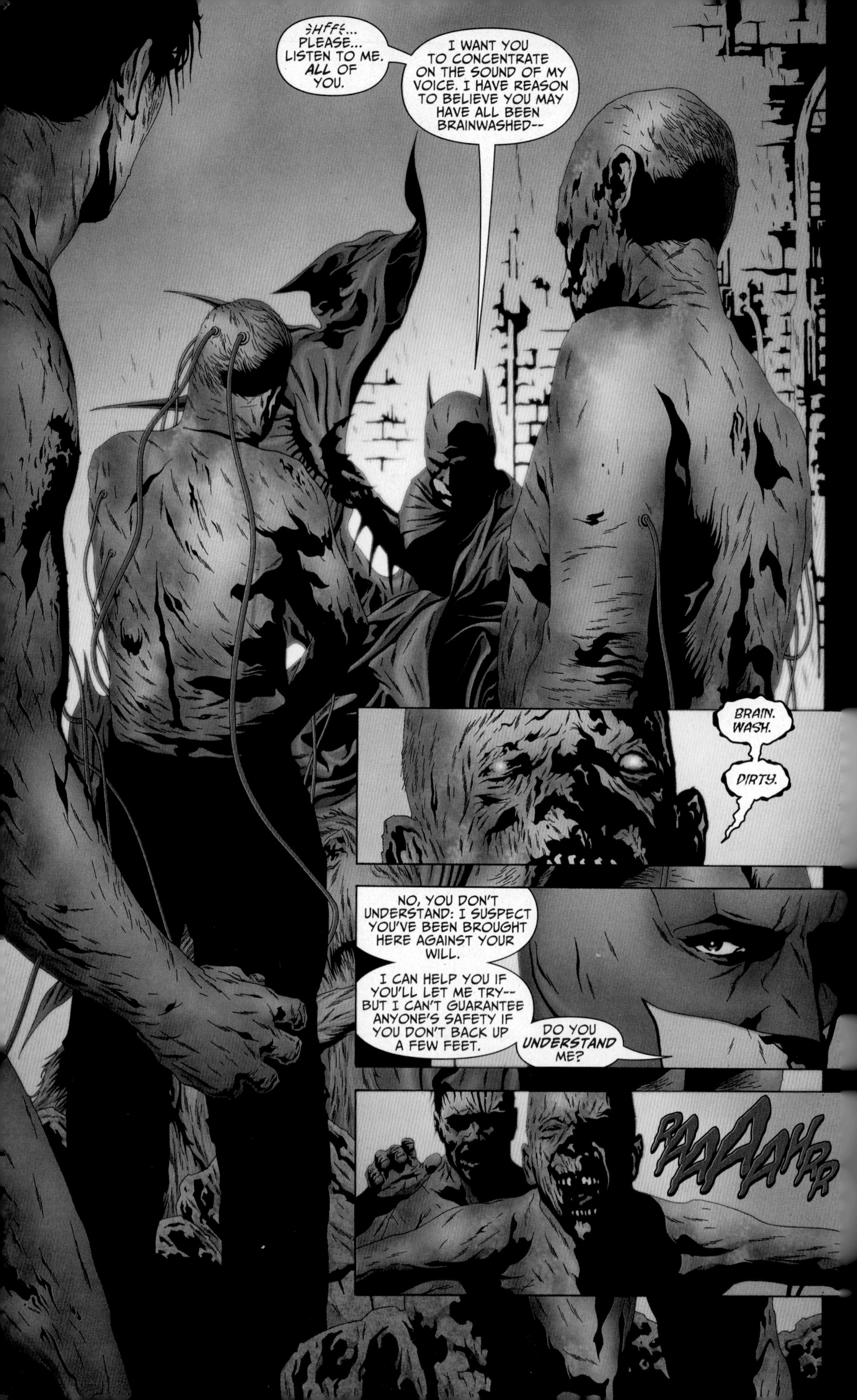
HFF... PLEASE... LISTEN TO ME. **ALL** OF YOU.
I WANT YOU TO CONCENTRATE ON THE SOUND OF MY VOICE. I HAVE REASON TO BELIEVE YOU MAY HAVE ALL BEEN BRAINWASHED--
BRAIN. WASH.
DIRTY.
NO, YOU DON'T UNDERSTAND: I SUSPECT YOU'VE BEEN BROUGHT HERE AGAINST YOUR WILL.
I CAN HELP YOU IF YOU'LL LET ME TRY-- BUT I CAN'T GUARANTEE ANYONE'S SAFETY IF YOU DON'T BACK UP A FEW FEET.
DO YOU **UNDERSTAND** ME?
RAAAAHRR

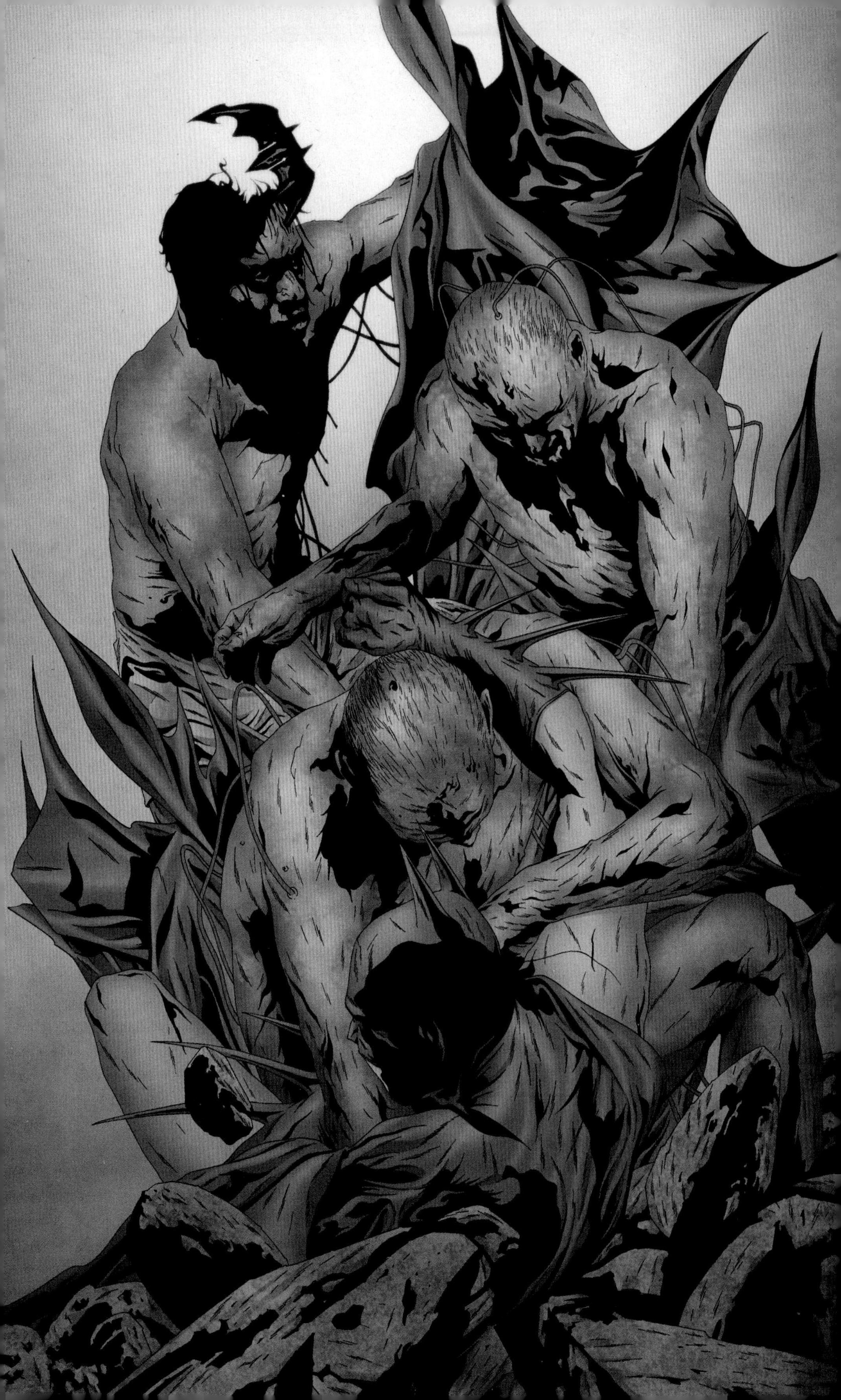

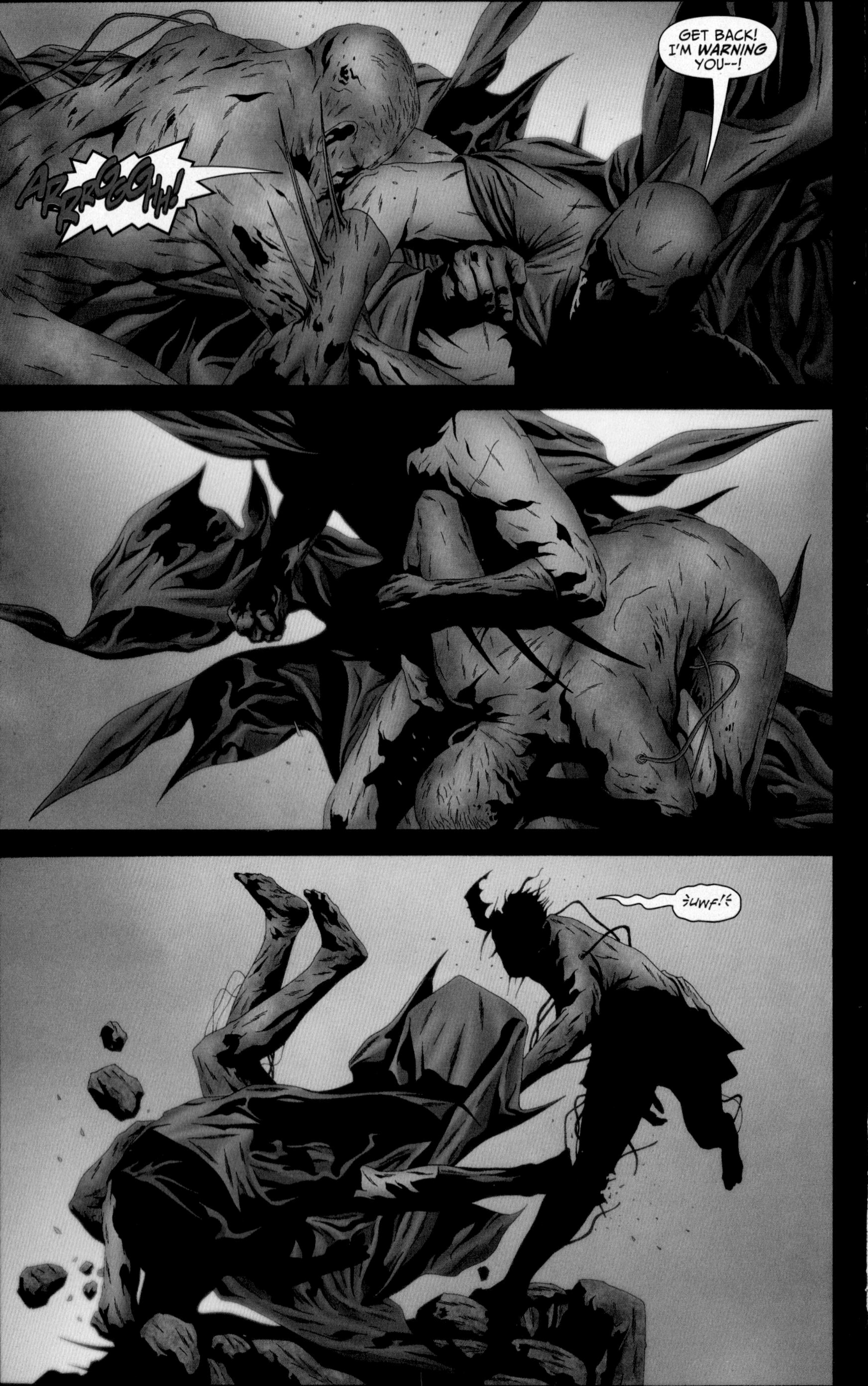
GET BACK! I'M WARNING YOU--!
ARRRGGGHH!
UWF!

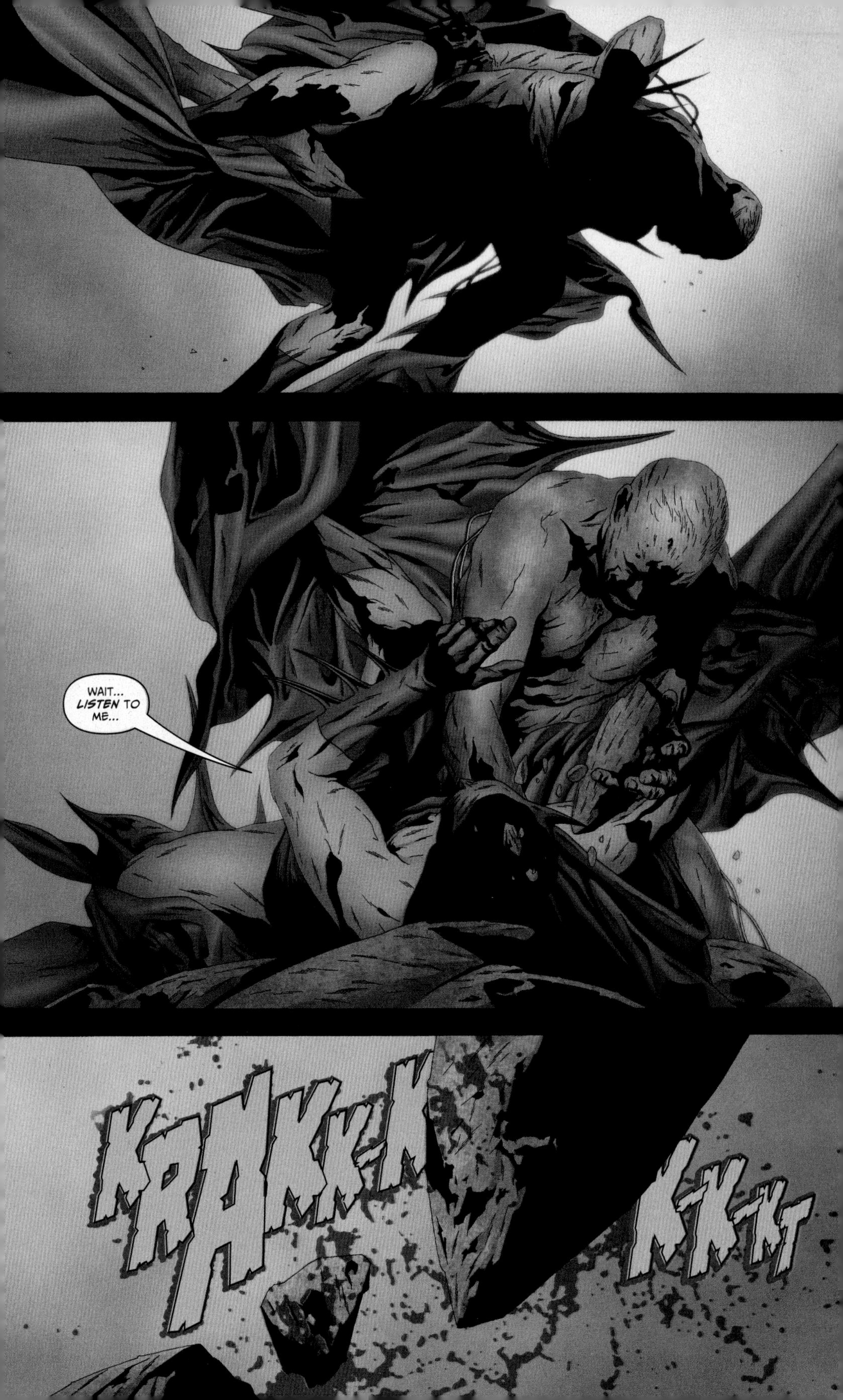
WAIT... LISTEN TO ME...
KRAKKK
KKKT

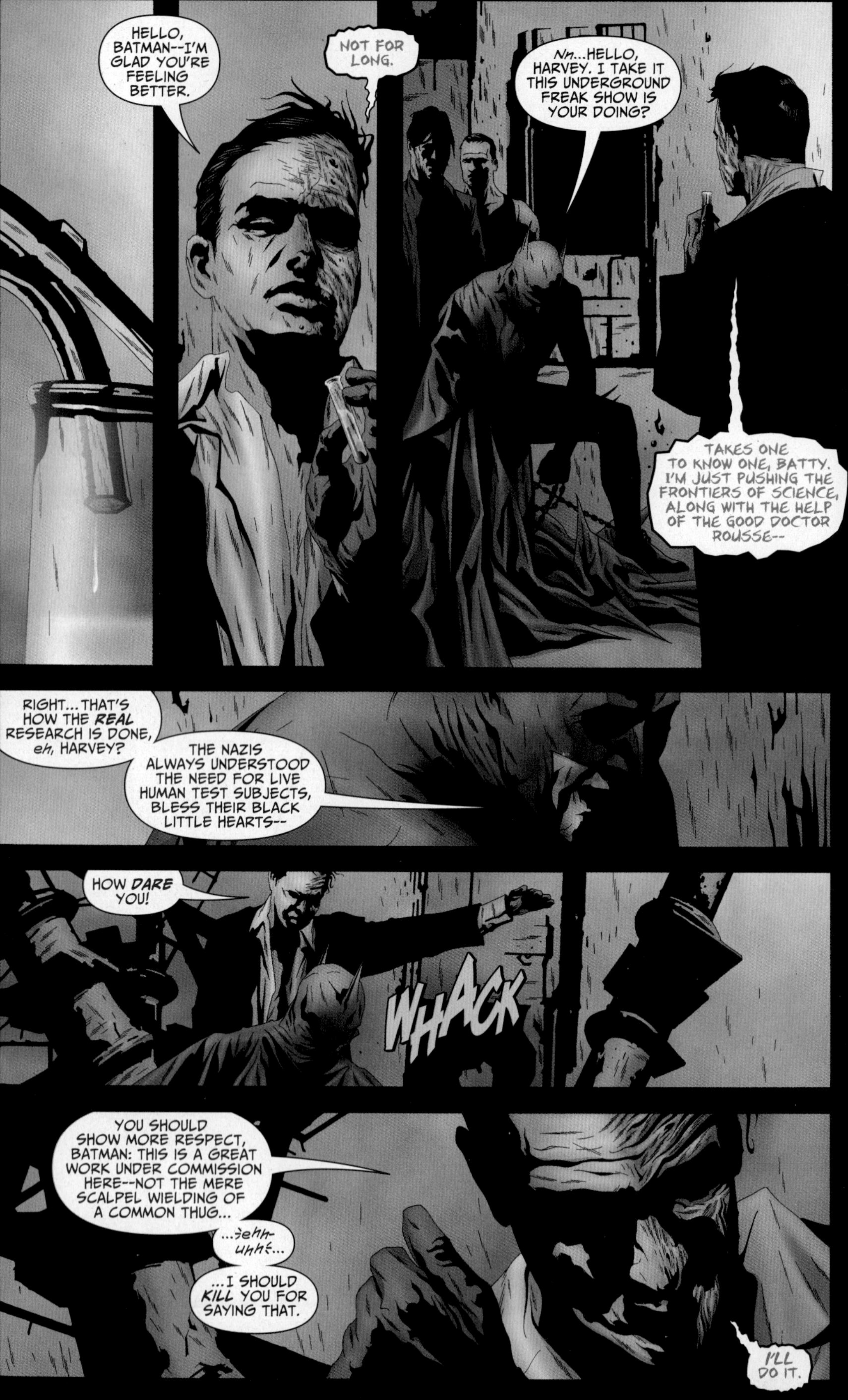
HELLO, BATMAN--I'M GLAD YOU'RE FEELING BETTER.
NOT FOR LONG.
Nn...HELLO, HARVEY. I TAKE IT THIS UNDERGROUND FREAK SHOW IS YOUR DOING?
TAKES ONE TO KNOW ONE, BATTY. I'M JUST PUSHING THE FRONTIERS OF SCIENCE, ALONG WITH THE HELP OF THE GOOD DOCTOR ROUSSE--
RIGHT...THAT'S HOW THE REAL RESEARCH IS DONE, eh, HARVEY?
THE NAZIS ALWAYS UNDERSTOOD THE NEED FOR LIVE HUMAN TEST SUBJECTS, BLESS THEIR BLACK LITTLE HEARTS--
HOW DARE YOU!
WHACK
YOU SHOULD SHOW MORE RESPECT, BATMAN: THIS IS A GREAT WORK UNDER COMMISSION HERE--NOT THE MERE SCALPEL WIELDING OF A COMMON THUG...
...ehh-uhh...
...I SHOULD KILL YOU FOR SAYING THAT.
I'LL DO IT.

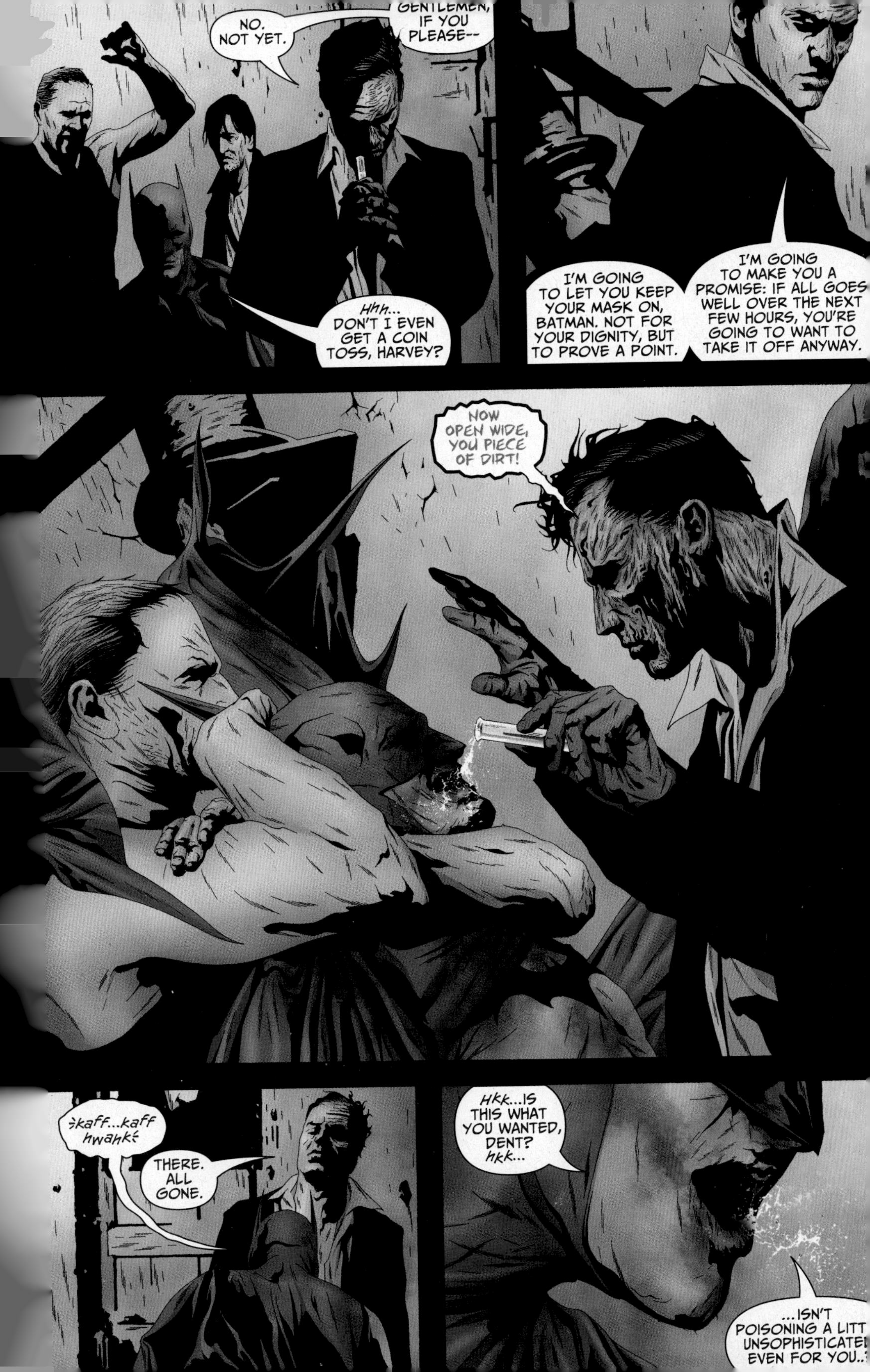
GENTLEMEN, IF YOU PLEASE--
NO. NOT YET.
Hhh... DON'T I EVEN GET A COIN TOSS, HARVEY?
I'M GOING TO LET YOU KEEP YOUR MASK ON, BATMAN. NOT FOR YOUR DIGNITY, BUT TO PROVE A POINT.
I'M GOING TO MAKE YOU A PROMISE: IF ALL GOES WELL OVER THE NEXT FEW HOURS, YOU'RE GOING TO WANT TO TAKE IT OFF ANYWAY.
NOW OPEN WIDE, YOU PIECE OF DIRT!
kaff...kaff hwahk
THERE. ALL GONE.
HKK...IS THIS WHAT YOU WANTED, DENT? hkk...
...ISN'T POISONING A LITT UNSOPHISTICATE EVEN FOR YOU..

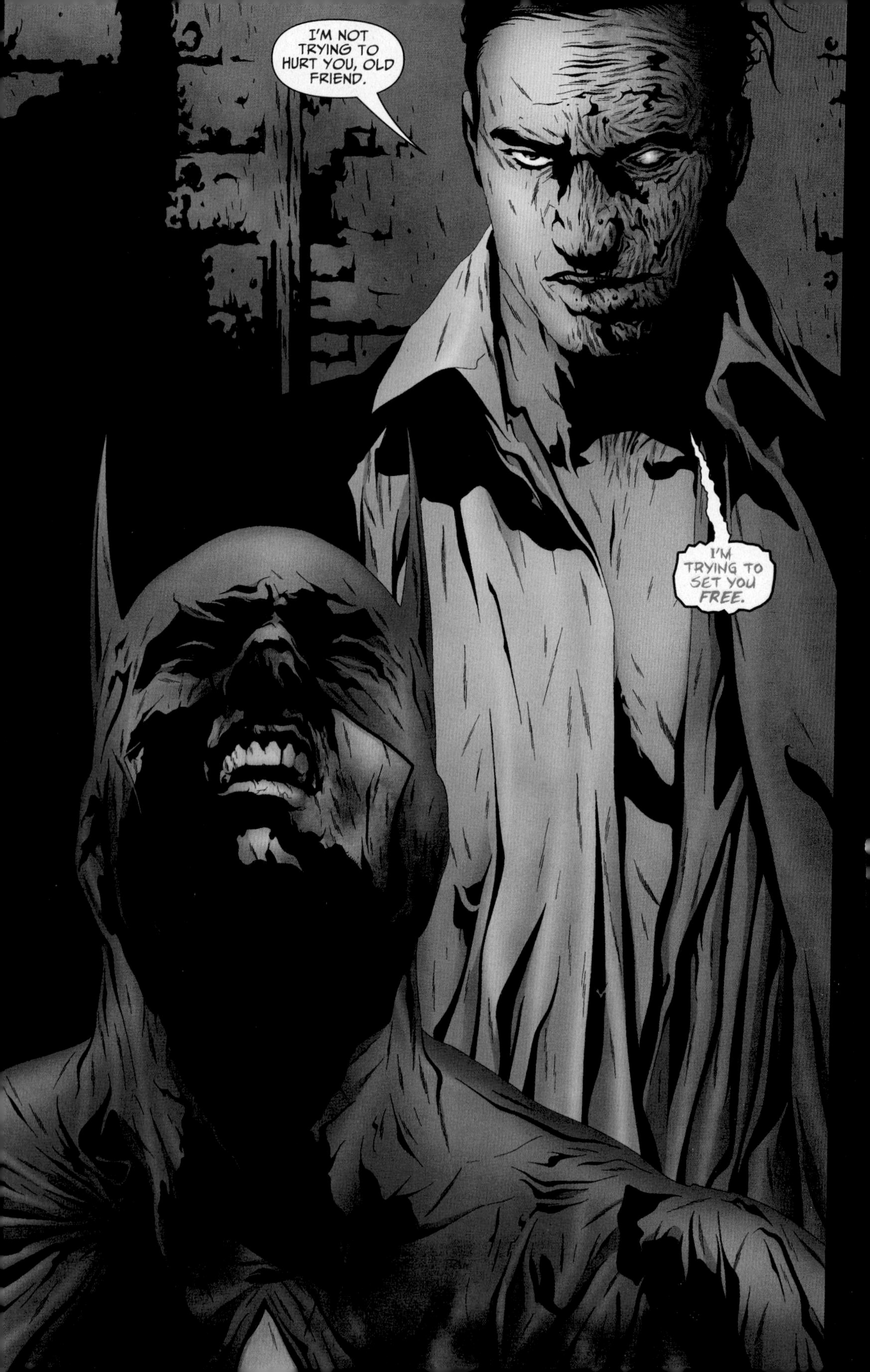
I'M NOT TRYING TO HURT YOU, OLD FRIEND.
I'M TRYING TO SET YOU FREE.

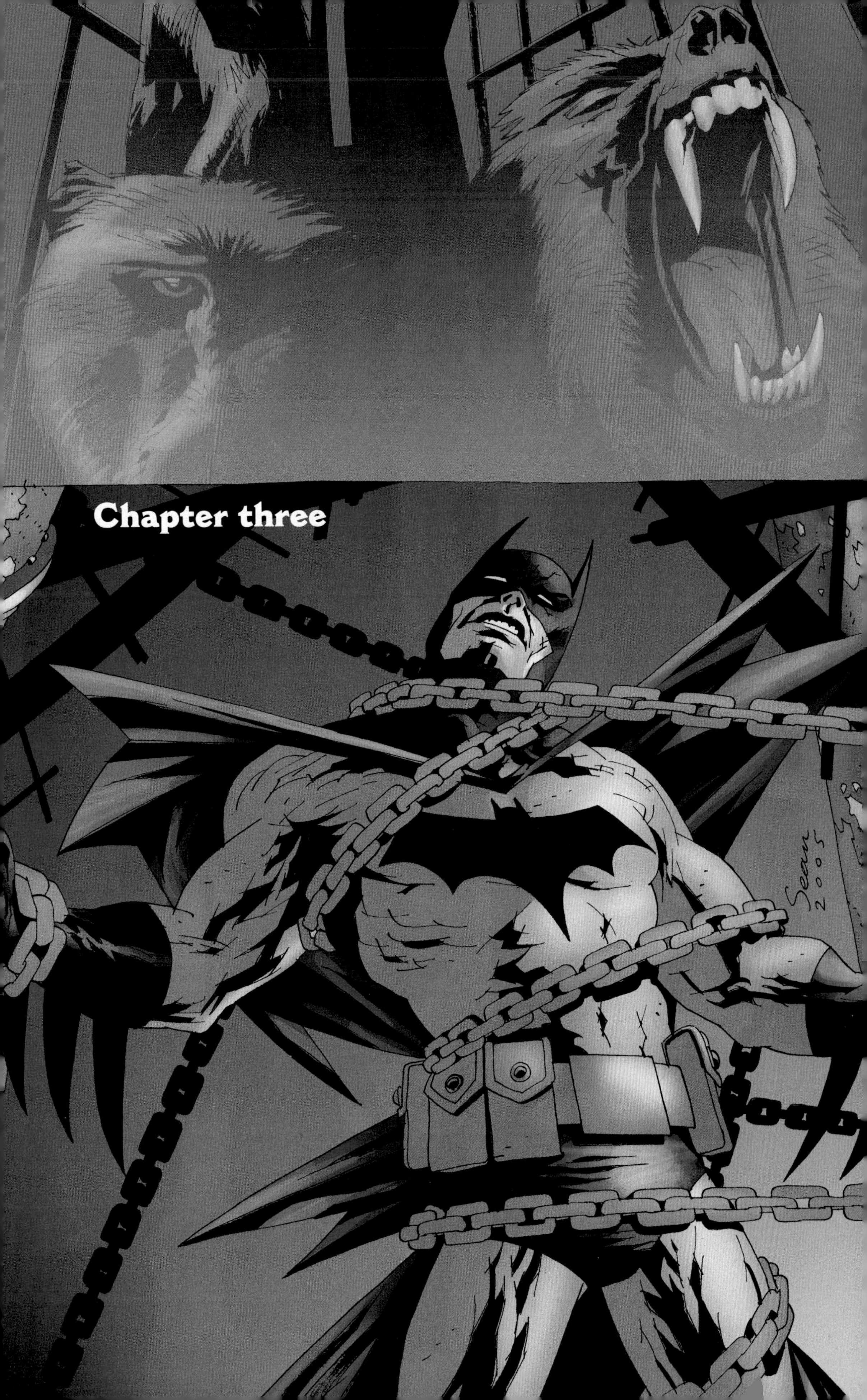
Chapter three
Sean
2005

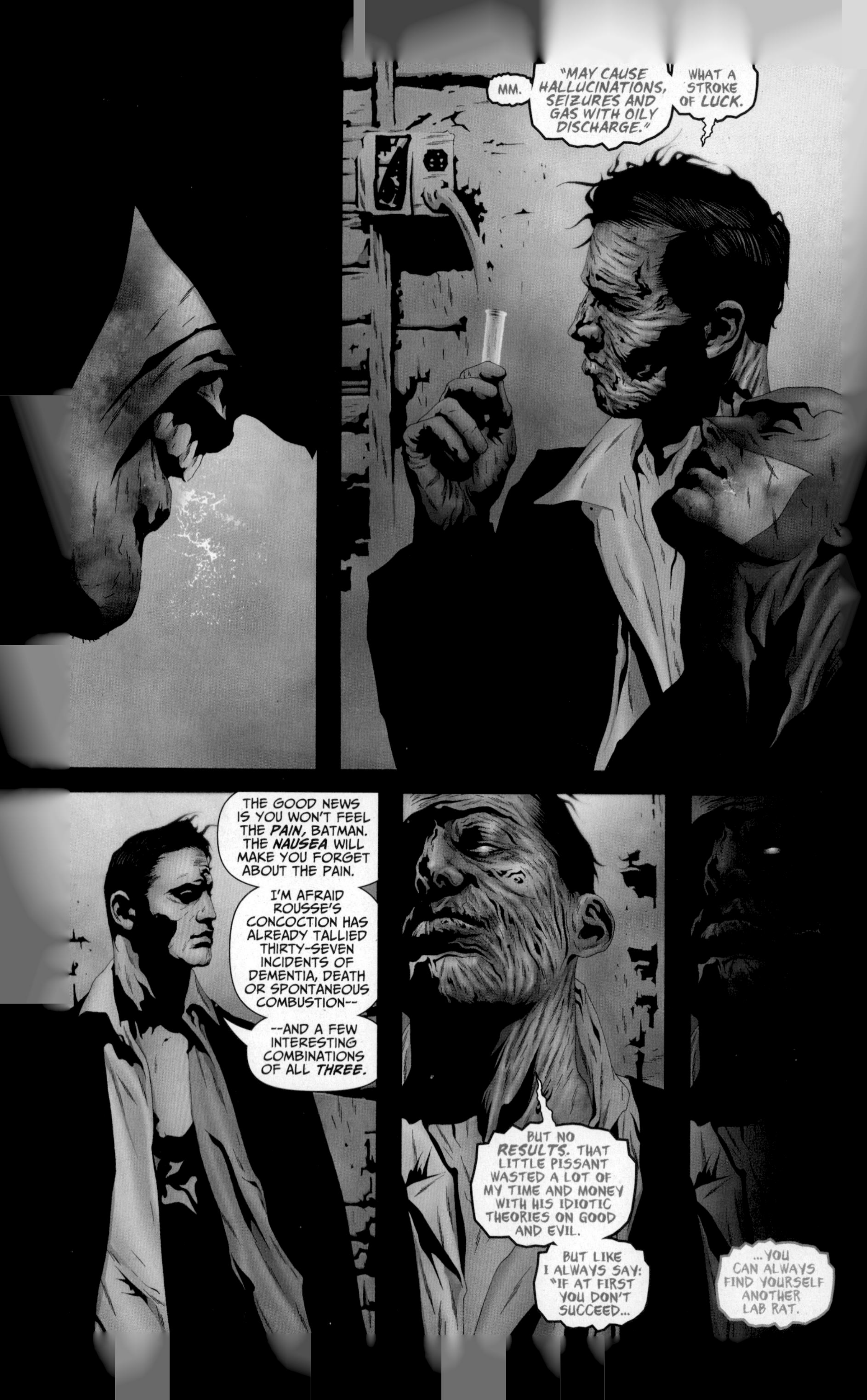
MM.
"MAY CAUSE HALLUCINATIONS, SEIZURES AND GAS WITH OILY DISCHARGE."
WHAT A STROKE OF LUCK.
THE GOOD NEWS IS YOU WON'T FEEL THE PAIN, BATMAN. THE NAUSEA WILL MAKE YOU FORGET ABOUT THE PAIN.
I'M AFRAID ROUSSE'S CONCOCTION HAS ALREADY TALLIED THIRTY-SEVEN INCIDENTS OF DEMENTIA, DEATH OR SPONTANEOUS COMBUSTION--
--AND A FEW INTERESTING COMBINATIONS OF ALL THREE.
BUT NO RESULTS. THAT LITTLE PISSANT WASTED A LOT OF MY TIME AND MONEY WITH HIS IDIOTIC THEORIES ON GOOD AND EVIL.
BUT LIKE I ALWAYS SAY: "IF AT FIRST YOU DON'T SUCCEED...
...YOU CAN ALWAYS FIND YOURSELF ANOTHER LAB RAT.

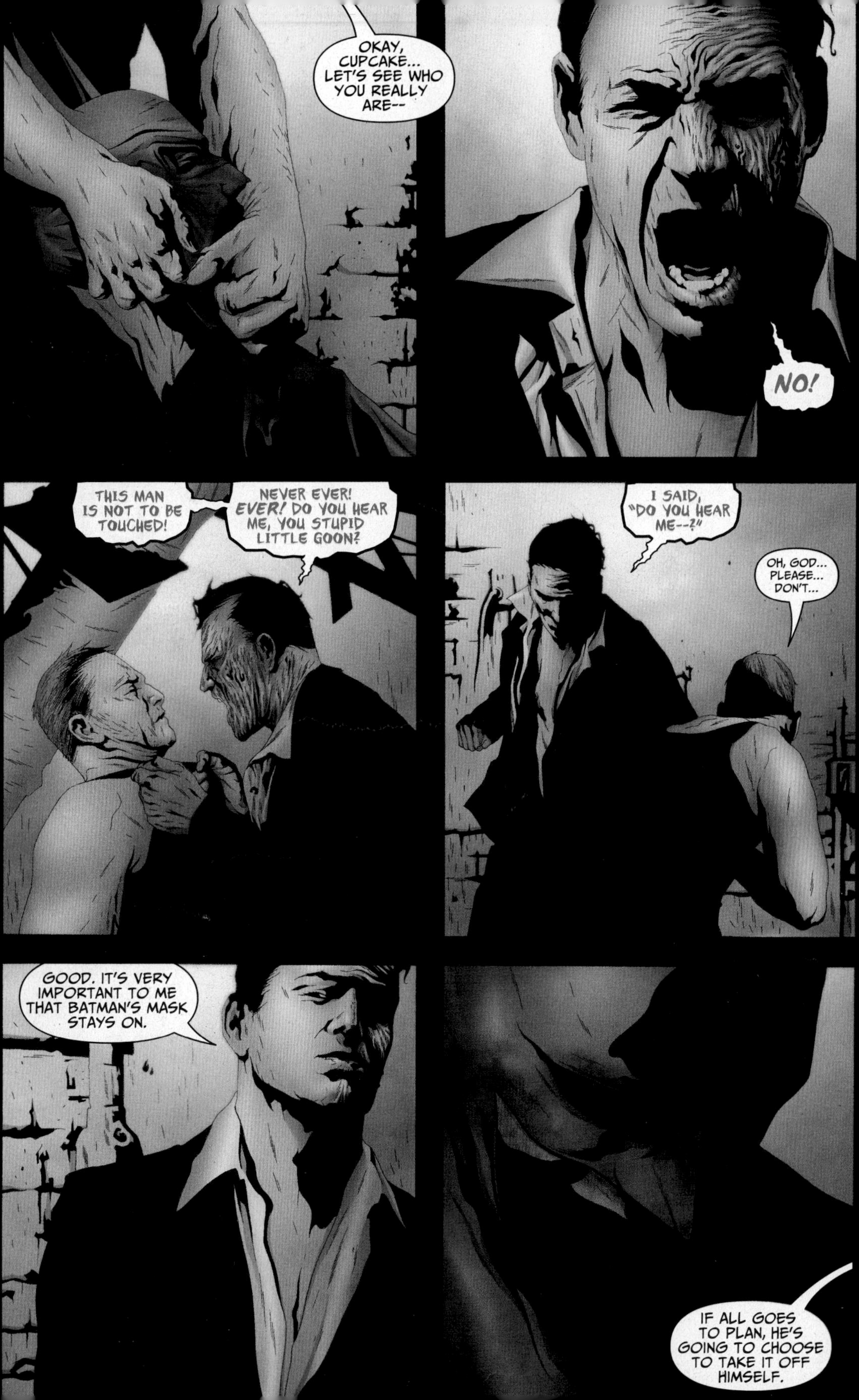
OKAY, CUPCAKE... LET'S SEE WHO YOU REALLY ARE--
NO!
THIS MAN IS NOT TO BE TOUCHED!
NEVER EVER! EVER! DO YOU HEAR ME, YOU STUPID LITTLE GOON?
I SAID, "DO YOU HEAR ME--?"
OH, GOD... PLEASE... DON'T...
GOOD. IT'S VERY IMPORTANT TO ME THAT BATMAN'S MASK STAYS ON.
IF ALL GOES TO PLAN, HE'S GOING TO CHOOSE TO TAKE IT OFF HIMSELF.

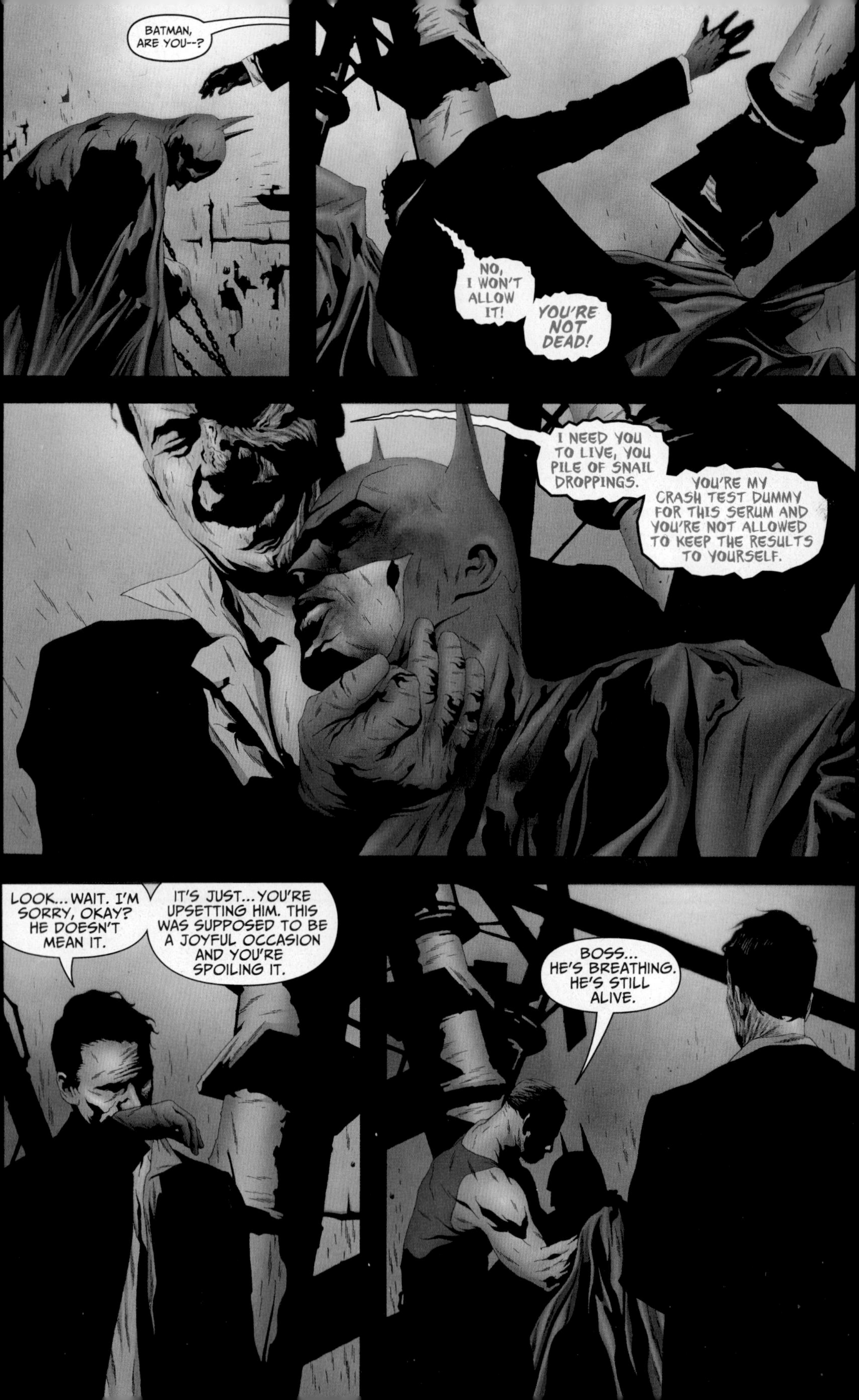
BATMAN, ARE YOU--?
NO, I WON'T ALLOW IT!
YOU'RE NOT DEAD!
I NEED YOU TO LIVE, YOU PILE OF SNAIL DROPPINGS.
YOU'RE MY CRASH TEST DUMMY FOR THIS SERUM AND YOU'RE NOT ALLOWED TO KEEP THE RESULTS TO YOURSELF.
LOOK... WAIT. I'M SORRY, OKAY? HE DOESN'T MEAN IT.
IT'S JUST... YOU'RE UPSETTING HIM. THIS WAS SUPPOSED TO BE A JOYFUL OCCASION AND YOU'RE SPOILING IT.
BOSS... HE'S BREATHING. HE'S STILL ALIVE.

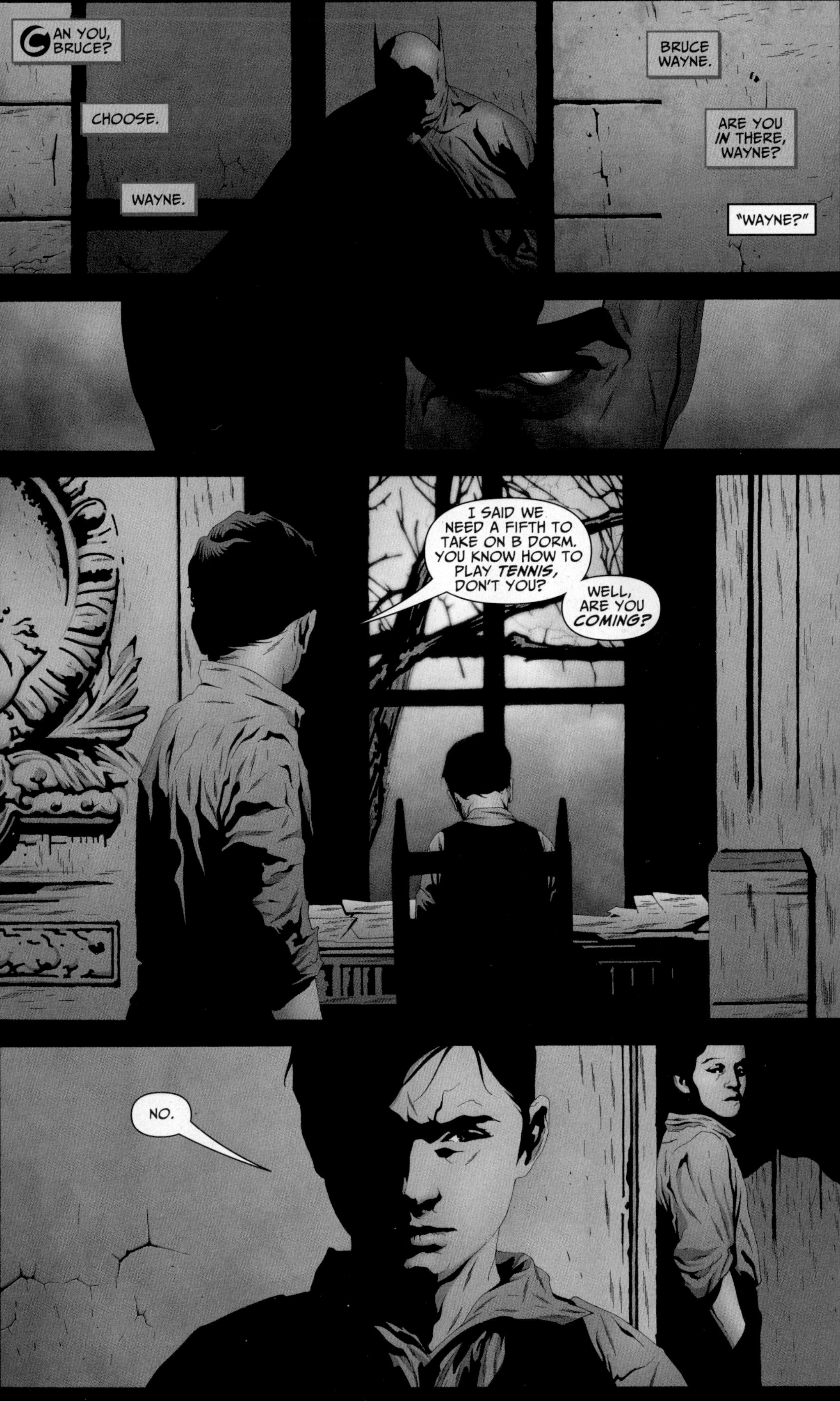
CAN YOU, BRUCE?
CHOOSE.
WAYNE.
BRUCE WAYNE.
ARE YOU IN THERE, WAYNE?
"WAYNE?"
I SAID WE NEED A FIFTH TO TAKE ON B DORM. YOU KNOW HOW TO PLAY TENNIS, DON'T YOU?
WELL, ARE YOU COMING?
NO.

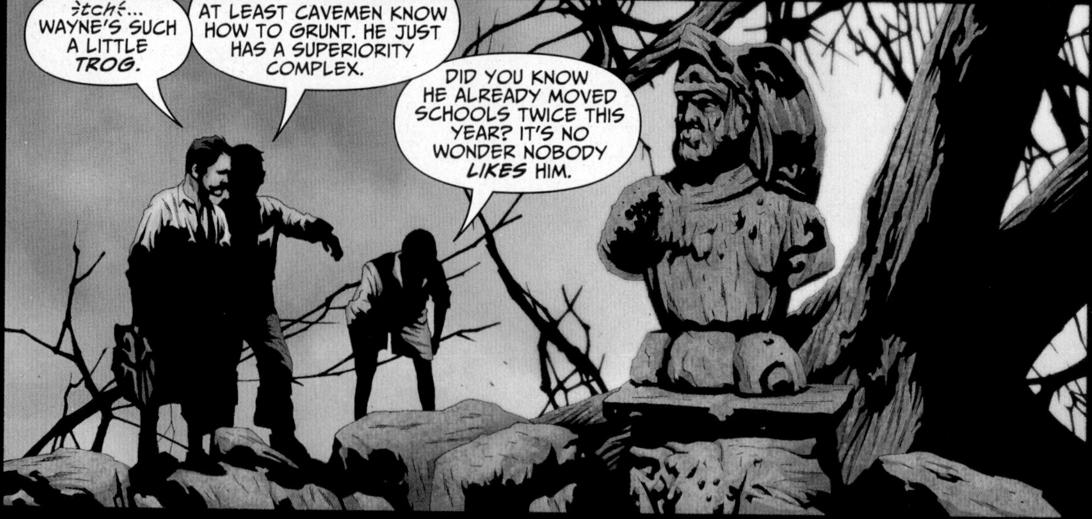

≈tch≈... WAYNE'S SUCH A LITTLE TROG.
AT LEAST CAVEMEN KNOW HOW TO GRUNT. HE JUST HAS A SUPERIORITY COMPLEX.
DID YOU KNOW HE ALREADY MOVED SCHOOLS TWICE THIS YEAR? IT'S NO WONDER NOBODY LIKES HIM.

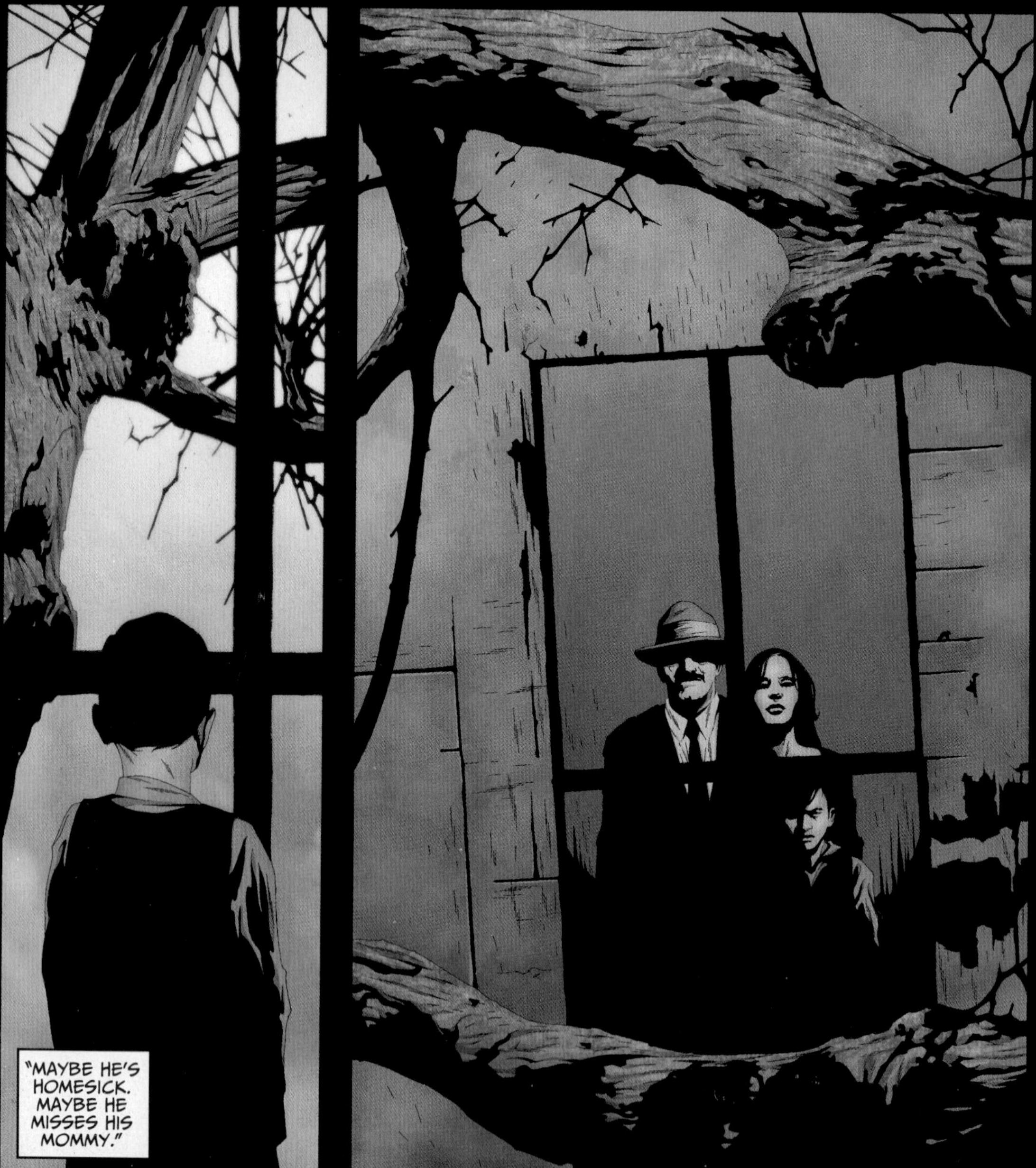

"MAYBE HE'S HOMESICK. MAYBE HE MISSES HIS MOMMY."

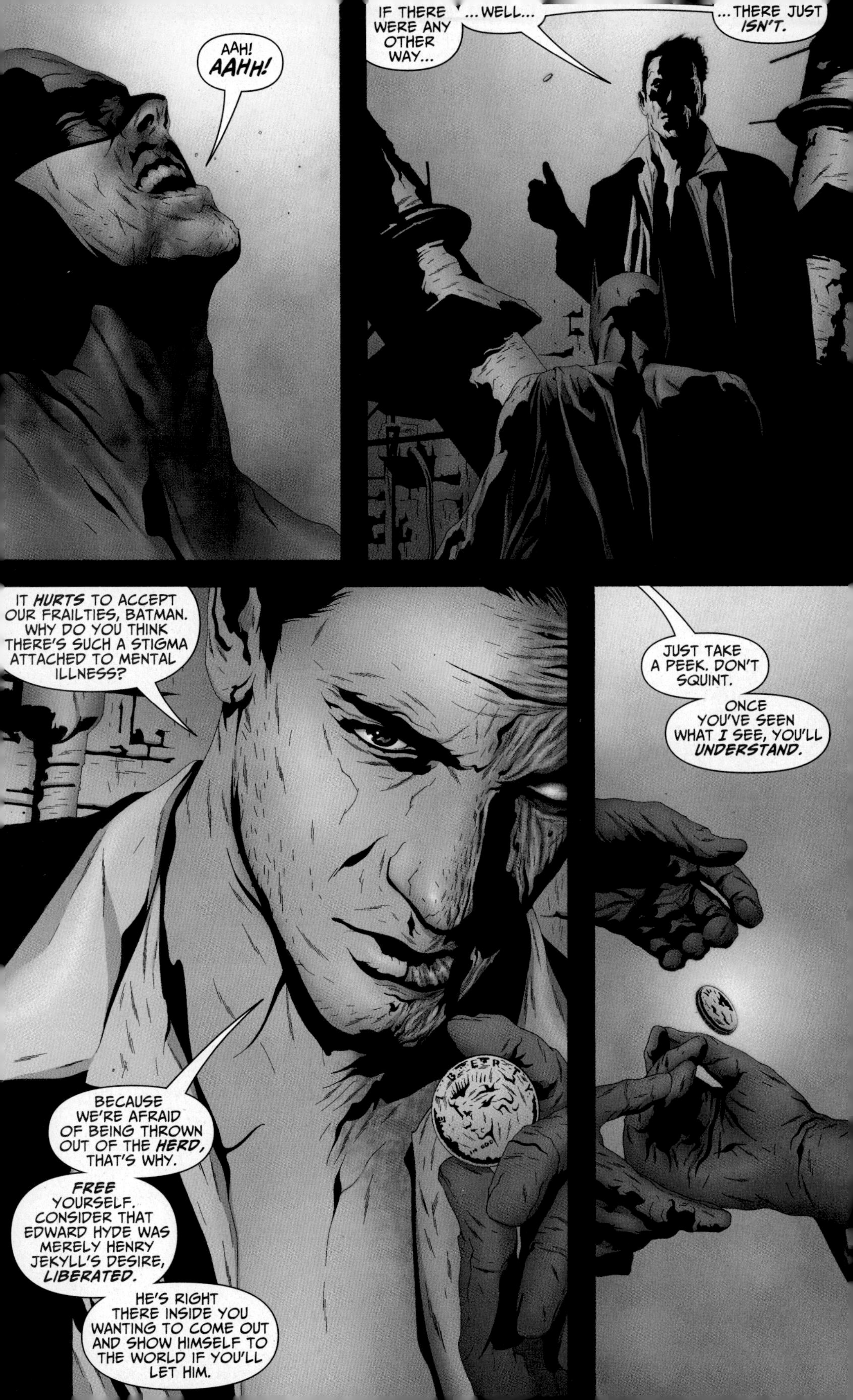
AAH! AAHH!
IF THERE WERE ANY OTHER WAY...
...WELL...
...THERE JUST ISN'T.
IT HURTS TO ACCEPT OUR FRAILTIES, BATMAN. WHY DO YOU THINK THERE'S SUCH A STIGMA ATTACHED TO MENTAL ILLNESS?
BECAUSE WE'RE AFRAID OF BEING THROWN OUT OF THE HERD, THAT'S WHY.
FREE YOURSELF. CONSIDER THAT EDWARD HYDE WAS MERELY HENRY JEKYLL'S DESIRE, LIBERATED.
HE'S RIGHT THERE INSIDE YOU WANTING TO COME OUT AND SHOW HIMSELF TO THE WORLD IF YOU'LL LET HIM.
JUST TAKE A PEEK. DON'T SQUINT.
ONCE YOU'VE SEEN WHAT I SEE, YOU'LL UNDERSTAND.

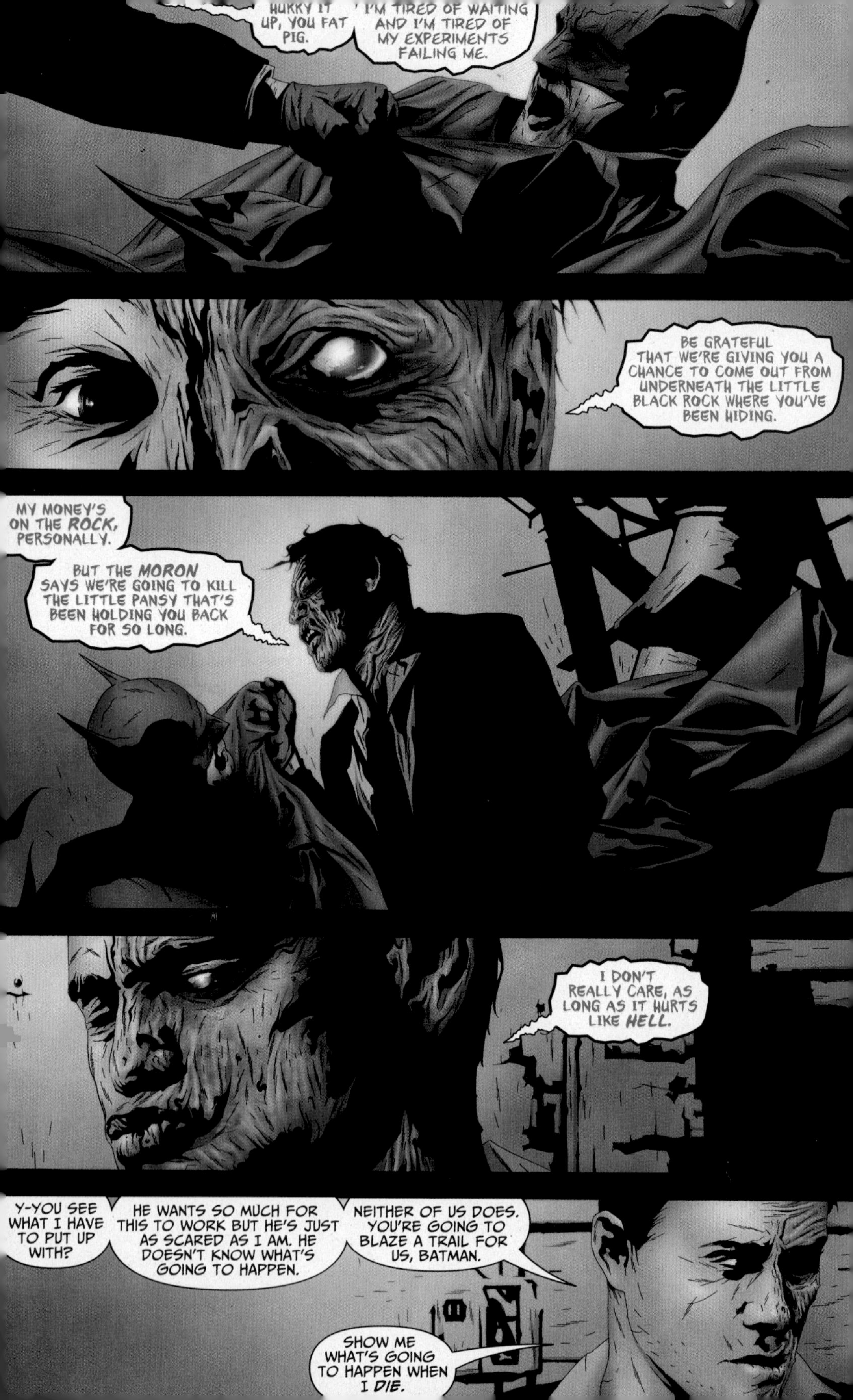
HURRY IT UP, YOU FAT PIG.
I'M TIRED OF WAITING AND I'M TIRED OF MY EXPERIMENTS FAILING ME.
BE GRATEFUL THAT WE'RE GIVING YOU A CHANCE TO COME OUT FROM UNDERNEATH THE LITTLE BLACK ROCK WHERE YOU'VE BEEN HIDING.
MY MONEY'S ON THE ROCK, PERSONALLY.
BUT THE MORON SAYS WE'RE GOING TO KILL THE LITTLE PANSY THAT'S BEEN HOLDING YOU BACK FOR SO LONG.
I DON'T REALLY CARE, AS LONG AS IT HURTS LIKE HELL.
Y-YOU SEE WHAT I HAVE TO PUT UP WITH?
HE WANTS SO MUCH FOR THIS TO WORK BUT HE'S JUST AS SCARED AS I AM. HE DOESN'T KNOW WHAT'S GOING TO HAPPEN.
NEITHER OF US DOES. YOU'RE GOING TO BLAZE A TRAIL FOR US, BATMAN.
SHOW ME WHAT'S GOING TO HAPPEN WHEN I DIE.

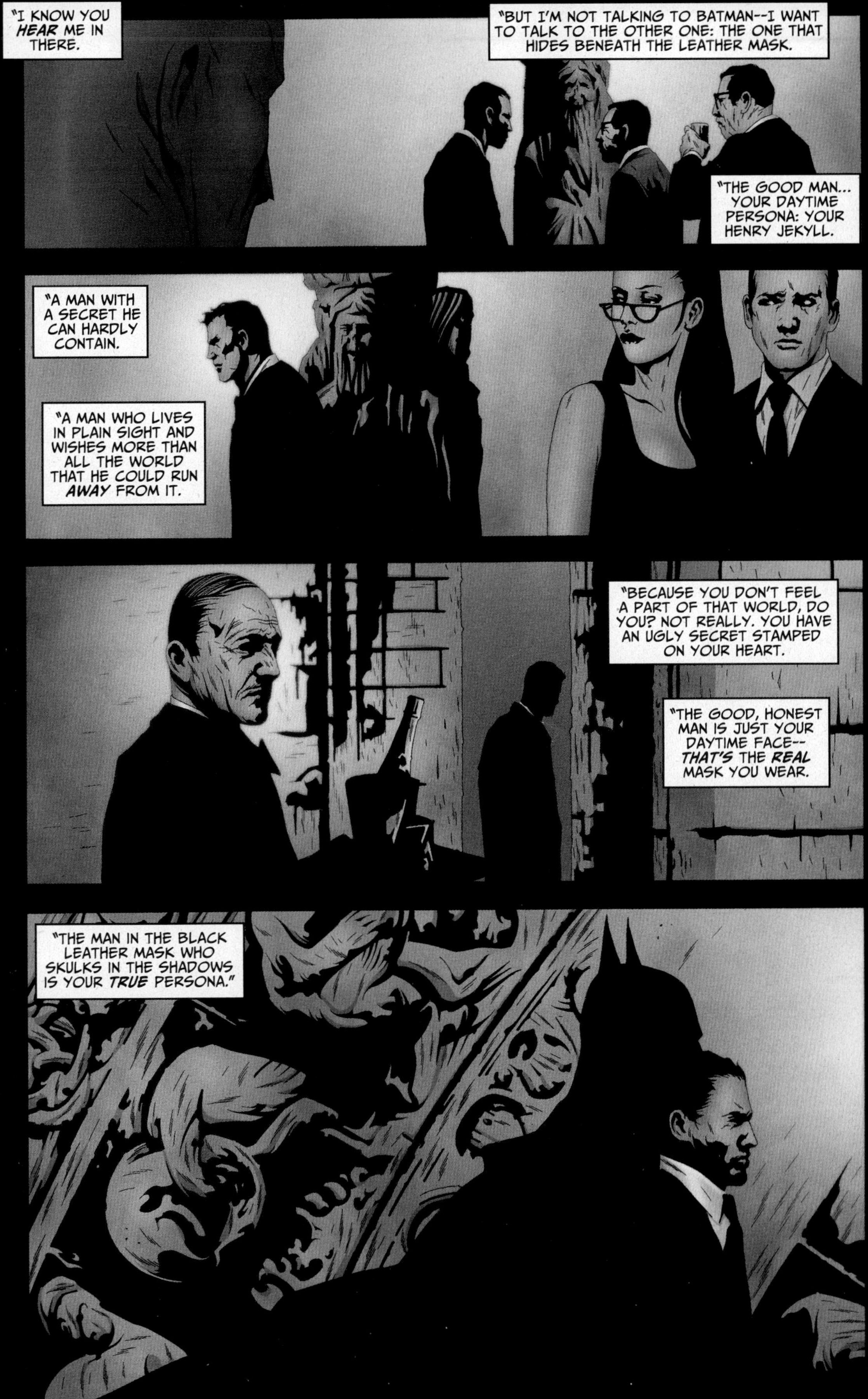
"I KNOW YOU HEAR ME IN THERE.
"BUT I'M NOT TALKING TO BATMAN--I WANT TO TALK TO THE OTHER ONE: THE ONE THAT HIDES BENEATH THE LEATHER MASK.
"THE GOOD MAN... YOUR DAYTIME PERSONA: YOUR HENRY JEKYLL.
"A MAN WITH A SECRET HE CAN HARDLY CONTAIN.
"A MAN WHO LIVES IN PLAIN SIGHT AND WISHES MORE THAN ALL THE WORLD THAT HE COULD RUN AWAY FROM IT.
"BECAUSE YOU DON'T FEEL A PART OF THAT WORLD, DO YOU? NOT REALLY. YOU HAVE AN UGLY SECRET STAMPED ON YOUR HEART.
"THE GOOD, HONEST MAN IS JUST YOUR DAYTIME FACE--THAT'S THE REAL MASK YOU WEAR.
"THE MAN IN THE BLACK LEATHER MASK WHO SKULKS IN THE SHADOWS IS YOUR TRUE PERSONA."

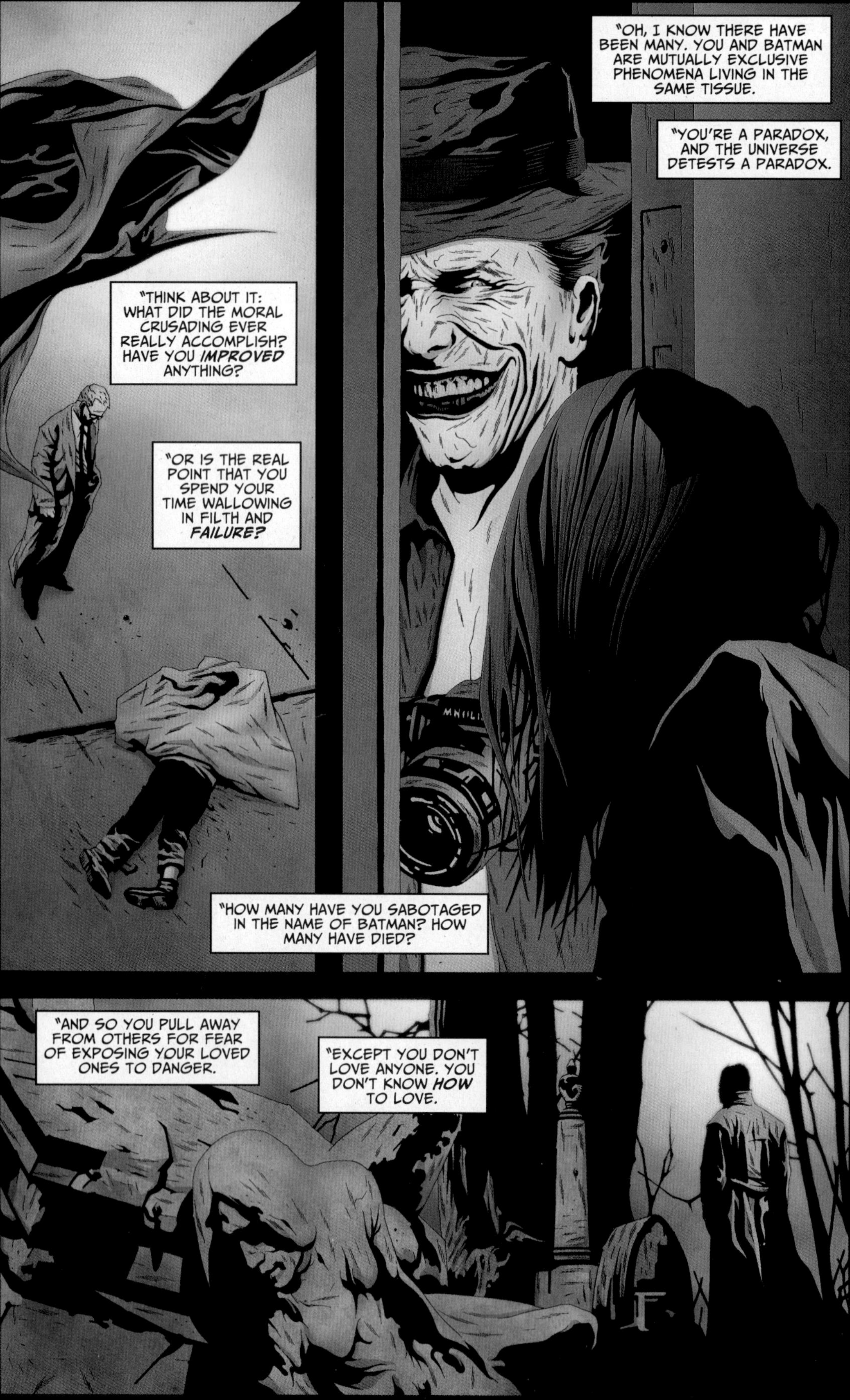

"THINK ABOUT IT: WHAT DID THE MORAL CRUSADING EVER REALLY ACCOMPLISH? HAVE YOU *IMPROVED* ANYTHING?
"OR IS THE REAL POINT THAT YOU SPEND YOUR TIME WALLOWING IN FILTH AND ***FAILURE?***
"OH, I KNOW THERE HAVE BEEN MANY. YOU AND BATMAN ARE MUTUALLY EXCLUSIVE PHENOMENA LIVING IN THE SAME TISSUE.
"YOU'RE A PARADOX, AND THE UNIVERSE DETESTS A PARADOX.
"HOW MANY HAVE YOU SABOTAGED IN THE NAME OF BATMAN? HOW MANY HAVE DIED?
"AND SO YOU PULL AWAY FROM OTHERS FOR FEAR OF EXPOSING YOUR LOVED ONES TO DANGER.
"EXCEPT YOU DON'T LOVE ANYONE. YOU DON'T KNOW ***HOW*** TO LOVE.

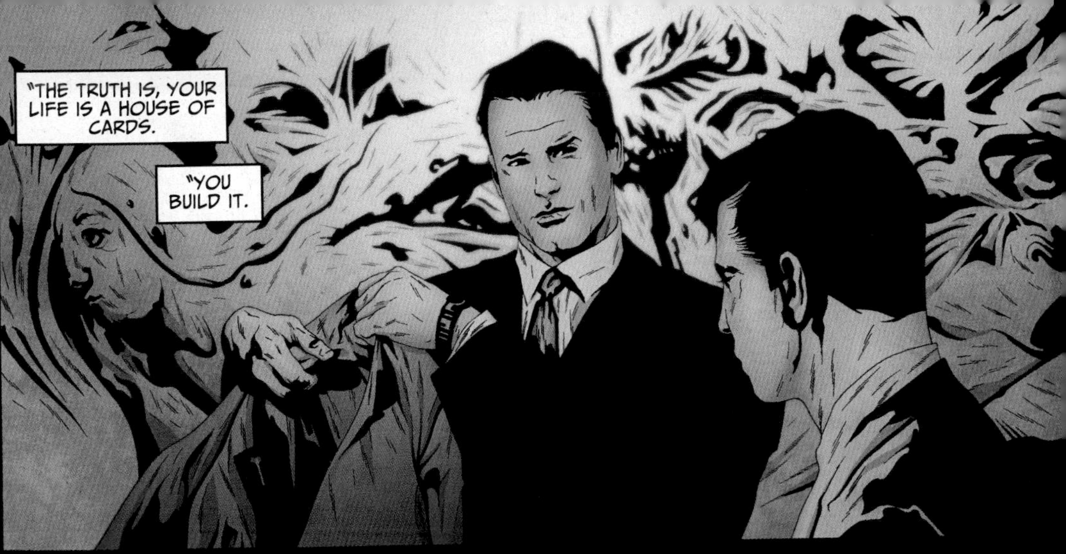
"THE TRUTH IS, YOUR LIFE IS A HOUSE OF CARDS.
"YOU BUILD IT.

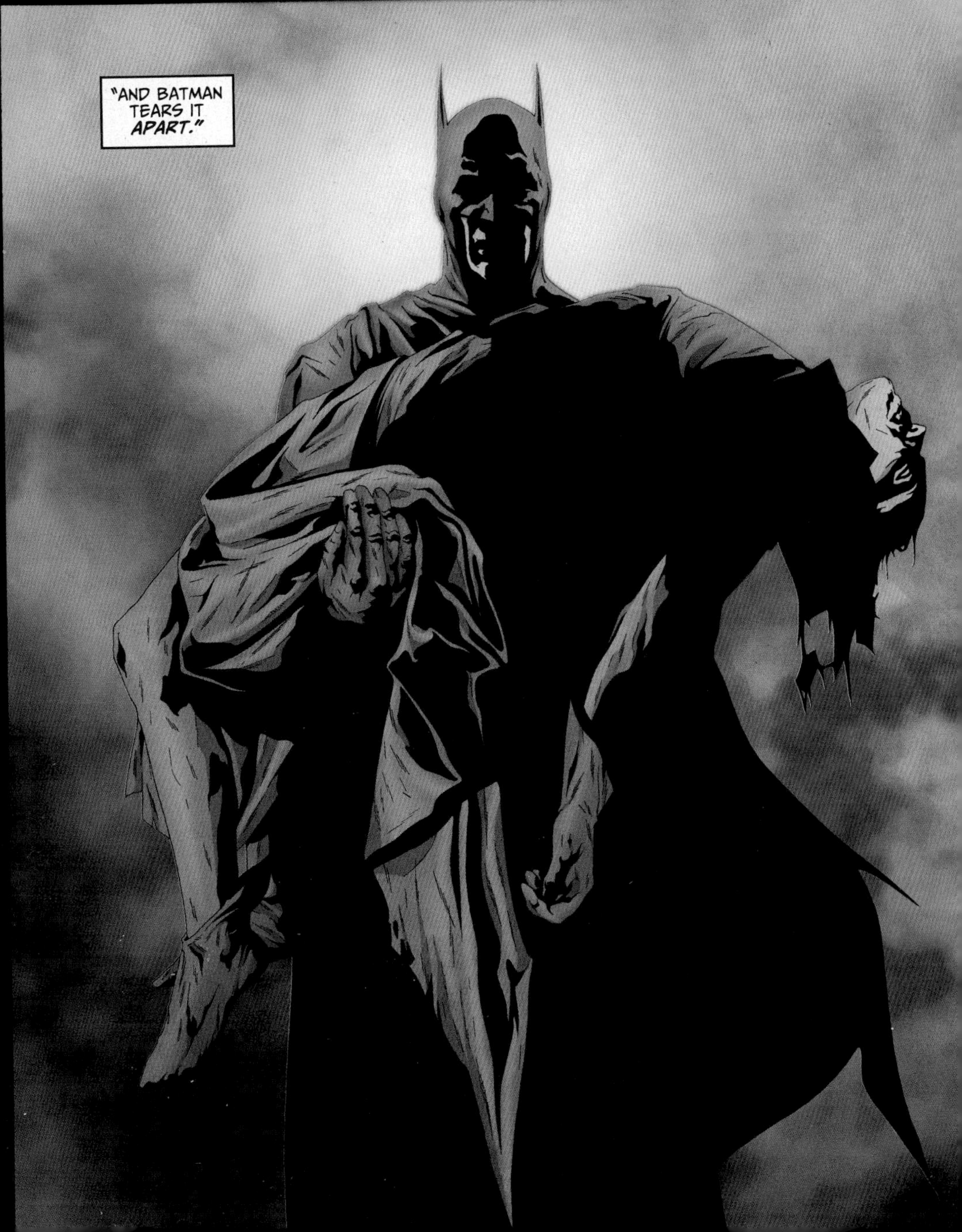
"AND BATMAN TEARS IT APART."

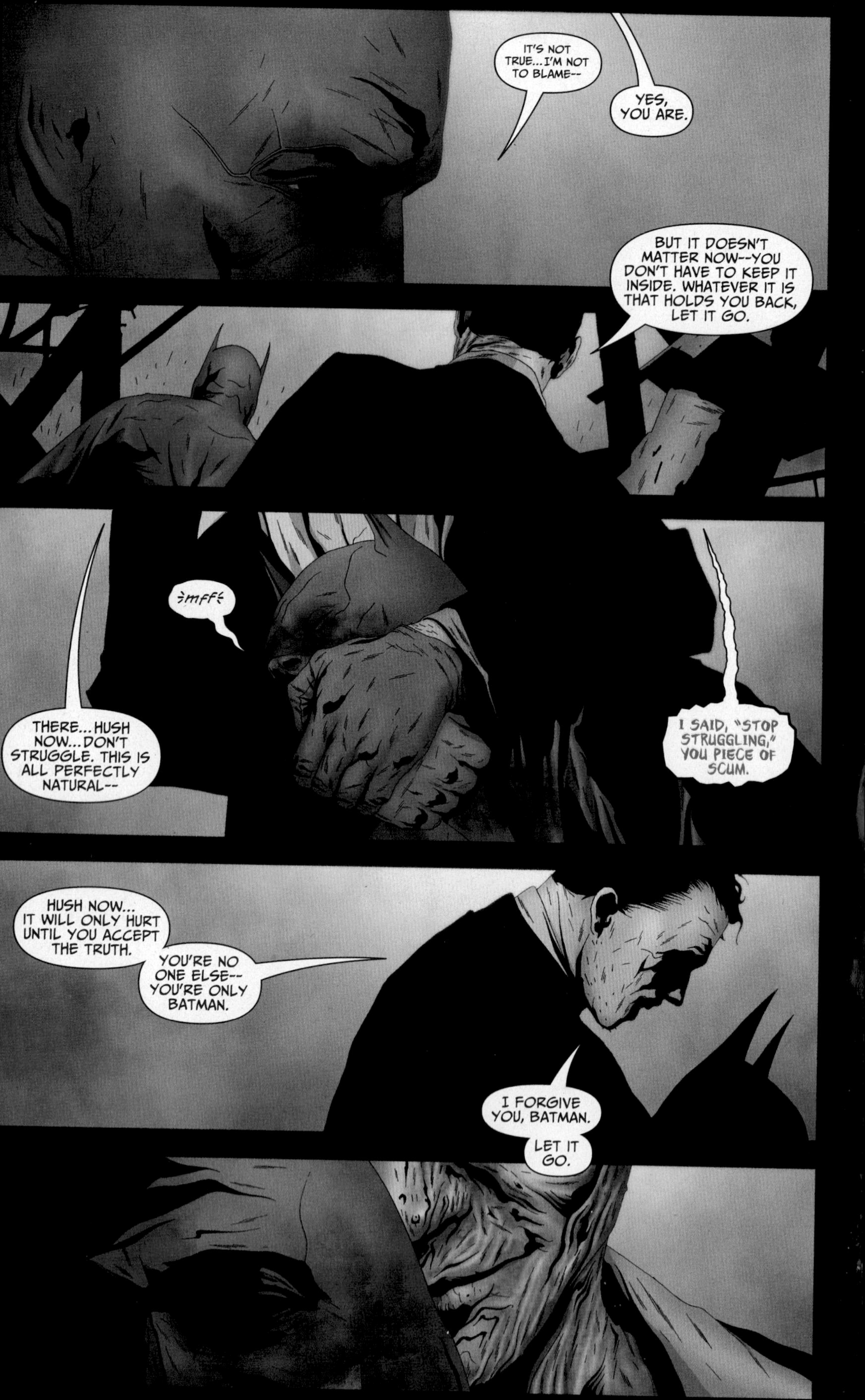
IT'S NOT TRUE... I'M NOT TO BLAME--
YES, YOU ARE.
BUT IT DOESN'T MATTER NOW--YOU DON'T HAVE TO KEEP IT INSIDE. WHATEVER IT IS THAT HOLDS YOU BACK, LET IT GO.
mff
THERE... HUSH NOW... DON'T STRUGGLE. THIS IS ALL PERFECTLY NATURAL--
I SAID, "STOP STRUGGLING," YOU PIECE OF SCUM.
HUSH NOW... IT WILL ONLY HURT UNTIL YOU ACCEPT THE TRUTH.
YOU'RE NO ONE ELSE-- YOU'RE ONLY BATMAN.
I FORGIVE YOU, BATMAN.
LET IT GO.

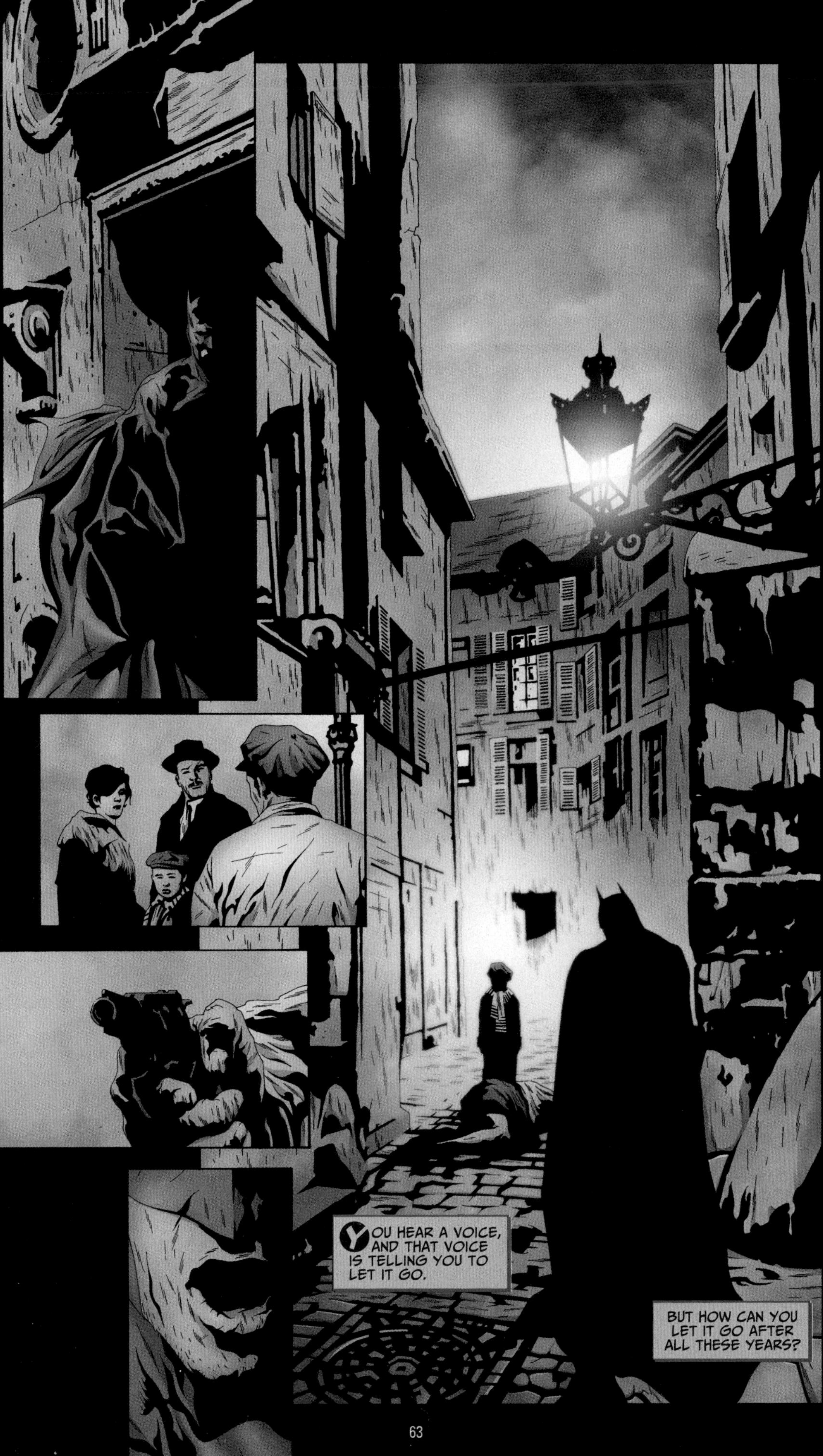
YOU HEAR A VOICE, AND THAT VOICE IS TELLING YOU TO LET IT GO.
BUT HOW CAN YOU LET IT GO AFTER ALL THESE YEARS?

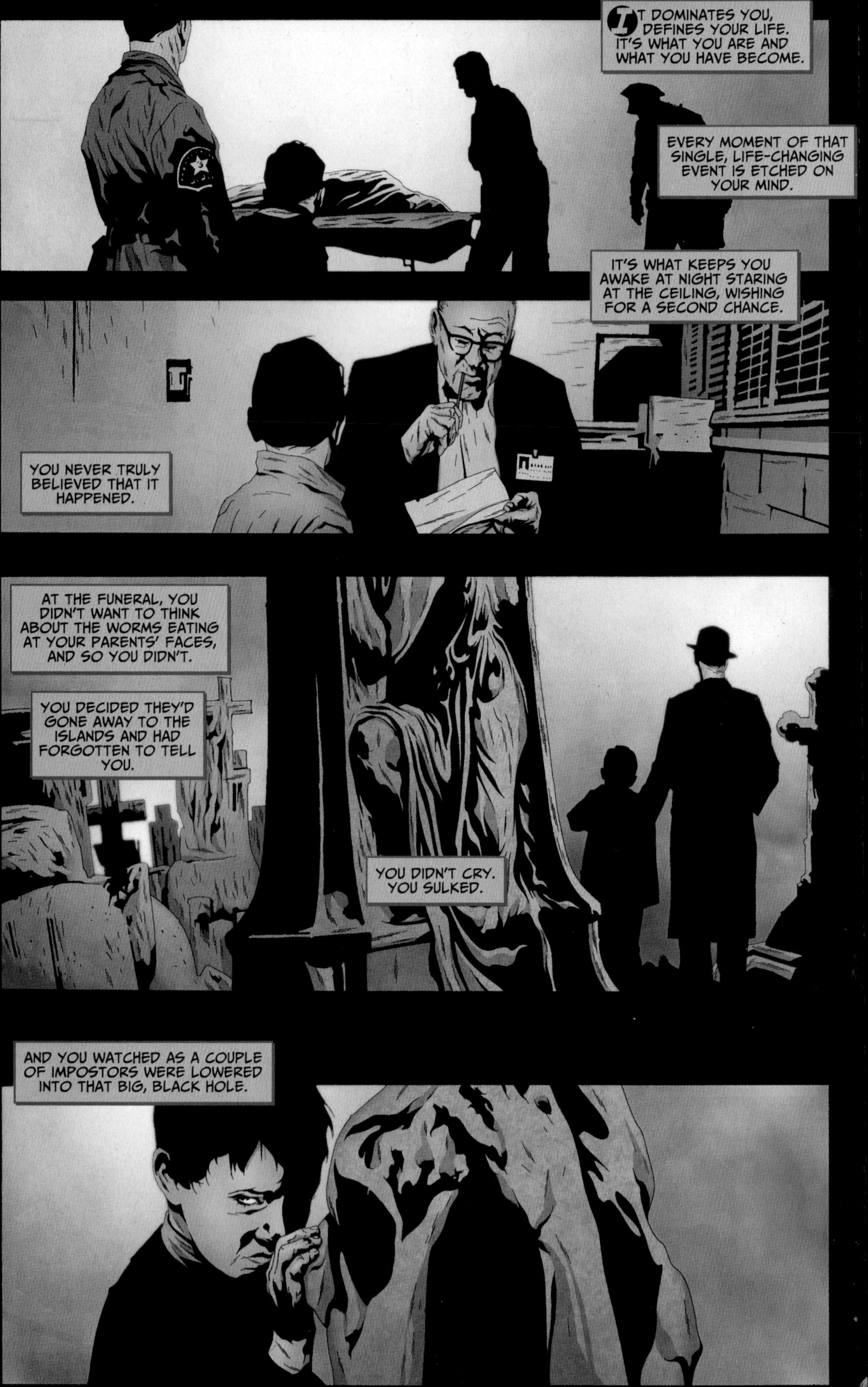
IT DOMINATES YOU, DEFINES YOUR LIFE. IT'S WHAT YOU ARE AND WHAT YOU HAVE BECOME.
EVERY MOMENT OF THAT SINGLE, LIFE-CHANGING EVENT IS ETCHED ON YOUR MIND.
IT'S WHAT KEEPS YOU AWAKE AT NIGHT STARING AT THE CEILING, WISHING FOR A SECOND CHANCE.
YOU NEVER TRULY BELIEVED THAT IT HAPPENED.
AT THE FUNERAL, YOU DIDN'T WANT TO THINK ABOUT THE WORMS EATING AT YOUR PARENTS' FACES, AND SO YOU DIDN'T.
YOU DECIDED THEY'D GONE AWAY TO THE ISLANDS AND HAD FORGOTTEN TO TELL YOU.
YOU DIDN'T CRY. YOU SULKED.
AND YOU WATCHED AS A COUPLE OF IMPOSTORS WERE LOWERED INTO THAT BIG, BLACK HOLE.

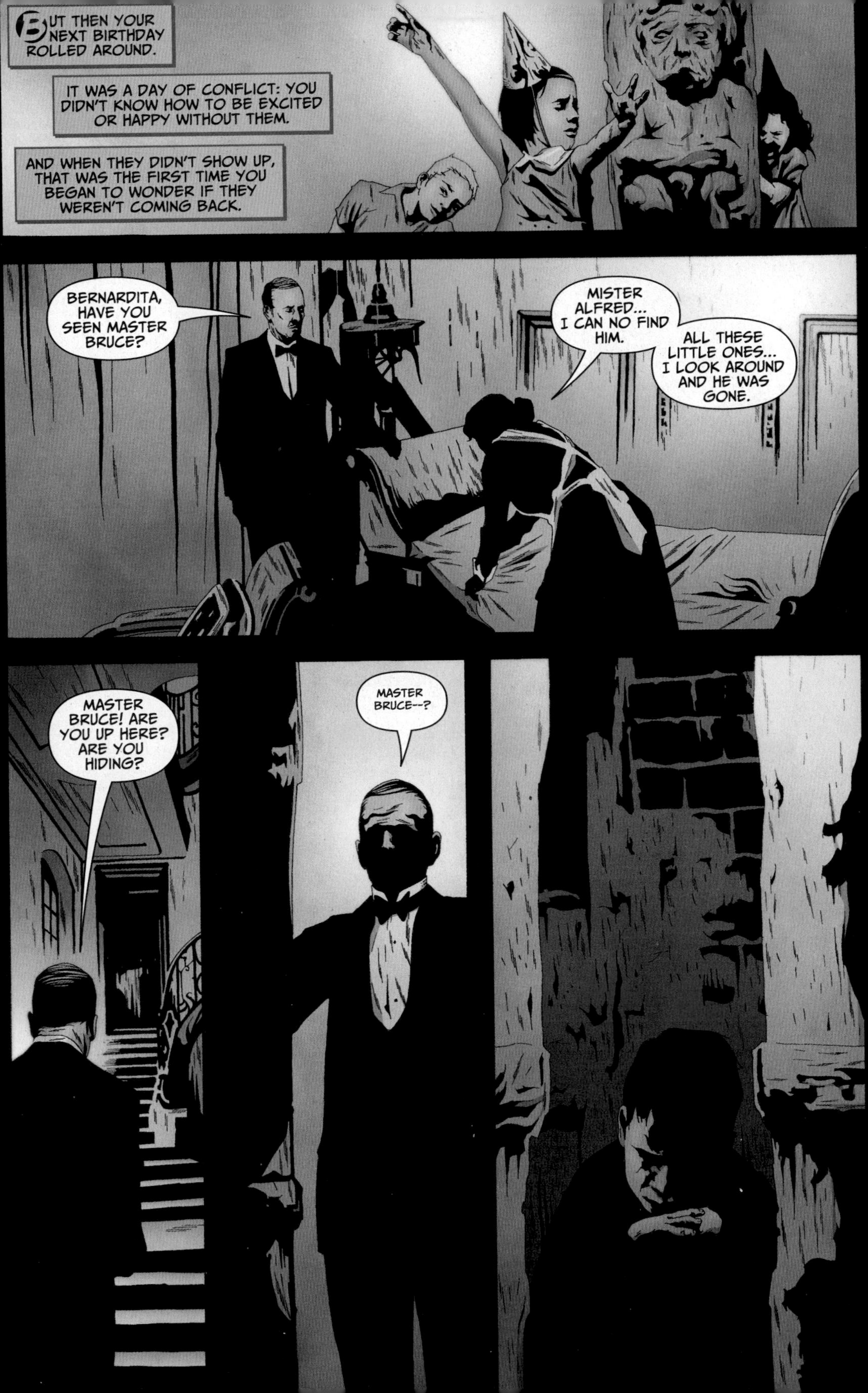
BUT THEN YOUR NEXT BIRTHDAY ROLLED AROUND.
IT WAS A DAY OF CONFLICT: YOU DIDN'T KNOW HOW TO BE EXCITED OR HAPPY WITHOUT THEM.
AND WHEN THEY DIDN'T SHOW UP, THAT WAS THE FIRST TIME YOU BEGAN TO WONDER IF THEY WEREN'T COMING BACK.
BERNARDITA, HAVE YOU SEEN MASTER BRUCE?
MISTER ALFRED... I CAN NO FIND HIM.
ALL THESE LITTLE ONES... I LOOK AROUND AND HE WAS GONE.
MASTER BRUCE! ARE YOU UP HERE? ARE YOU HIDING?
MASTER BRUCE--?

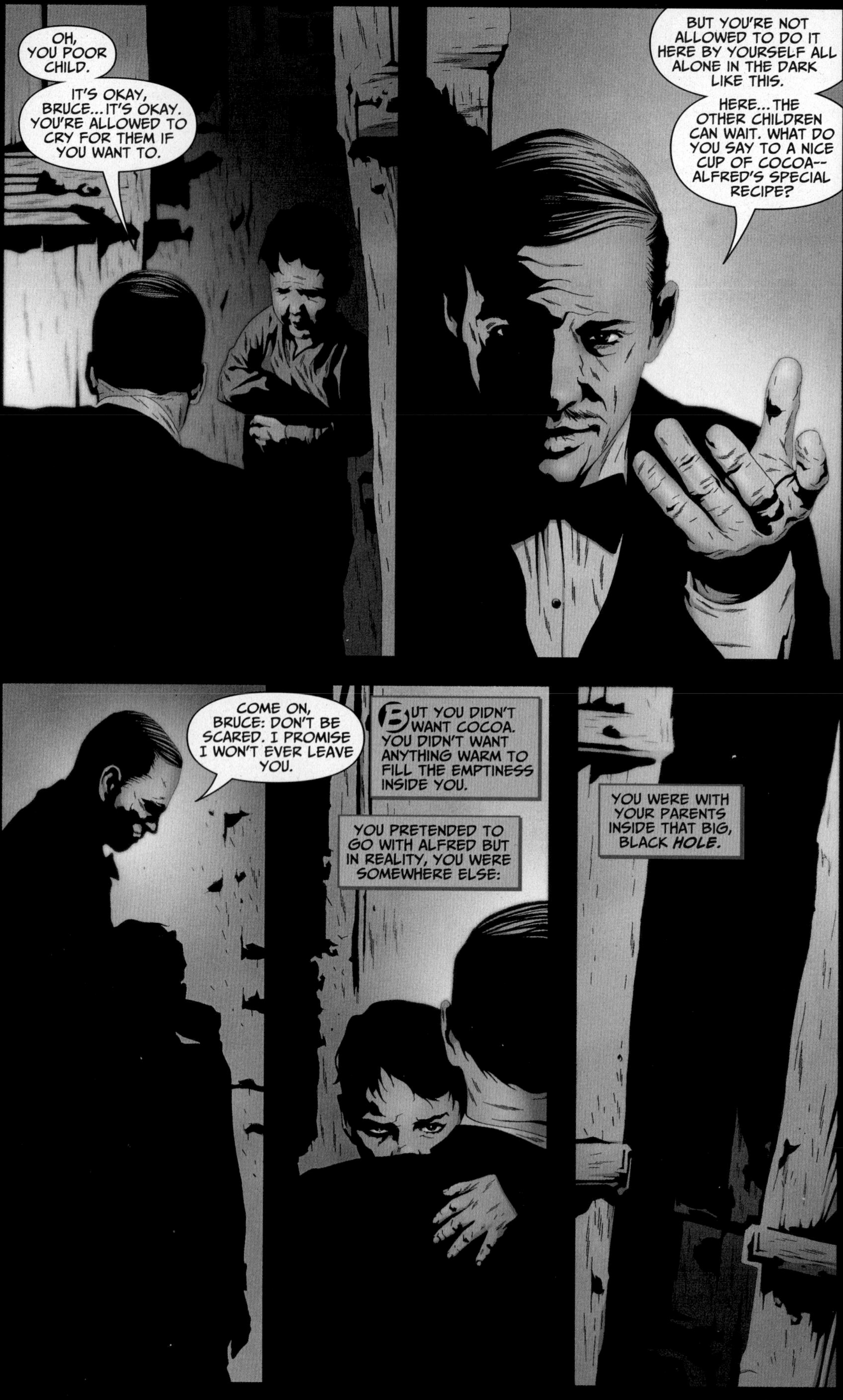
OH, YOU POOR CHILD.
IT'S OKAY, BRUCE... IT'S OKAY. YOU'RE ALLOWED TO CRY FOR THEM IF YOU WANT TO.
BUT YOU'RE NOT ALLOWED TO DO IT HERE BY YOURSELF ALL ALONE IN THE DARK LIKE THIS.
HERE... THE OTHER CHILDREN CAN WAIT. WHAT DO YOU SAY TO A NICE CUP OF COCOA-- ALFRED'S SPECIAL RECIPE?
COME ON, BRUCE: DON'T BE SCARED. I PROMISE I WON'T EVER LEAVE YOU.
BUT YOU DIDN'T WANT COCOA. YOU DIDN'T WANT ANYTHING WARM TO FILL THE EMPTINESS INSIDE YOU.
YOU PRETENDED TO GO WITH ALFRED BUT IN REALITY, YOU WERE SOMEWHERE ELSE:
YOU WERE WITH YOUR PARENTS INSIDE THAT BIG, BLACK *HOLE*.

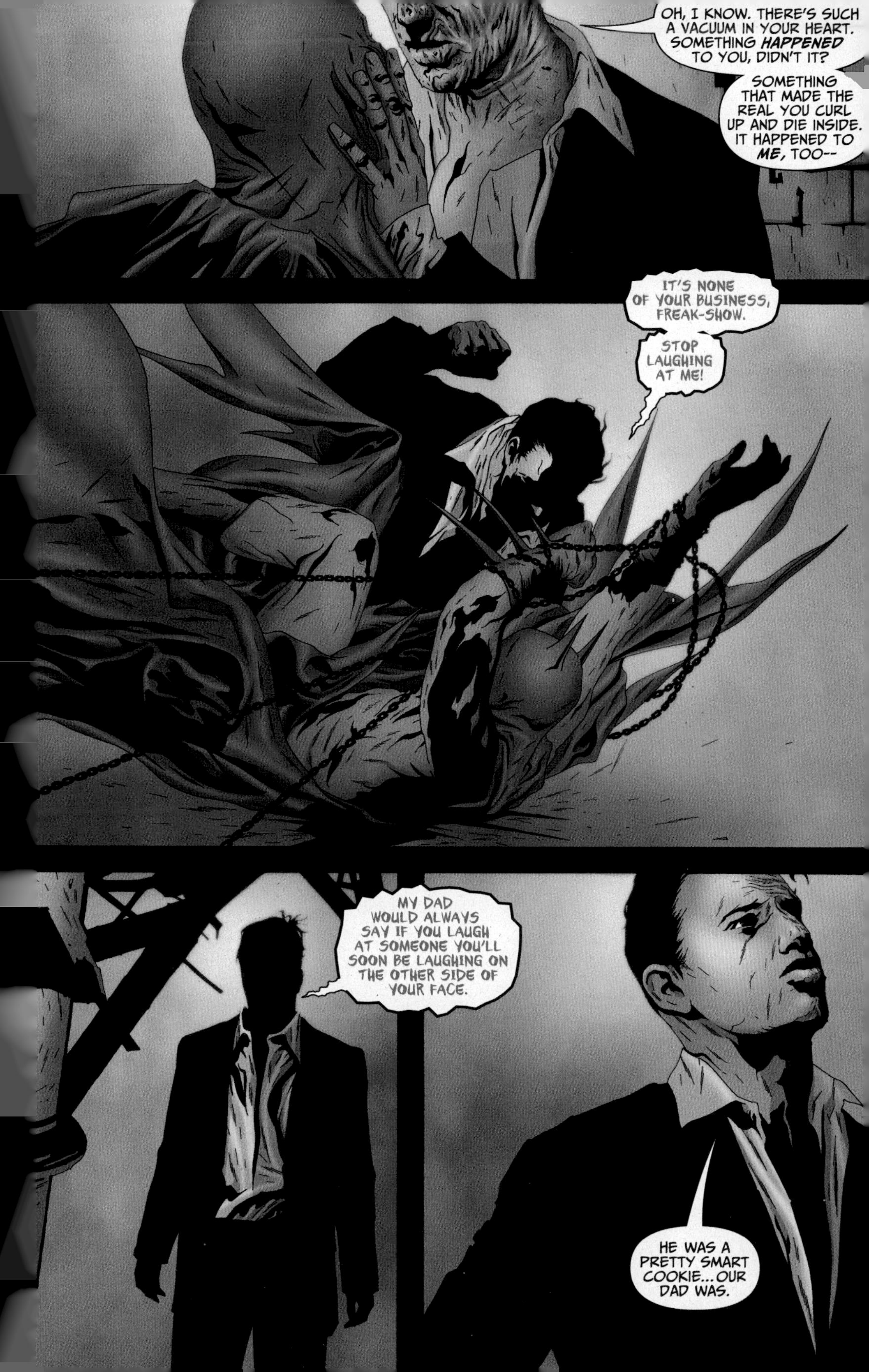
OH, I KNOW. THERE'S SUCH A VACUUM IN YOUR HEART. SOMETHING HAPPENED TO YOU, DIDN'T IT?
SOMETHING THAT MADE THE REAL YOU CURL UP AND DIE INSIDE. IT HAPPENED TO ME, TOO--
IT'S NONE OF YOUR BUSINESS, FREAK-SHOW.
STOP LAUGHING AT ME!
MY DAD WOULD ALWAYS SAY IF YOU LAUGH AT SOMEONE YOU'LL SOON BE LAUGHING ON THE OTHER SIDE OF YOUR FACE.
HE WAS A PRETTY SMART COOKIE...OUR DAD WAS.

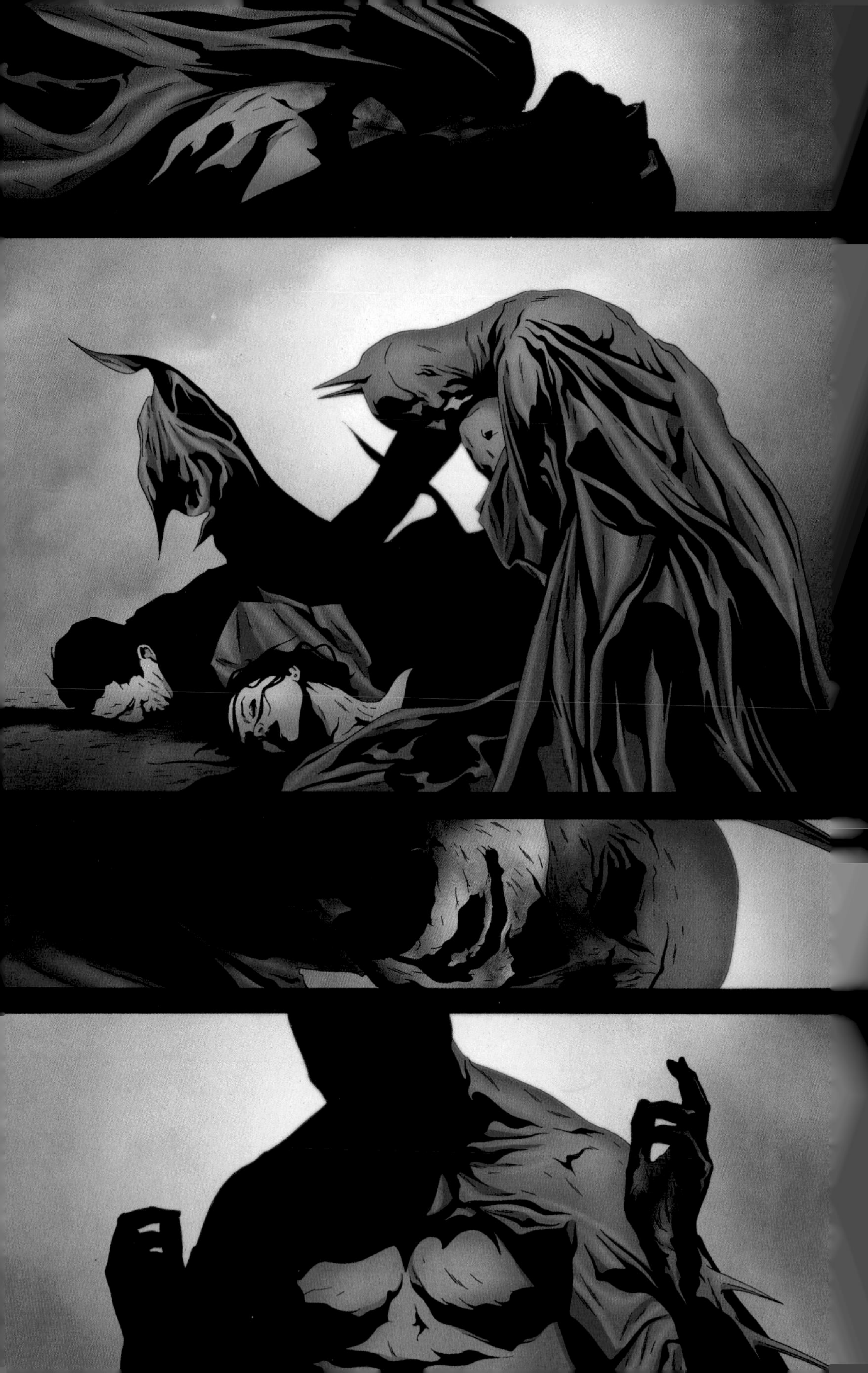

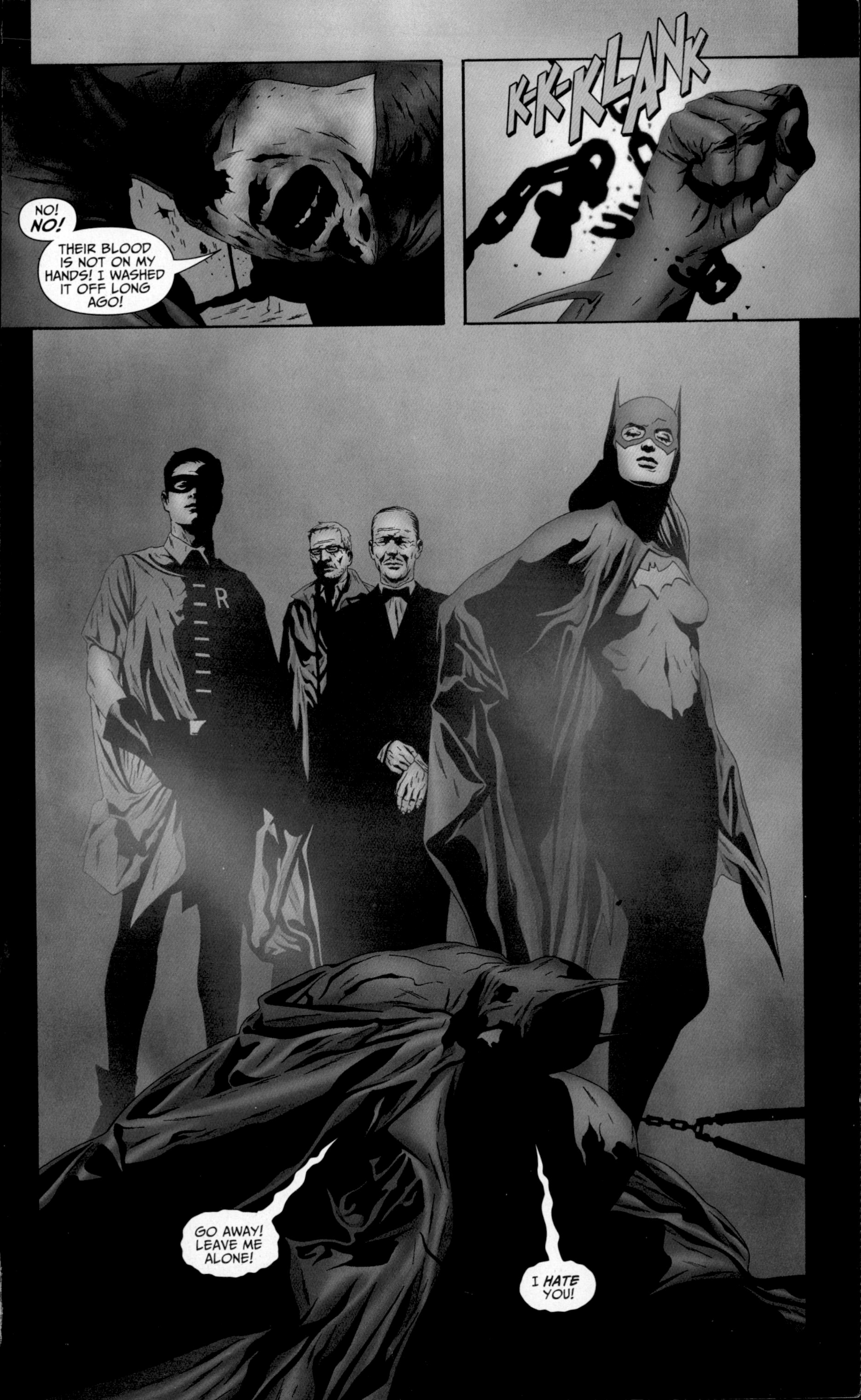
NO! NO!
THEIR BLOOD IS NOT ON MY HANDS! I WASHED IT OFF LONG AGO!
K-K-KLANK
GO AWAY! LEAVE ME ALONE!
I HATE YOU!

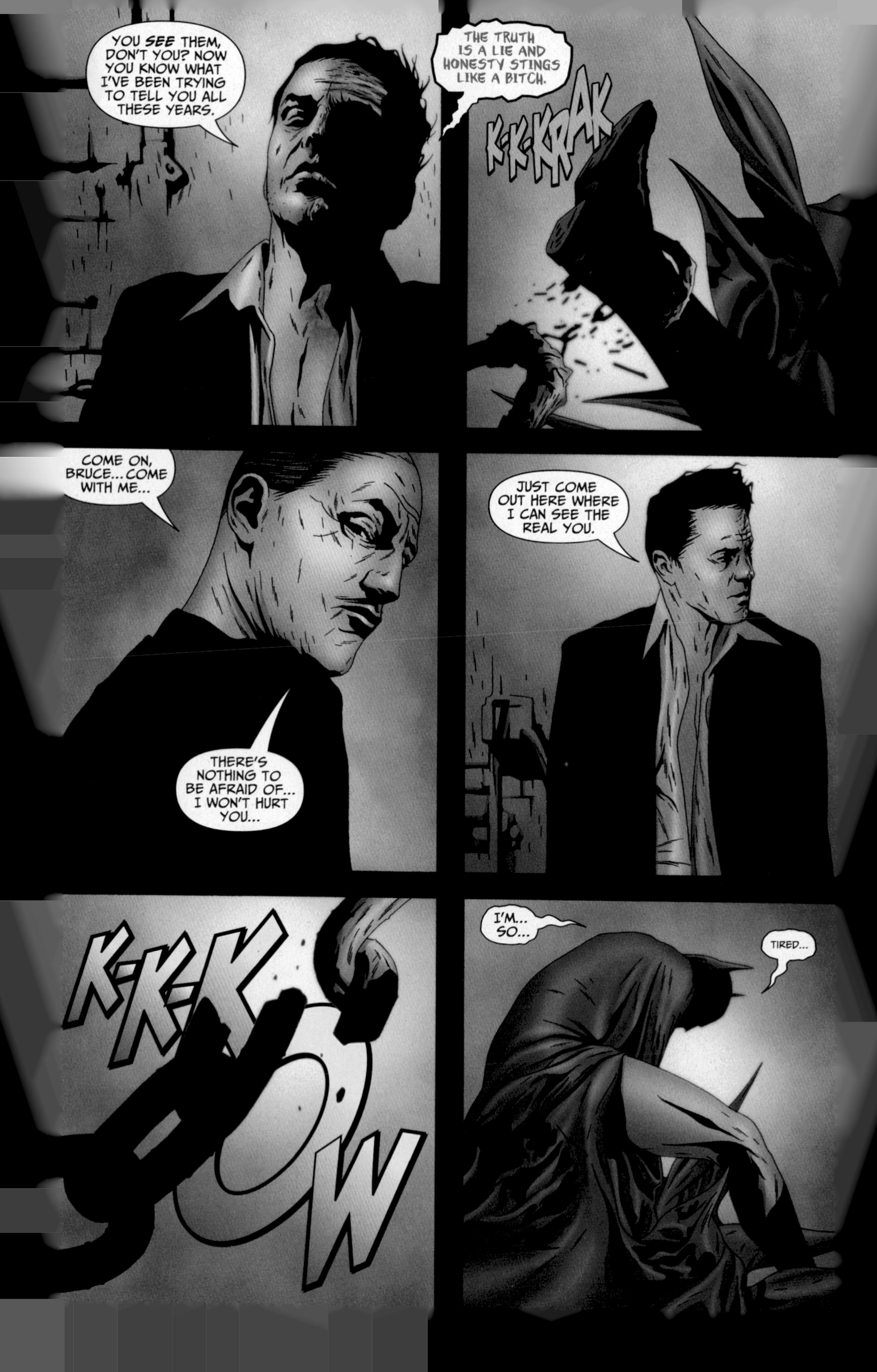
YOU SEE THEM, DON'T YOU? NOW YOU KNOW WHAT I'VE BEEN TRYING TO TELL YOU ALL THESE YEARS.
THE TRUTH IS A LIE AND HONESTY STINGS LIKE A BITCH.
K-K-KRAK
COME ON, BRUCE...COME WITH ME...
THERE'S NOTHING TO BE AFRAID OF... I WON'T HURT YOU...
JUST COME OUT HERE WHERE I CAN SEE THE REAL YOU.
K-K-K
OW
I'M... SO...
TIRED...

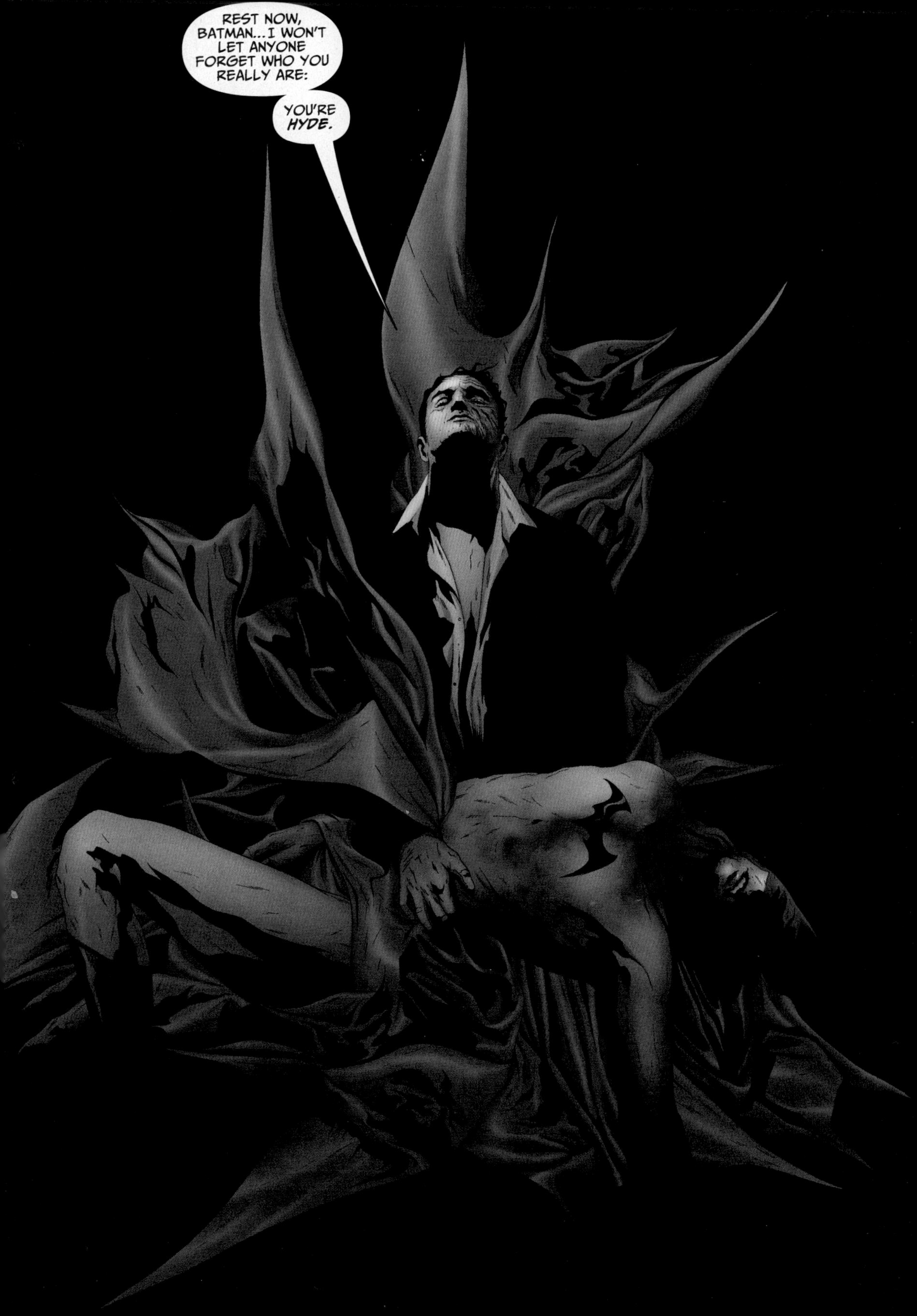
REST NOW, BATMAN... I WON'T LET ANYONE FORGET WHO YOU REALLY ARE:
YOU'RE *HYDE*.

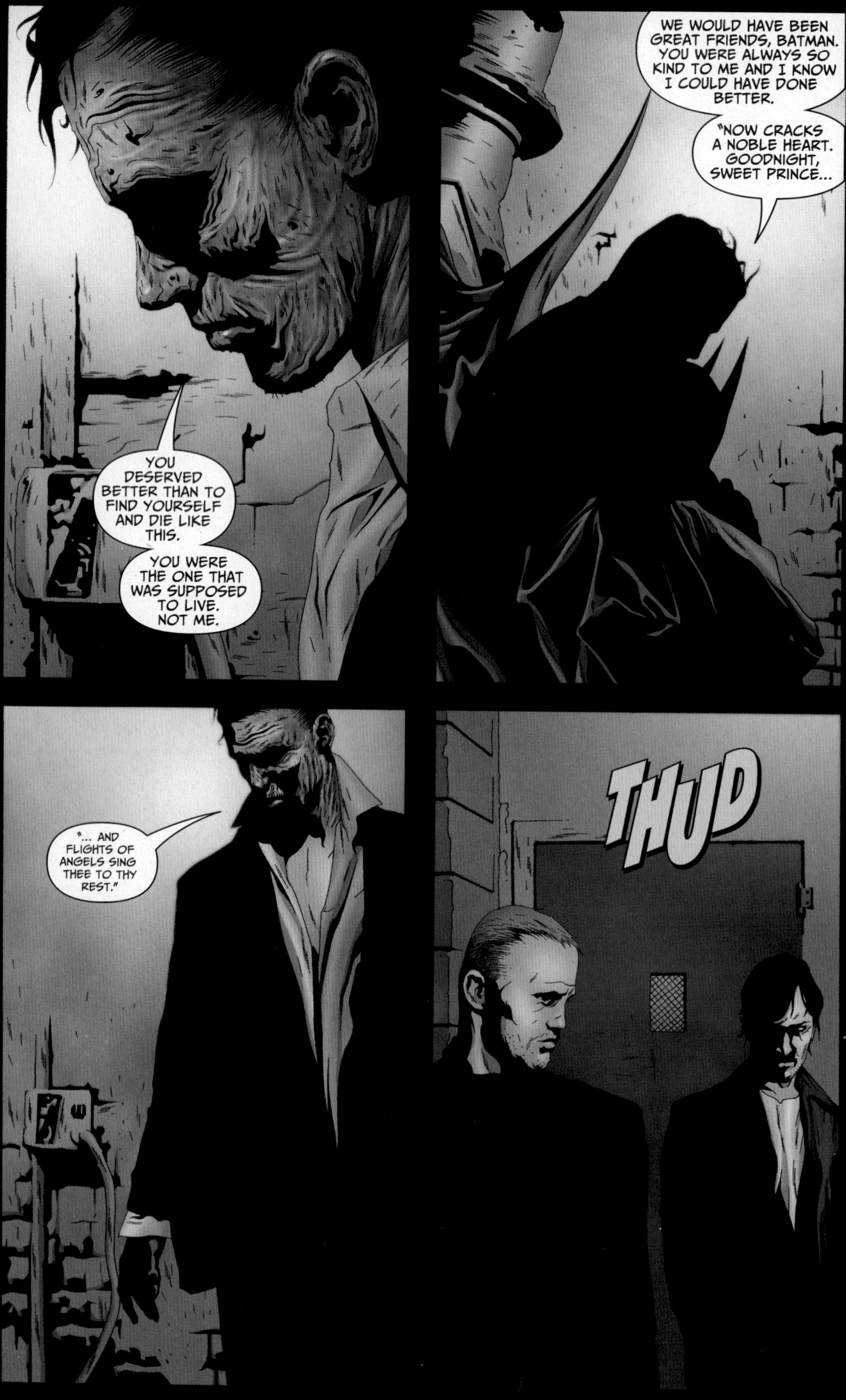
YOU DESERVED BETTER THAN TO FIND YOURSELF AND DIE LIKE THIS.
YOU WERE THE ONE THAT WAS SUPPOSED TO LIVE. NOT ME.
WE WOULD HAVE BEEN GREAT FRIENDS, BATMAN. YOU WERE ALWAYS SO KIND TO ME AND I KNOW I COULD HAVE DONE BETTER.
"NOW CRACKS A NOBLE HEART. GOODNIGHT, SWEET PRINCE...
"... AND FLIGHTS OF ANGELS SING THEE TO THY REST."
THUD

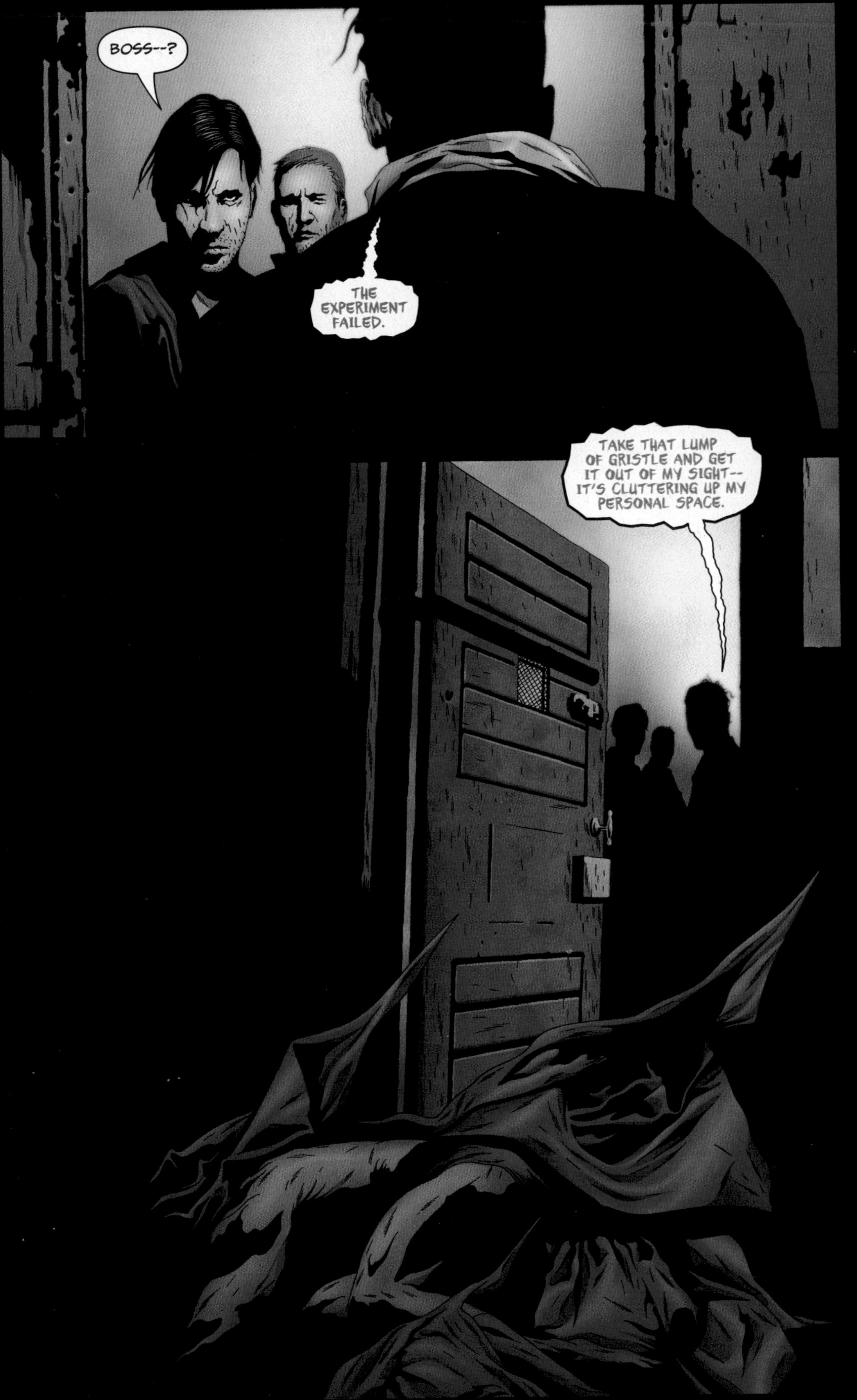
BOSS--?
THE EXPERIMENT FAILED.
TAKE THAT LUMP OF GRISTLE AND GET IT OUT OF MY SIGHT-- IT'S CLUTTERING UP MY PERSONAL SPACE.

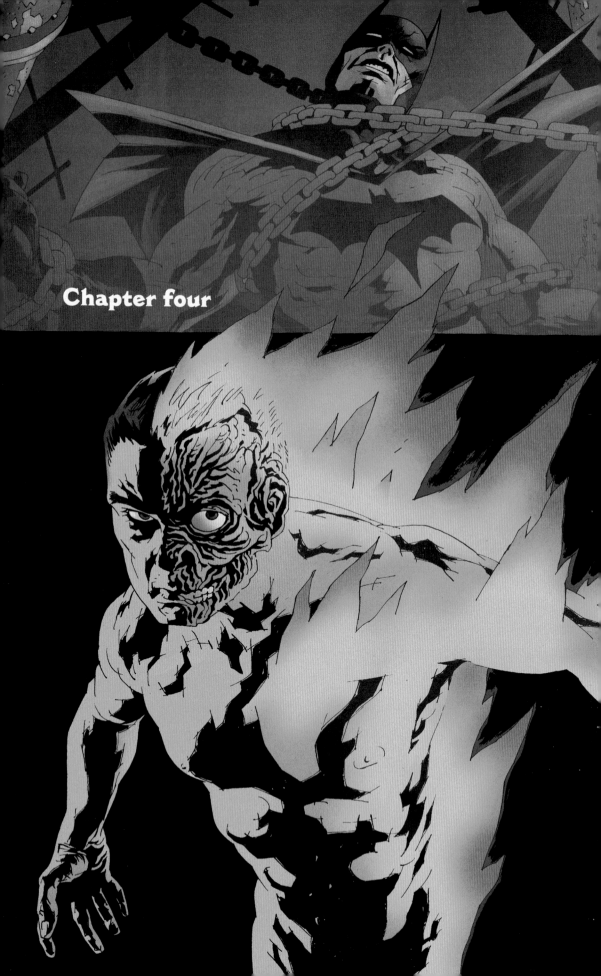

Chapter four

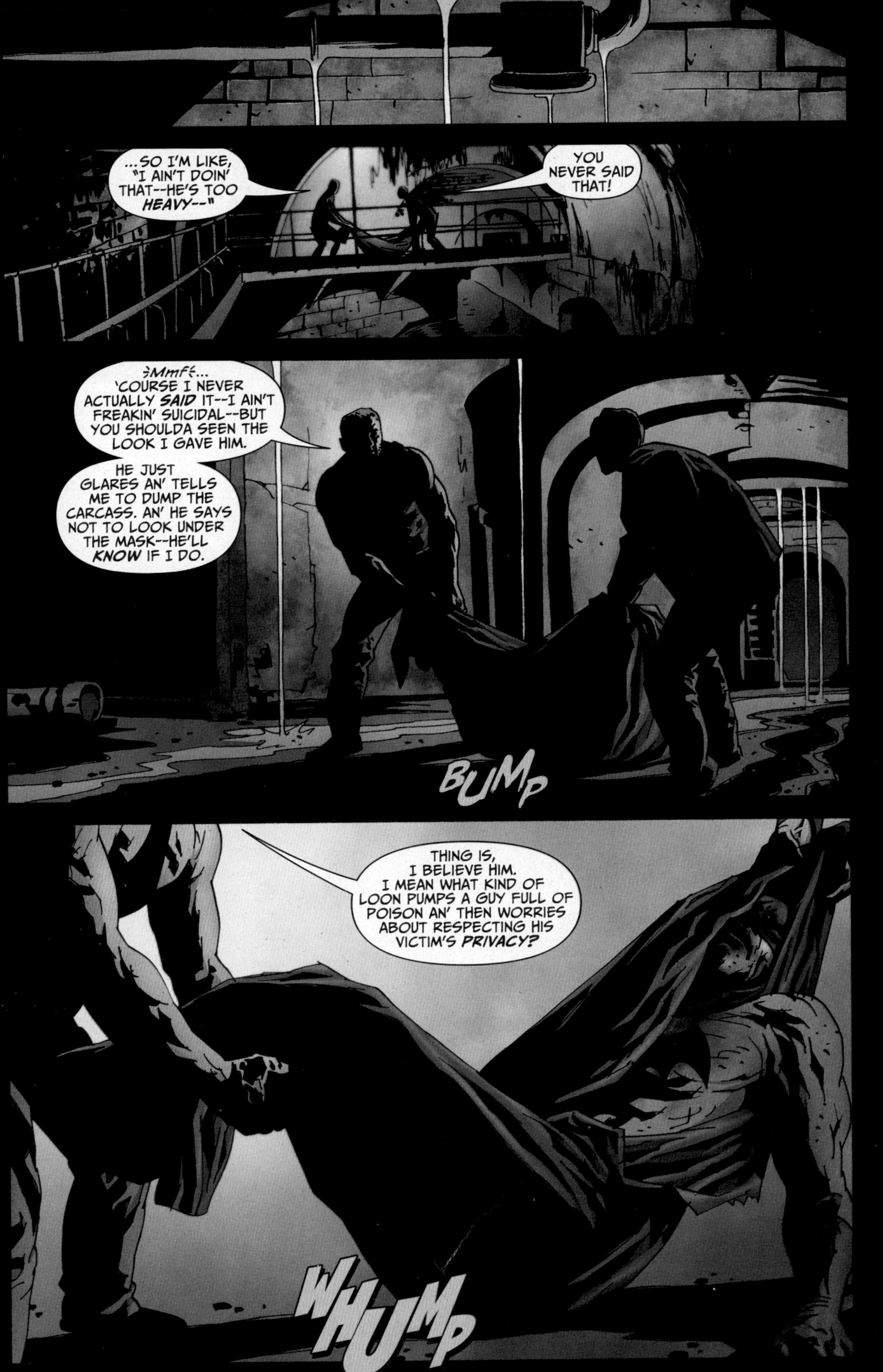
...SO I'M LIKE, "I AIN'T DOIN' THAT--HE'S TOO HEAVY--"
YOU NEVER SAID THAT!
Mmf... 'COURSE I NEVER ACTUALLY SAID IT--I AIN'T FREAKIN' SUICIDAL--BUT YOU SHOULDA SEEN THE LOOK I GAVE HIM.
HE JUST GLARES AN' TELLS ME TO DUMP THE CARCASS. AN' HE SAYS NOT TO LOOK UNDER THE MASK--HE'LL KNOW IF I DO.
BUMP
THING IS, I BELIEVE HIM. I MEAN WHAT KIND OF LOON PUMPS A GUY FULL OF POISON AN' THEN WORRIES ABOUT RESPECTING HIS VICTIM'S PRIVACY?
WHUMP

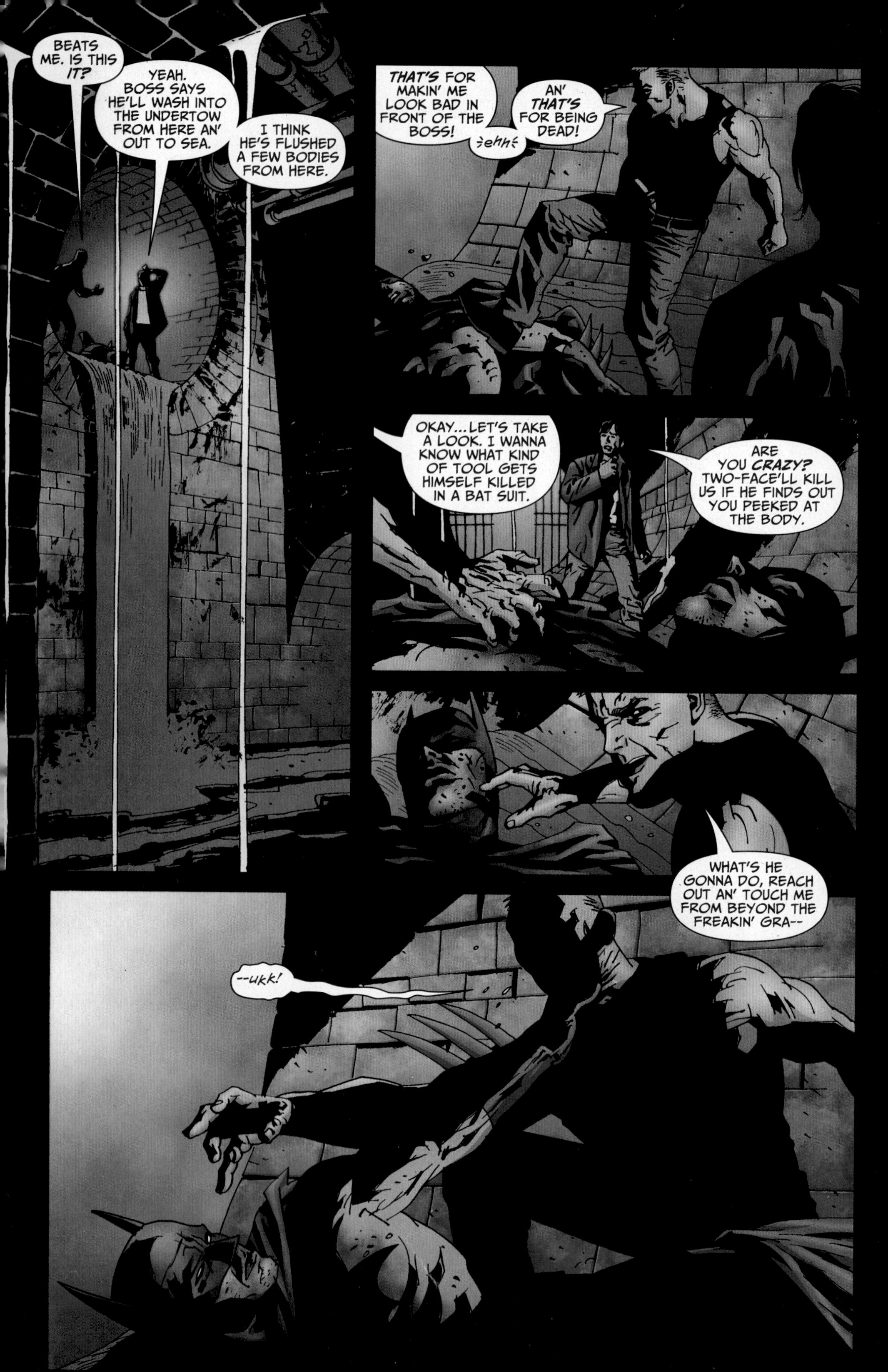
BEATS ME. IS THIS IT?
YEAH. BOSS SAYS HE'LL WASH INTO THE UNDERTOW FROM HERE AN' OUT TO SEA.
I THINK HE'S FLUSHED A FEW BODIES FROM HERE.
THAT'S FOR MAKIN' ME LOOK BAD IN FRONT OF THE BOSS!
ehh
AN' THAT'S FOR BEING DEAD!
OKAY...LET'S TAKE A LOOK. I WANNA KNOW WHAT KIND OF TOOL GETS HIMSELF KILLED IN A BAT SUIT.
ARE YOU CRAZY? TWO-FACE'LL KILL US IF HE FINDS OUT YOU PEEKED AT THE BODY.
WHAT'S HE GONNA DO, REACH OUT AN' TOUCH ME FROM BEYOND THE FREAKIN' GRA--
--ukk!

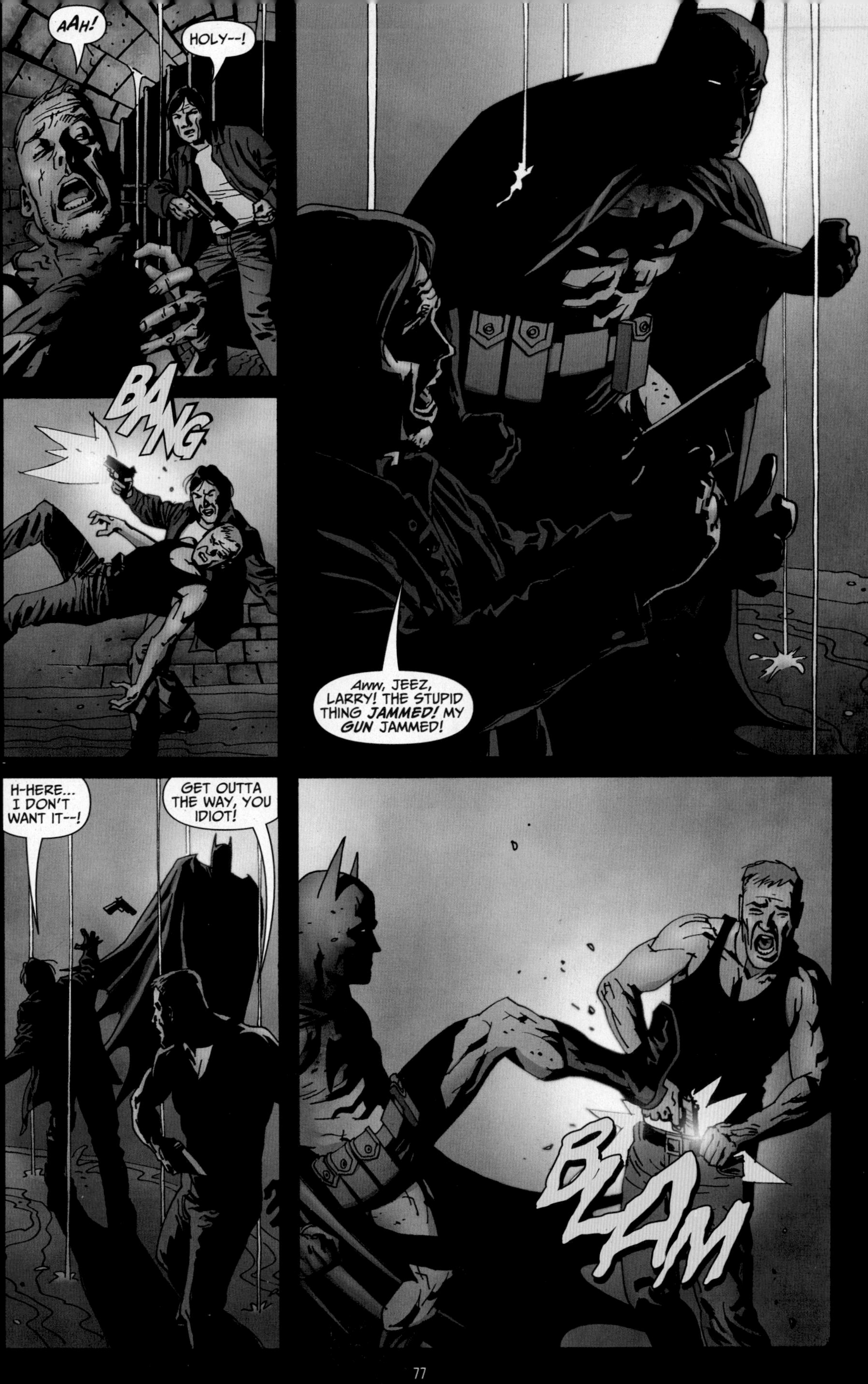
AAH!
HOLY--!
BANG
AWW, JEEZ, LARRY! THE STUPID THING JAMMED! MY GUN JAMMED!
H-HERE... I DON'T WANT IT--!
GET OUTTA THE WAY, YOU IDIOT!
BLAM

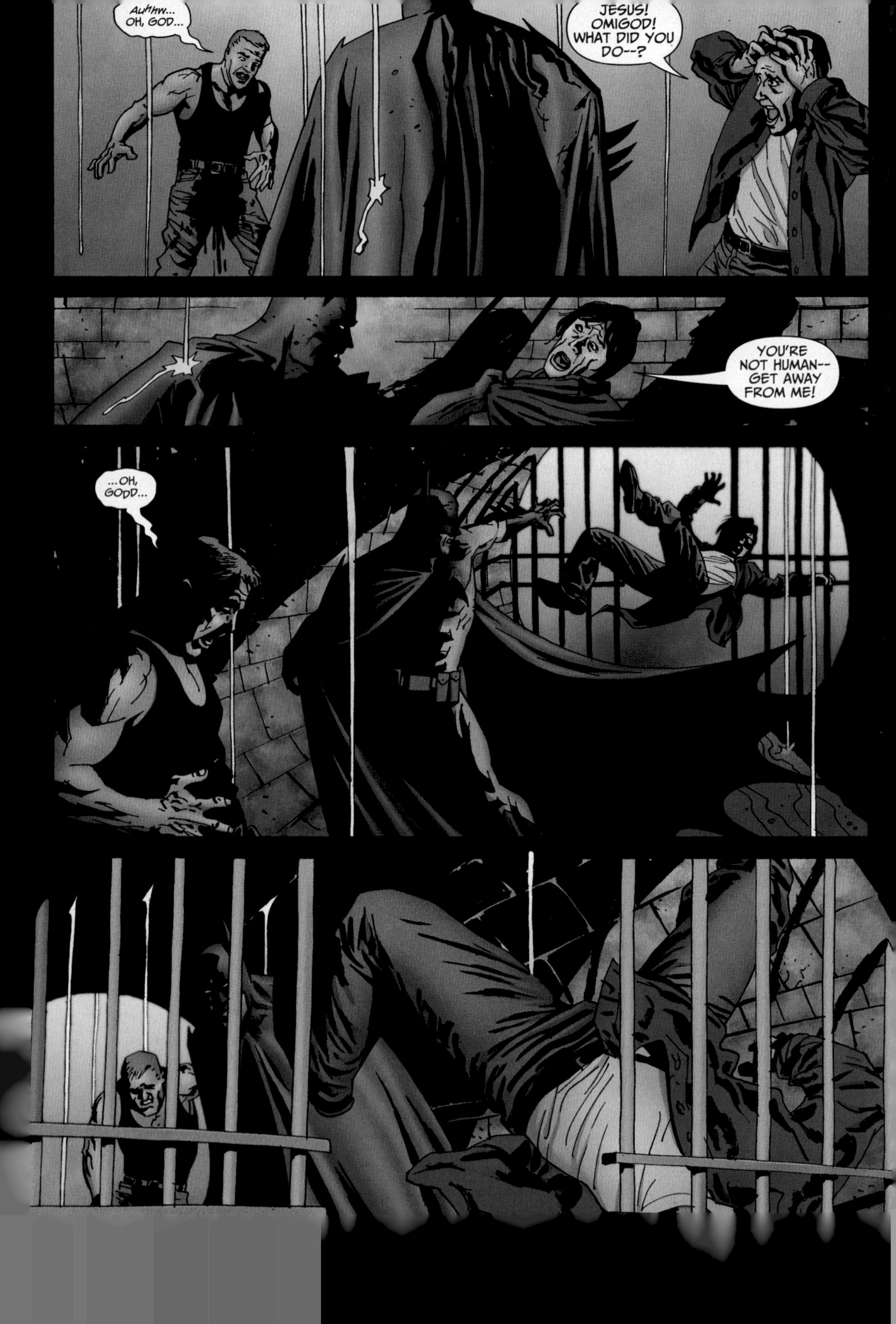
AUHHW... OH, GOD...
JESUS! OMIGOD! WHAT DID YOU DO--?
YOU'RE NOT HUMAN-- GET AWAY FROM ME!
...OH, GODD...

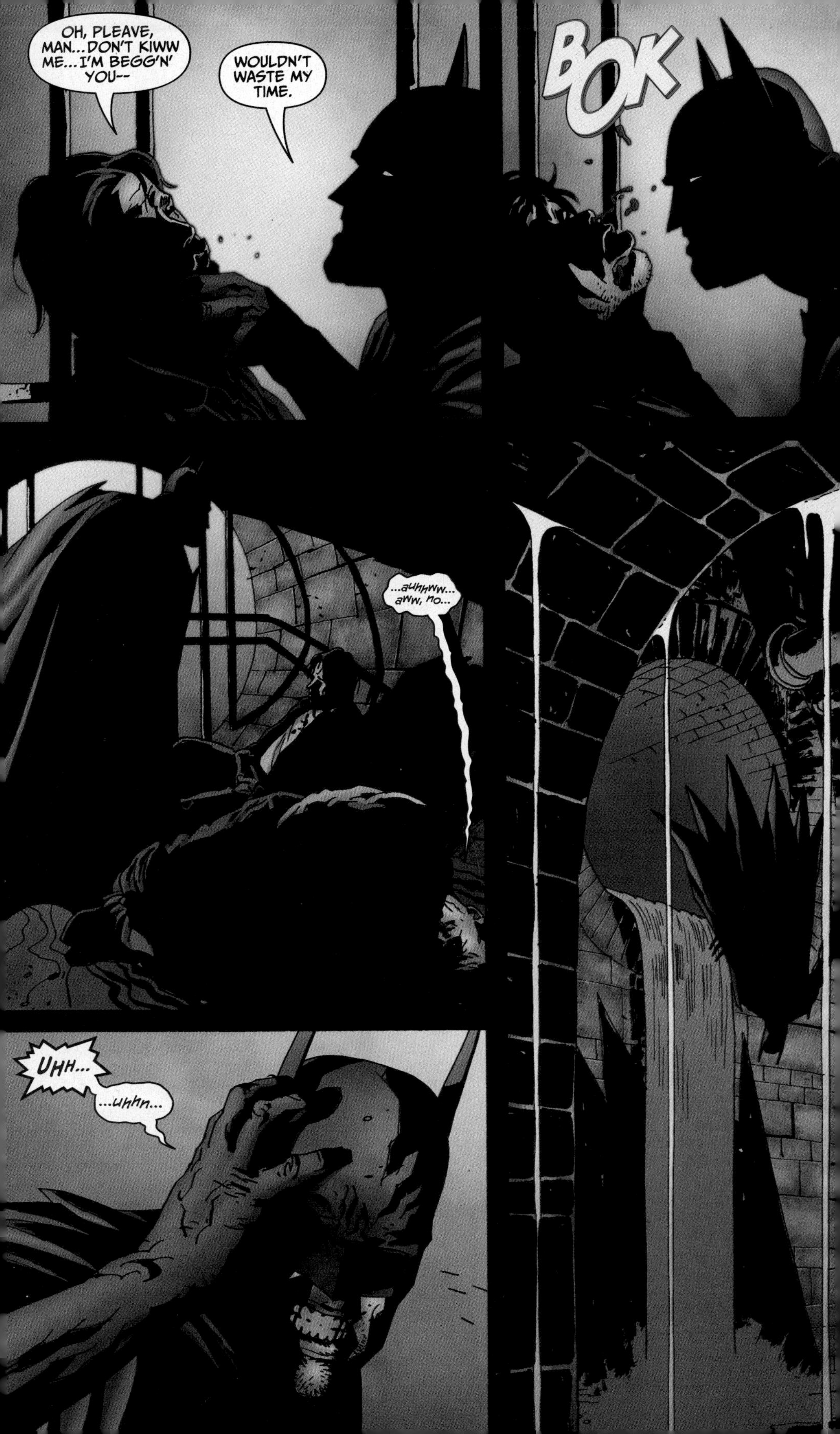
OH, PLEAVE, MAN...DON'T KIWW ME...I'M BEGG'N' YOU--
WOULDN'T WASTE MY TIME.
BOK
...auhhww... aww, no...
UHH...
...uhhn...

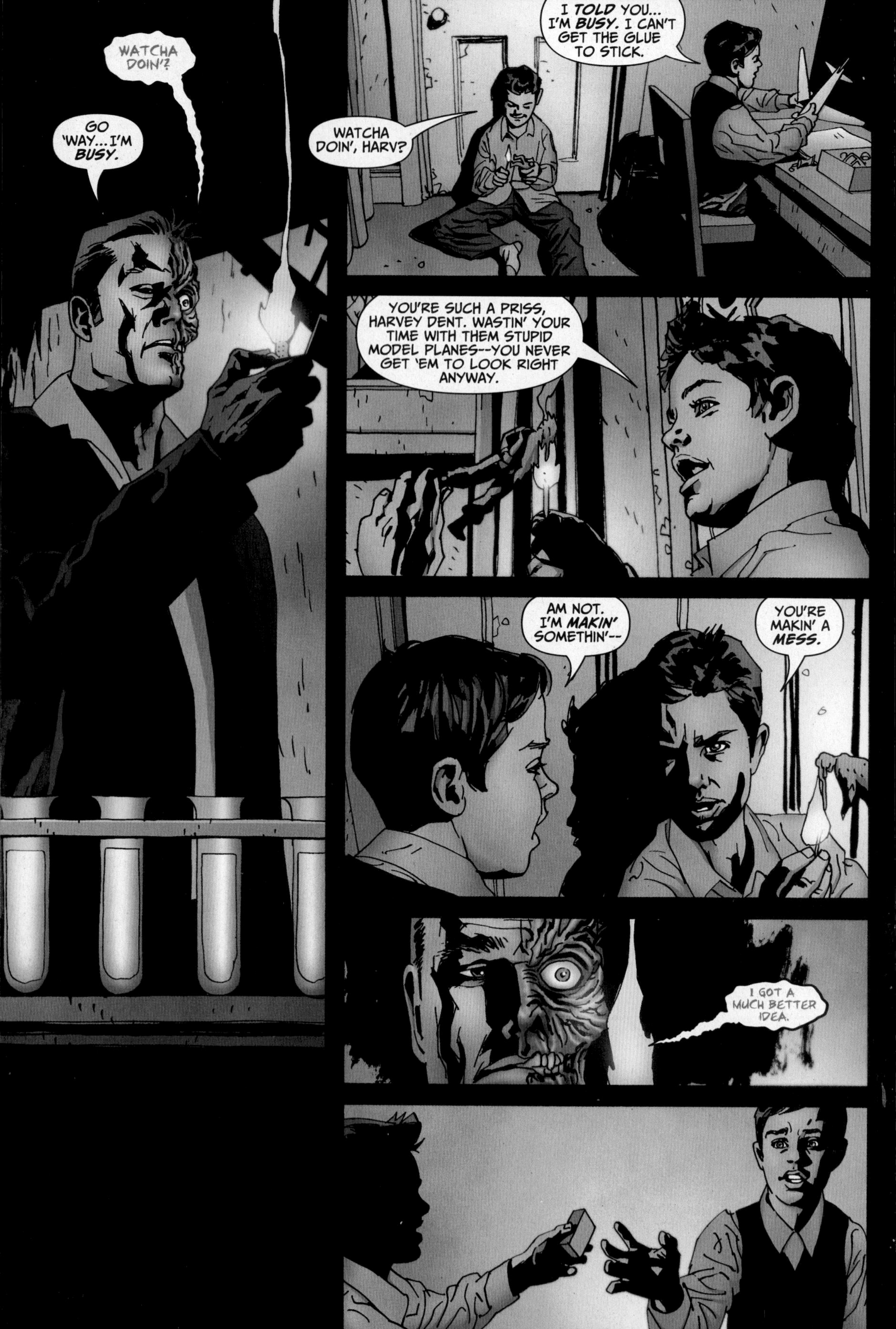
WATCHA DOIN'?
GO 'WAY...I'M BUSY.
WATCHA DOIN', HARV?
I TOLD YOU... I'M BUSY. I CAN'T GET THE GLUE TO STICK.
YOU'RE SUCH A PRISS, HARVEY DENT. WASTIN' YOUR TIME WITH THEM STUPID MODEL PLANES--YOU NEVER GET 'EM TO LOOK RIGHT ANYWAY.
AM NOT. I'M MAKIN' SOMETHIN'--
YOU'RE MAKIN' A MESS.
I GOT A MUCH BETTER IDEA.

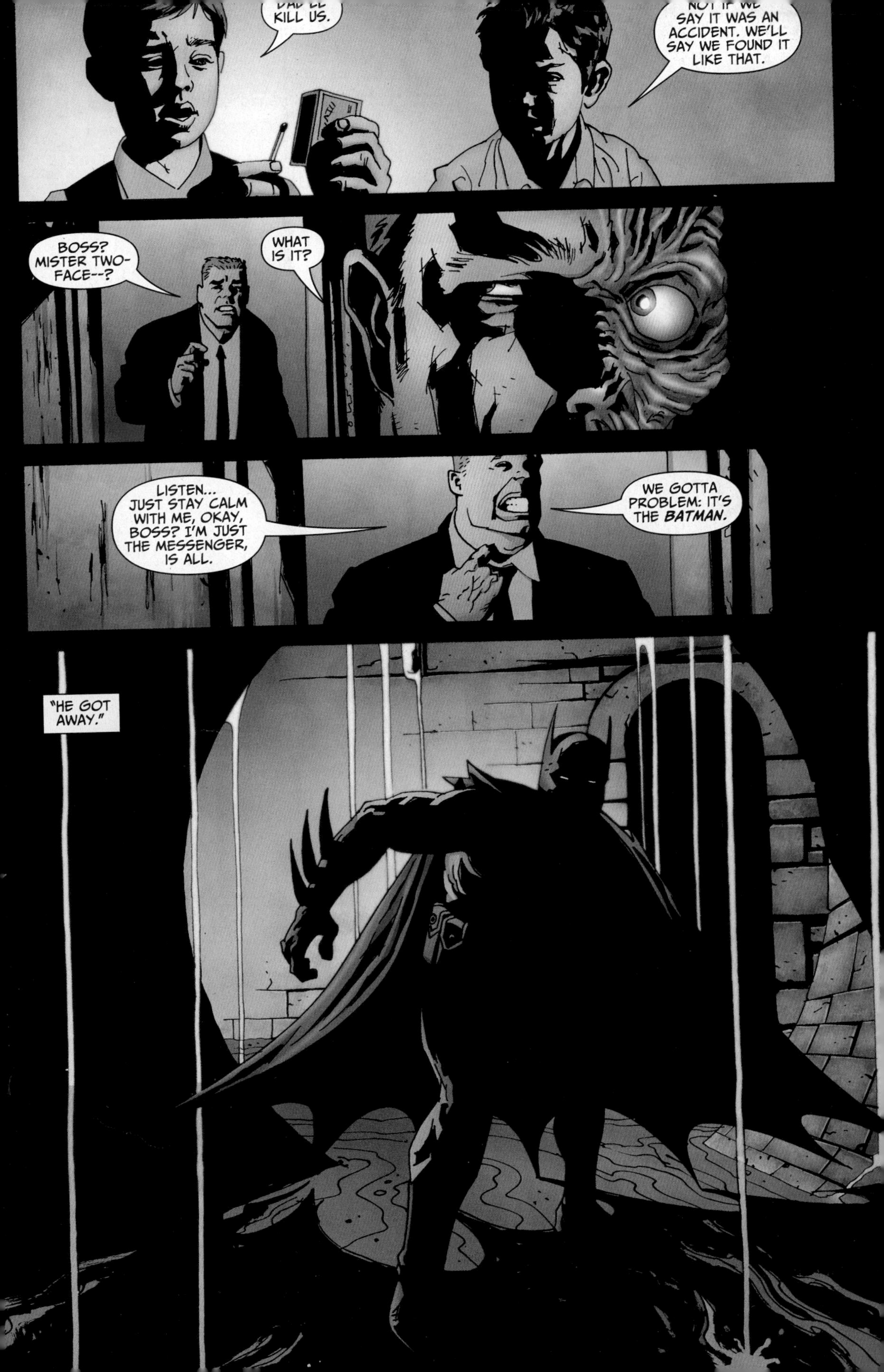
KILL US.
SAY IT WAS AN ACCIDENT. WE'LL SAY WE FOUND IT LIKE THAT.
BOSS? MISTER TWO-FACE--?
WHAT IS IT?
LISTEN... JUST STAY CALM WITH ME, OKAY, BOSS? I'M JUST THE MESSENGER, IS ALL.
WE GOTTA PROBLEM: IT'S THE BATMAN.
"HE GOT AWAY."

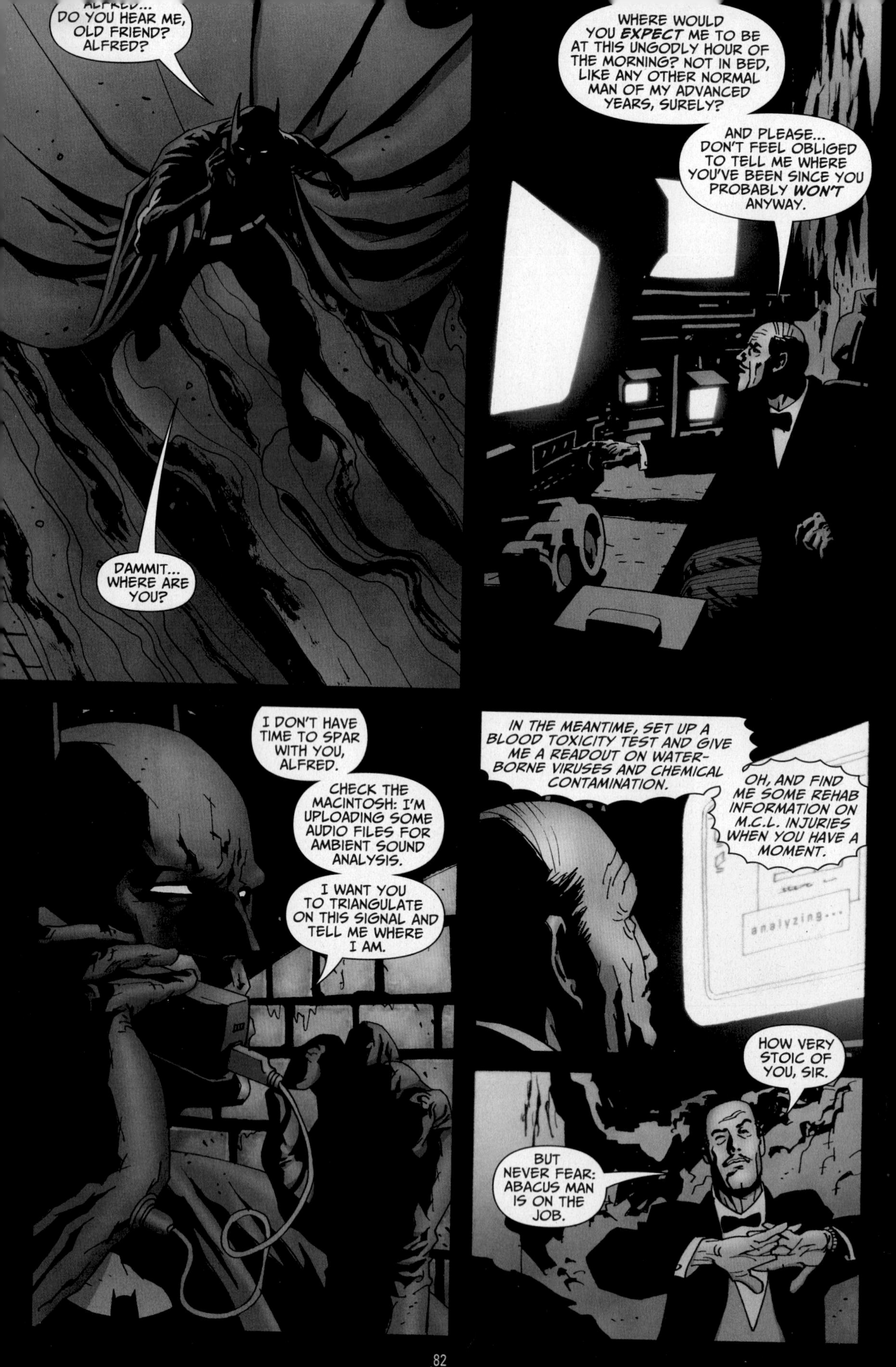
ALFRED... DO YOU HEAR ME, OLD FRIEND? ALFRED?
DAMMIT... WHERE ARE YOU?
WHERE WOULD YOU EXPECT ME TO BE AT THIS UNGODLY HOUR OF THE MORNING? NOT IN BED, LIKE ANY OTHER NORMAL MAN OF MY ADVANCED YEARS, SURELY?
AND PLEASE... DON'T FEEL OBLIGED TO TELL ME WHERE YOU'VE BEEN SINCE YOU PROBABLY WON'T ANYWAY.
I DON'T HAVE TIME TO SPAR WITH YOU, ALFRED.
CHECK THE MACINTOSH: I'M UPLOADING SOME AUDIO FILES FOR AMBIENT SOUND ANALYSIS.
I WANT YOU TO TRIANGULATE ON THIS SIGNAL AND TELL ME WHERE I AM.
IN THE MEANTIME, SET UP A BLOOD TOXICITY TEST AND GIVE ME A READOUT ON WATER-BORNE VIRUSES AND CHEMICAL CONTAMINATION.
OH, AND FIND ME SOME REHAB INFORMATION ON M.C.L. INJURIES WHEN YOU HAVE A MOMENT.
analyzing...
HOW VERY STOIC OF YOU, SIR.
BUT NEVER FEAR: ABACUS MAN IS ON THE JOB.

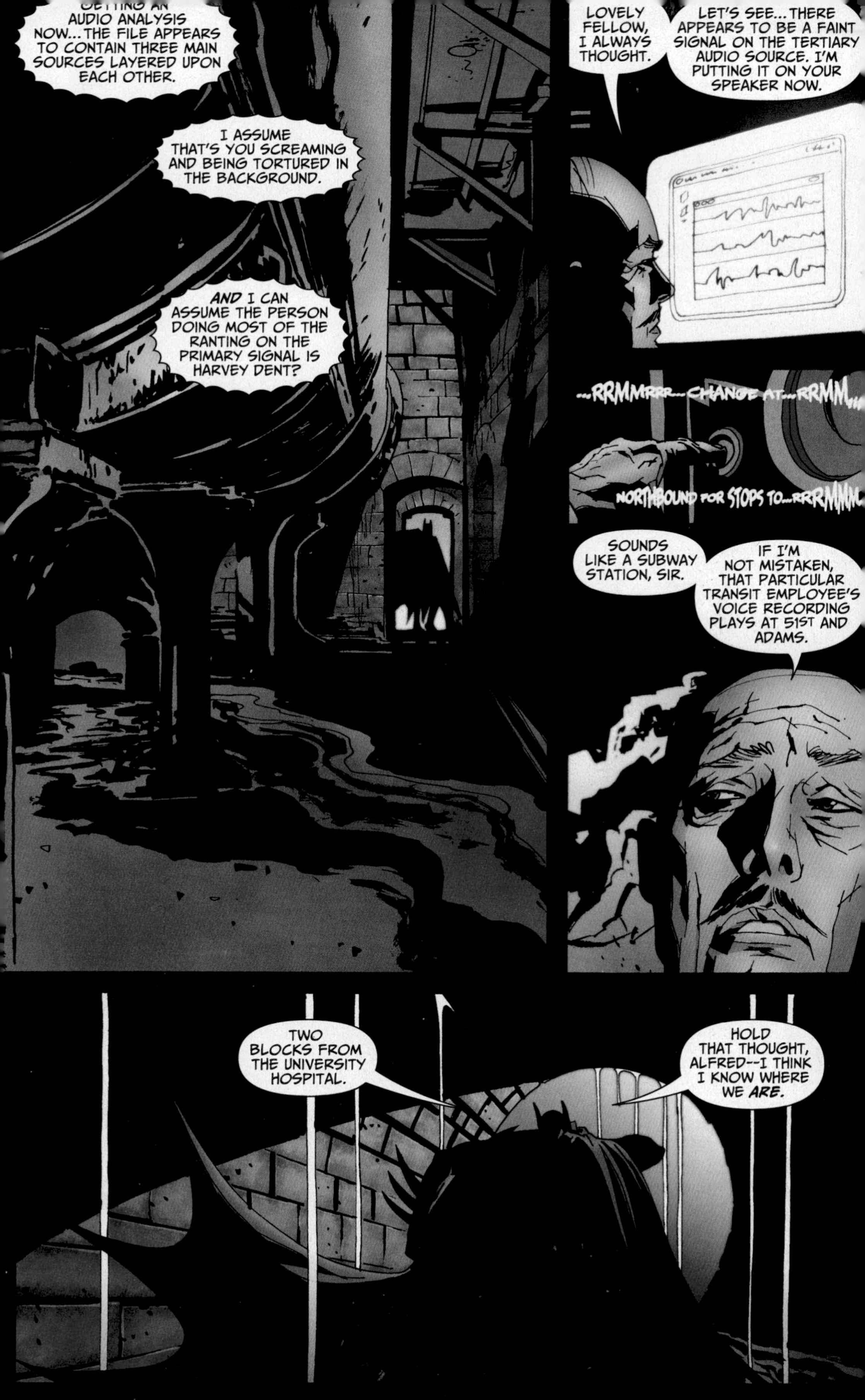
GETTING AN AUDIO ANALYSIS NOW... THE FILE APPEARS TO CONTAIN THREE MAIN SOURCES LAYERED UPON EACH OTHER.
I ASSUME THAT'S YOU SCREAMING AND BEING TORTURED IN THE BACKGROUND.
AND I CAN ASSUME THE PERSON DOING MOST OF THE RANTING ON THE PRIMARY SIGNAL IS HARVEY DENT?
LOVELY FELLOW, I ALWAYS THOUGHT.
LET'S SEE... THERE APPEARS TO BE A FAINT SIGNAL ON THE TERTIARY AUDIO SOURCE. I'M PUTTING IT ON YOUR SPEAKER NOW.
...RRMMRRR... CHANGE AT...RRMM...
NORTHBOUND FOR STOPS TO...RRRMMM...
SOUNDS LIKE A SUBWAY STATION, SIR.
IF I'M NOT MISTAKEN, THAT PARTICULAR TRANSIT EMPLOYEE'S VOICE RECORDING PLAYS AT 51ST AND ADAMS.
TWO BLOCKS FROM THE UNIVERSITY HOSPITAL.
HOLD THAT THOUGHT, ALFRED--I THINK I KNOW WHERE WE ARE.

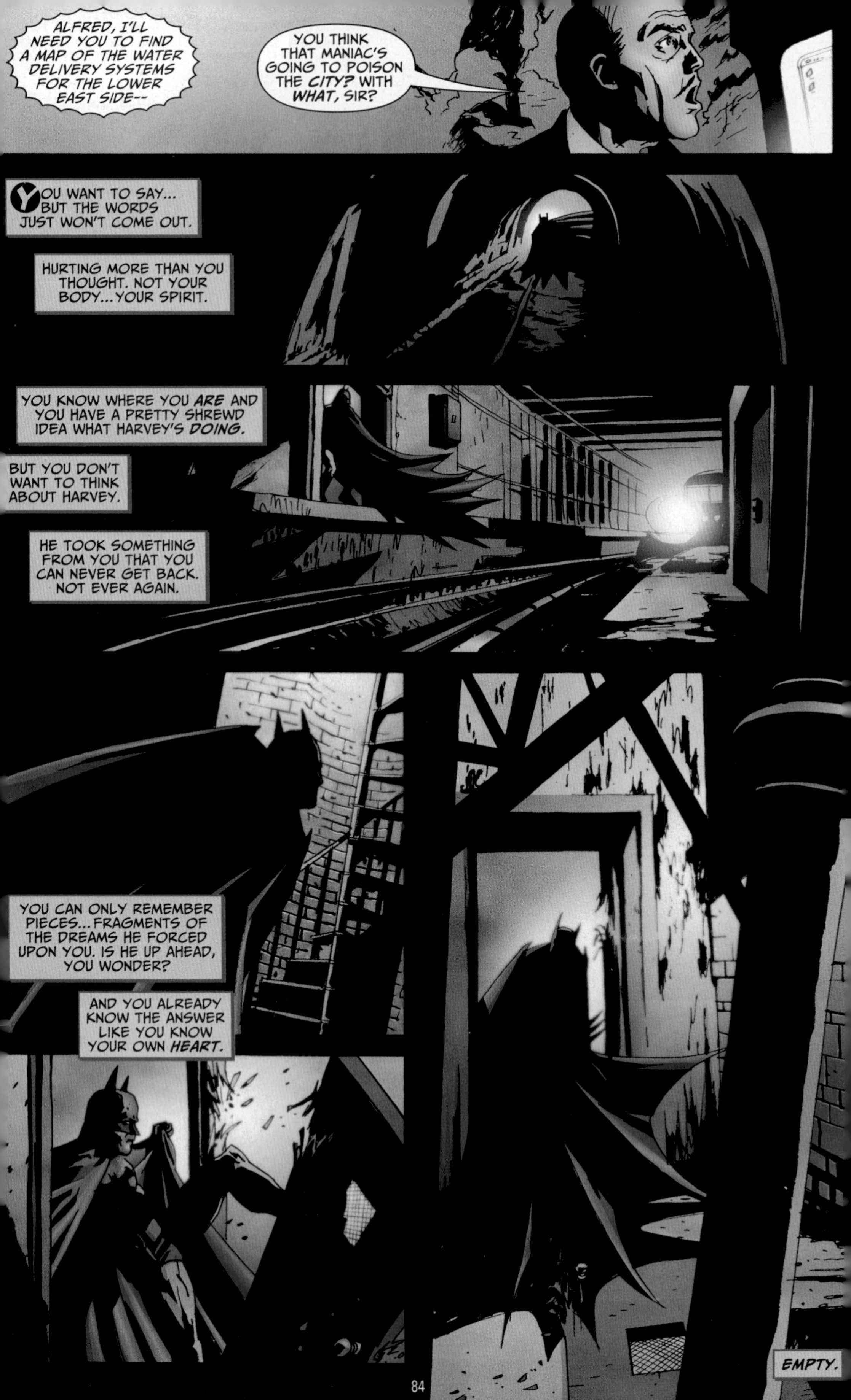
ALFRED, I'LL NEED YOU TO FIND A MAP OF THE WATER DELIVERY SYSTEMS FOR THE LOWER EAST SIDE--
YOU THINK THAT MANIAC'S GOING TO POISON THE CITY? WITH WHAT, SIR?
YOU WANT TO SAY... BUT THE WORDS JUST WON'T COME OUT.
HURTING MORE THAN YOU THOUGHT. NOT YOUR BODY... YOUR SPIRIT.
YOU KNOW WHERE YOU ARE AND YOU HAVE A PRETTY SHREWD IDEA WHAT HARVEY'S DOING.
BUT YOU DON'T WANT TO THINK ABOUT HARVEY.
HE TOOK SOMETHING FROM YOU THAT YOU CAN NEVER GET BACK. NOT EVER AGAIN.
YOU CAN ONLY REMEMBER PIECES... FRAGMENTS OF THE DREAMS HE FORCED UPON YOU. IS HE UP AHEAD, YOU WONDER?
AND YOU ALREADY KNOW THE ANSWER LIKE YOU KNOW YOUR OWN HEART.
EMPTY.

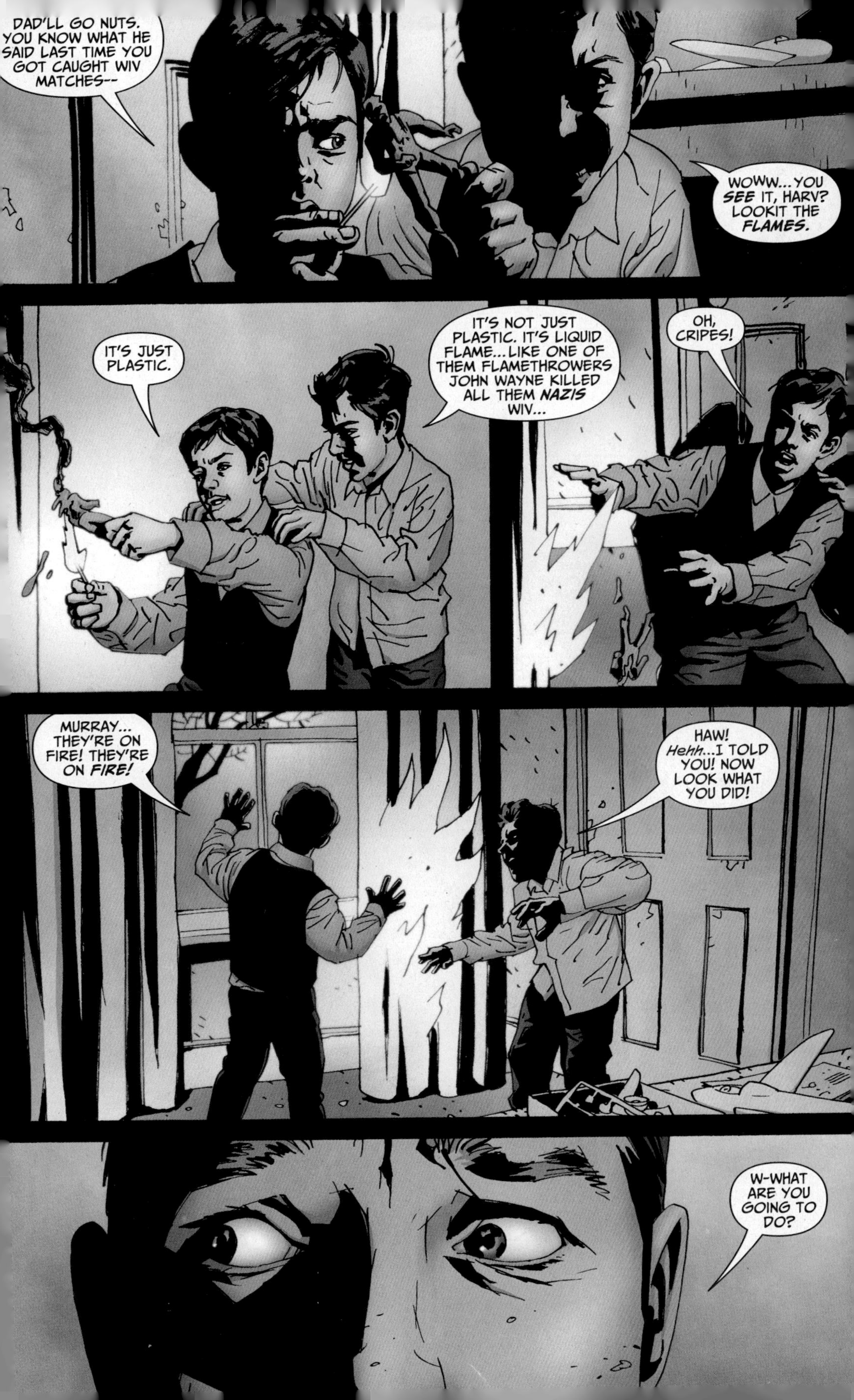
DAD'LL GO NUTS. YOU KNOW WHAT HE SAID LAST TIME YOU GOT CAUGHT WIV MATCHES--
WOWW...YOU *SEE* IT, HARV? LOOKIT THE *FLAMES.*
IT'S JUST PLASTIC.
IT'S NOT JUST PLASTIC. IT'S LIQUID FLAME...LIKE ONE OF THEM FLAMETHROWERS JOHN WAYNE KILLED ALL THEM *NAZIS* WIV...
OH, CRIPES!
MURRAY... THEY'RE ON FIRE! THEY'RE ON *FIRE!*
HAW! *Hehh*...I TOLD YOU! NOW LOOK WHAT YOU DID!
W-WHAT ARE YOU GOING TO DO?

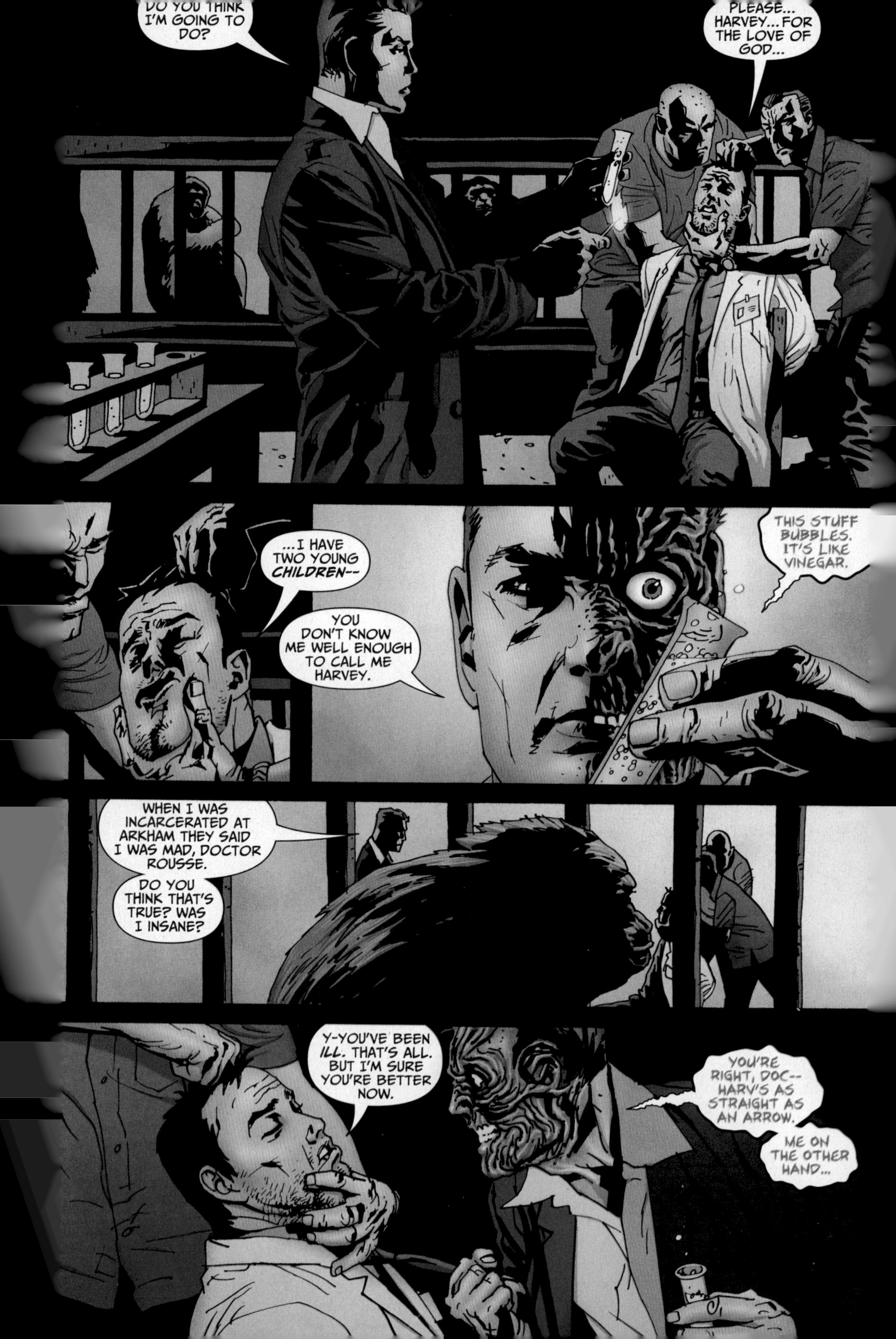

DO YOU THINK I'M GOING TO DO?
PLEASE... HARVEY... FOR THE LOVE OF GOD...
...I HAVE TWO YOUNG CHILDREN--
YOU DON'T KNOW ME WELL ENOUGH TO CALL ME HARVEY.
THIS STUFF BUBBLES. IT'S LIKE VINEGAR.
WHEN I WAS INCARCERATED AT ARKHAM THEY SAID I WAS MAD, DOCTOR ROUSSE.
DO YOU THINK THAT'S TRUE? WAS I INSANE?
Y-YOU'VE BEEN ILL. THAT'S ALL. BUT I'M SURE YOU'RE BETTER NOW.
YOU'RE RIGHT, DOC-- HARV'S AS STRAIGHT AS AN ARROW.
ME ON THE OTHER HAND...

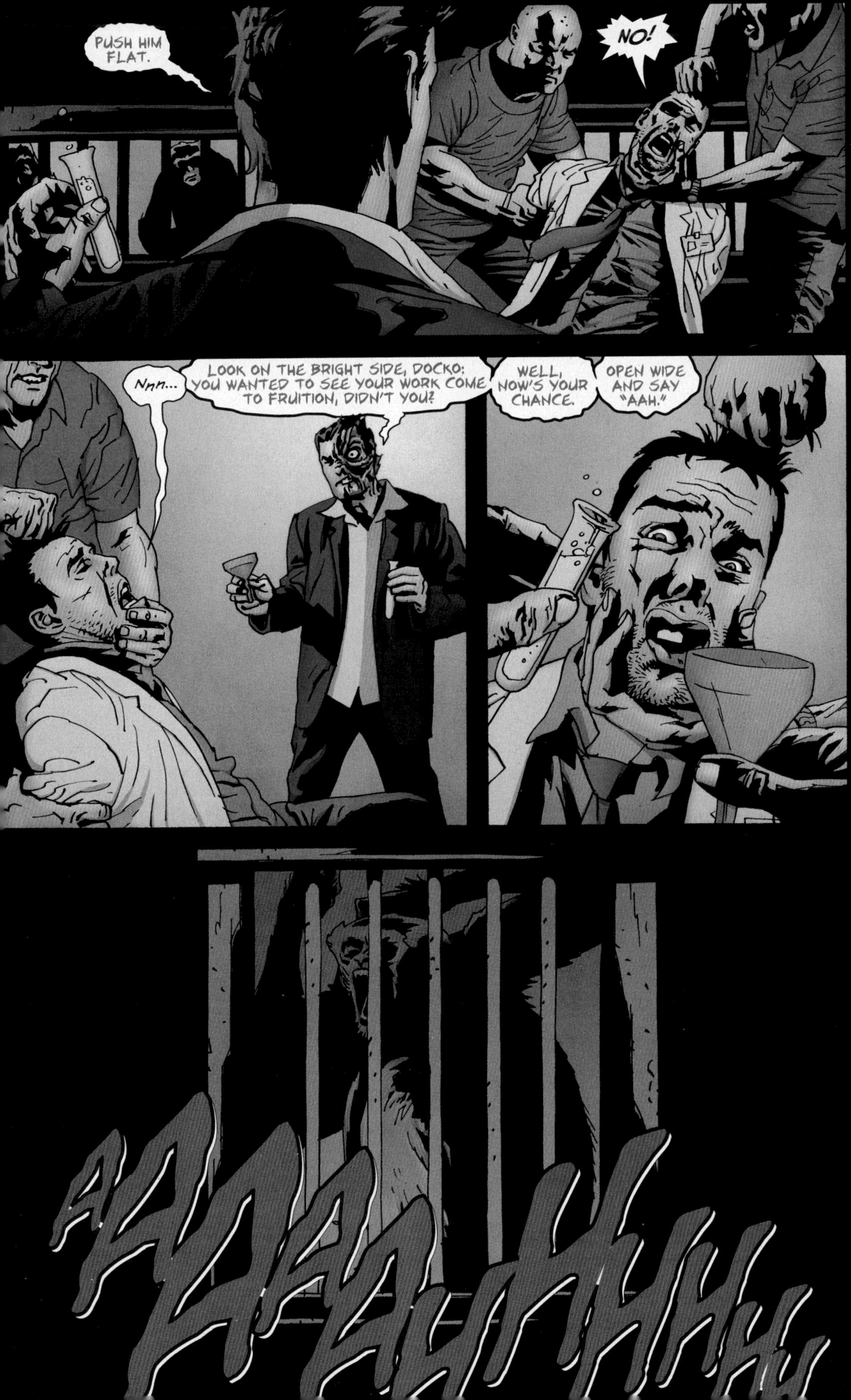
PUSH HIM FLAT.
NO!
Nnn...
LOOK ON THE BRIGHT SIDE, DOCKO: YOU WANTED TO SEE YOUR WORK COME TO FRUITION, DIDN'T YOU?
WELL, NOW'S YOUR CHANCE.
OPEN WIDE AND SAY "AAH."
AAAAAHHHHHH

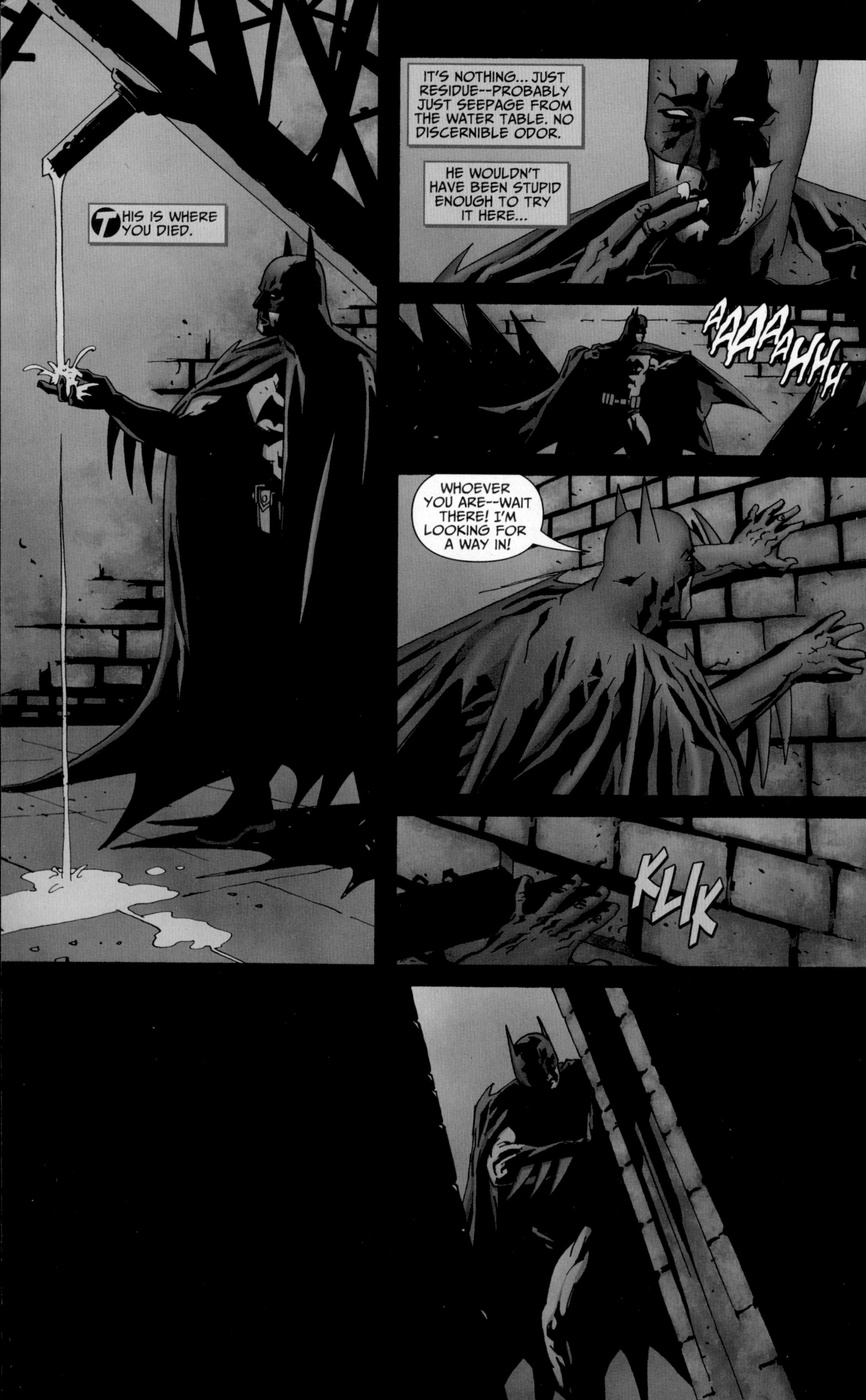
THIS IS WHERE YOU DIED.
IT'S NOTHING... JUST RESIDUE--PROBABLY JUST SEEPAGE FROM THE WATER TABLE. NO DISCERNIBLE ODOR.
HE WOULDN'T HAVE BEEN STUPID ENOUGH TO TRY IT HERE...
AAAAAAHHH
WHOEVER YOU ARE--WAIT THERE! I'M LOOKING FOR A WAY IN!
KLIK

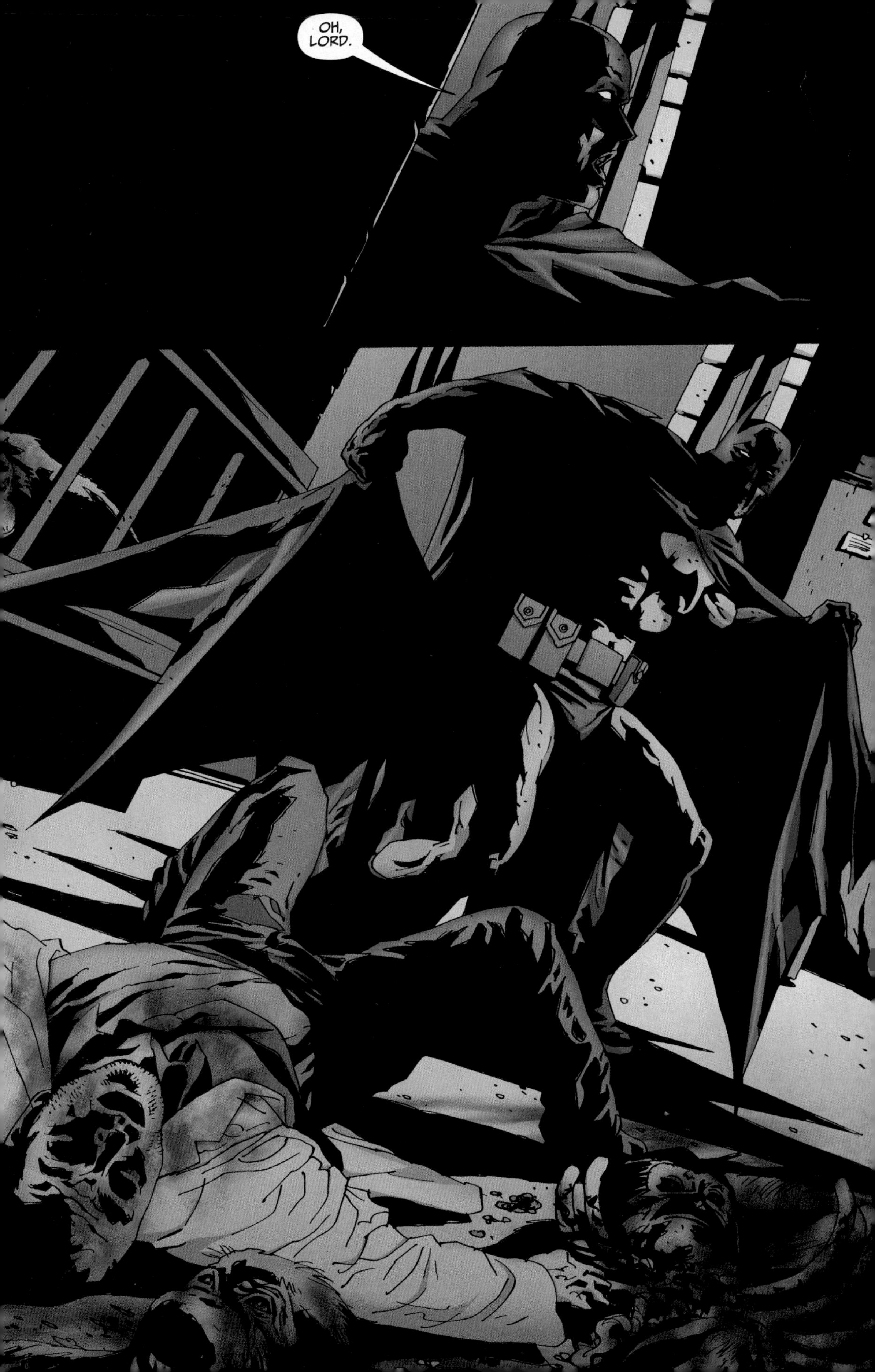
OH, LORD.

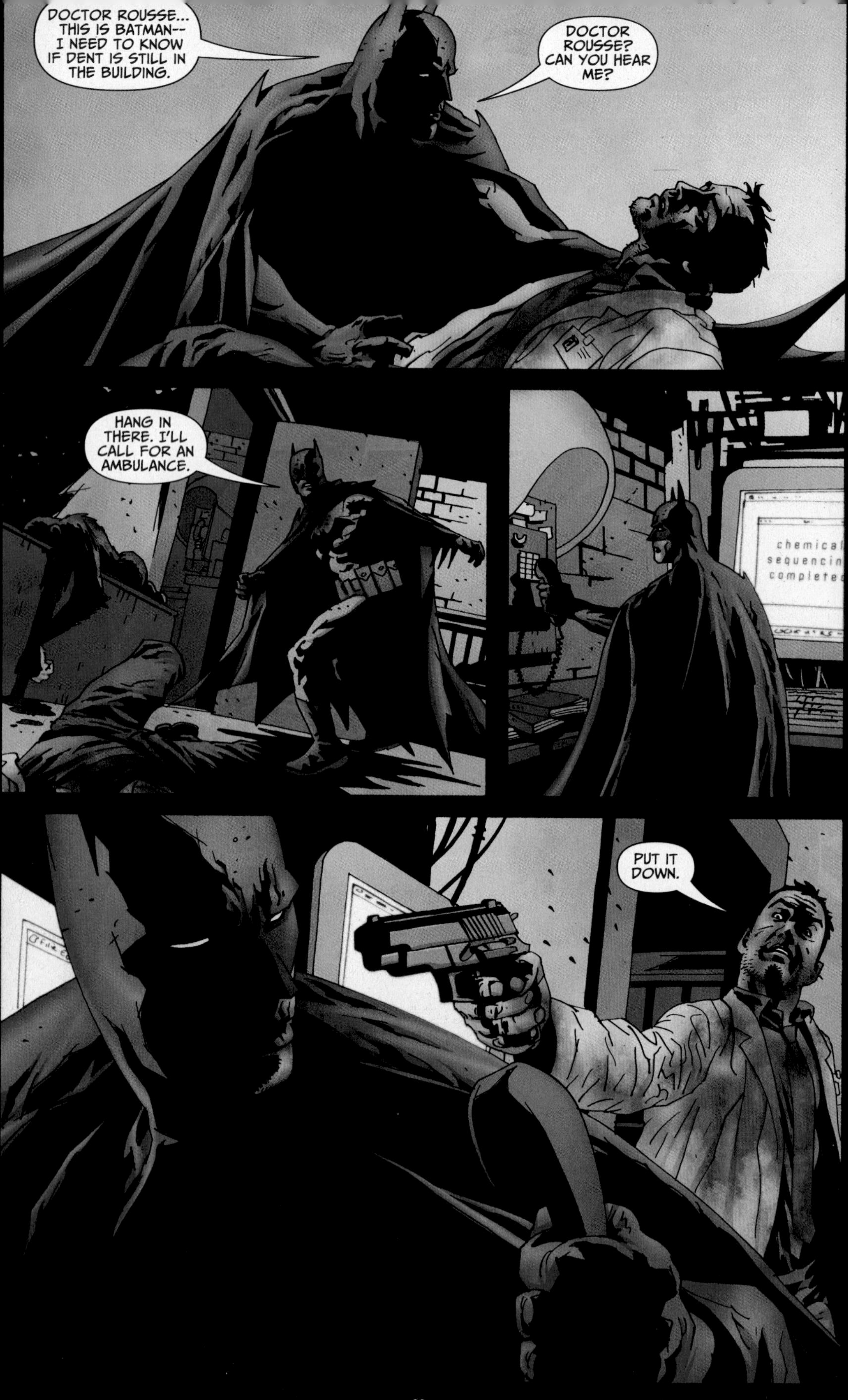
DOCTOR ROUSSE... THIS IS BATMAN-- I NEED TO KNOW IF DENT IS STILL IN THE BUILDING.
DOCTOR ROUSSE? CAN YOU HEAR ME?
HANG IN THERE. I'LL CALL FOR AN AMBULANCE.
chemical sequencin completed
PUT IT DOWN.

ROUSSE, LISTEN TO ME: I HAVE REASON TO BELIEVE YOU'VE BEEN POISONED BY A VARIATION OF YOUR OWN SERUM.

PUT THE GUN DOWN AND NO ONE GETS HURT--

BLAM

BLAM

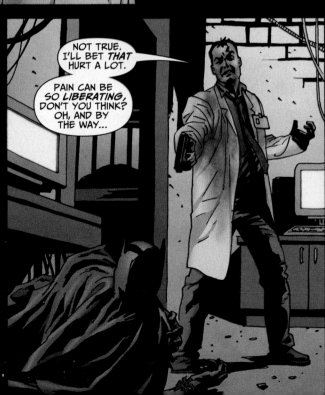

NOT TRUE. I'LL BET *THAT* HURT A LOT.

PAIN CAN BE SO *LIBERATING,* DON'T YOU THINK? OH, AND BY THE WAY...

...THE SERUM WORKS.

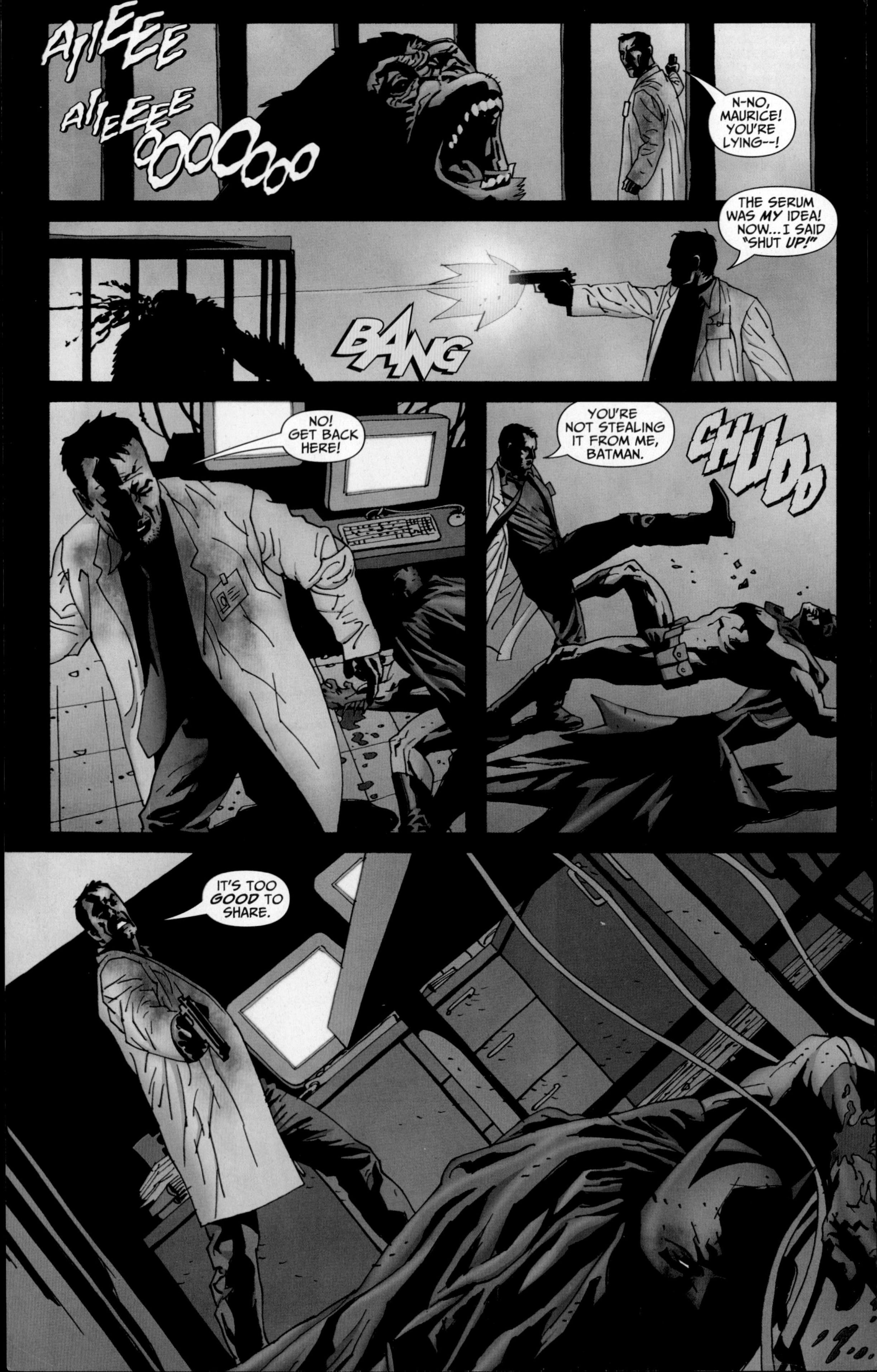
AIIEEE
AIIEEEE
OOOOOOO
N-NO, MAURICE! YOU'RE LYING--!
THE SERUM WAS MY IDEA! NOW... I SAID "SHUT UP!"
BANG
NO! GET BACK HERE!
YOU'RE NOT STEALING IT FROM ME, BATMAN.
CHUDD
IT'S TOO GOOD TO SHARE.

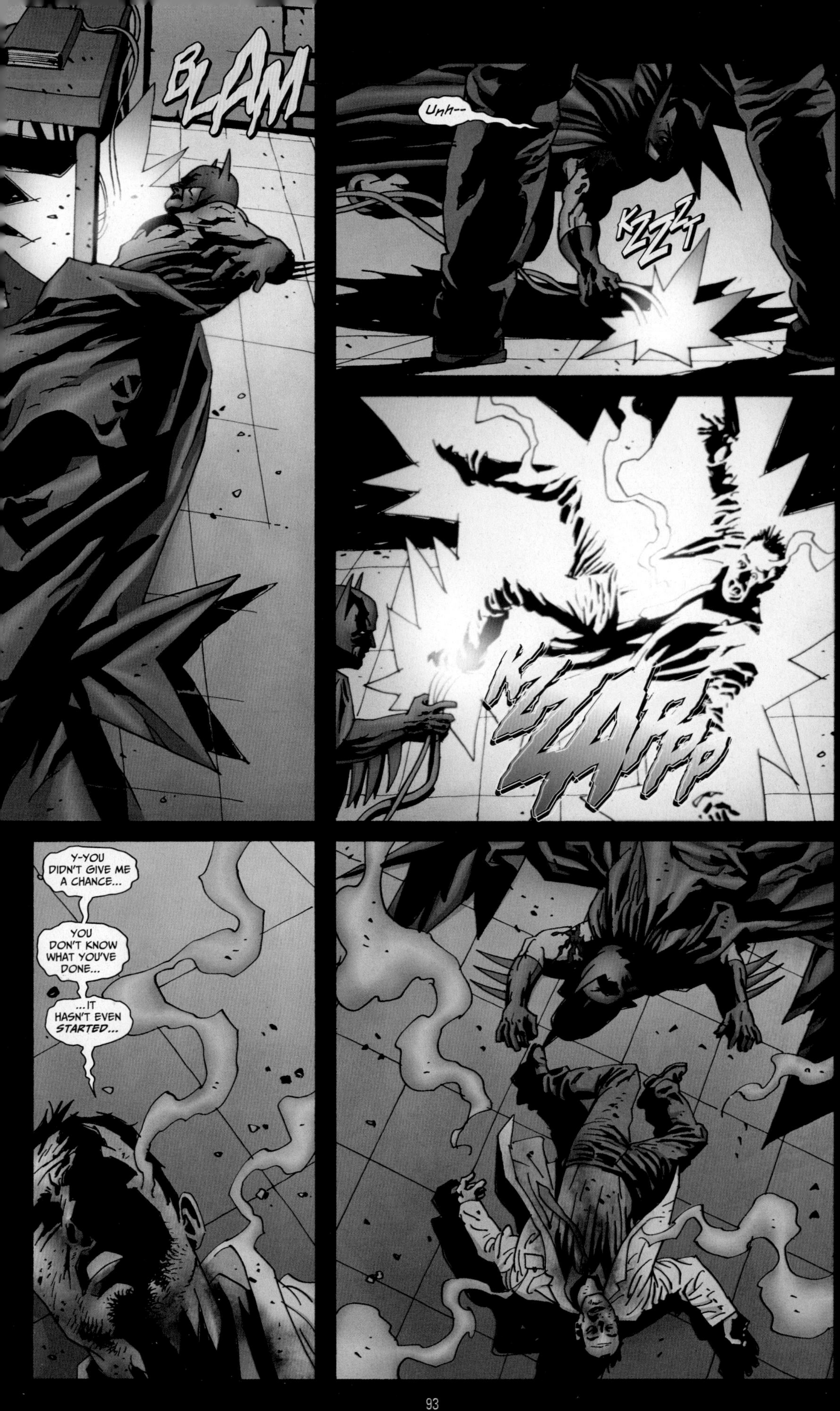
BLAM
Unh--
KZZZT
KZAPP
Y-YOU DIDN'T GIVE ME A CHANCE...
YOU DON'T KNOW WHAT YOU'VE DONE...
...IT HASN'T EVEN STARTED...

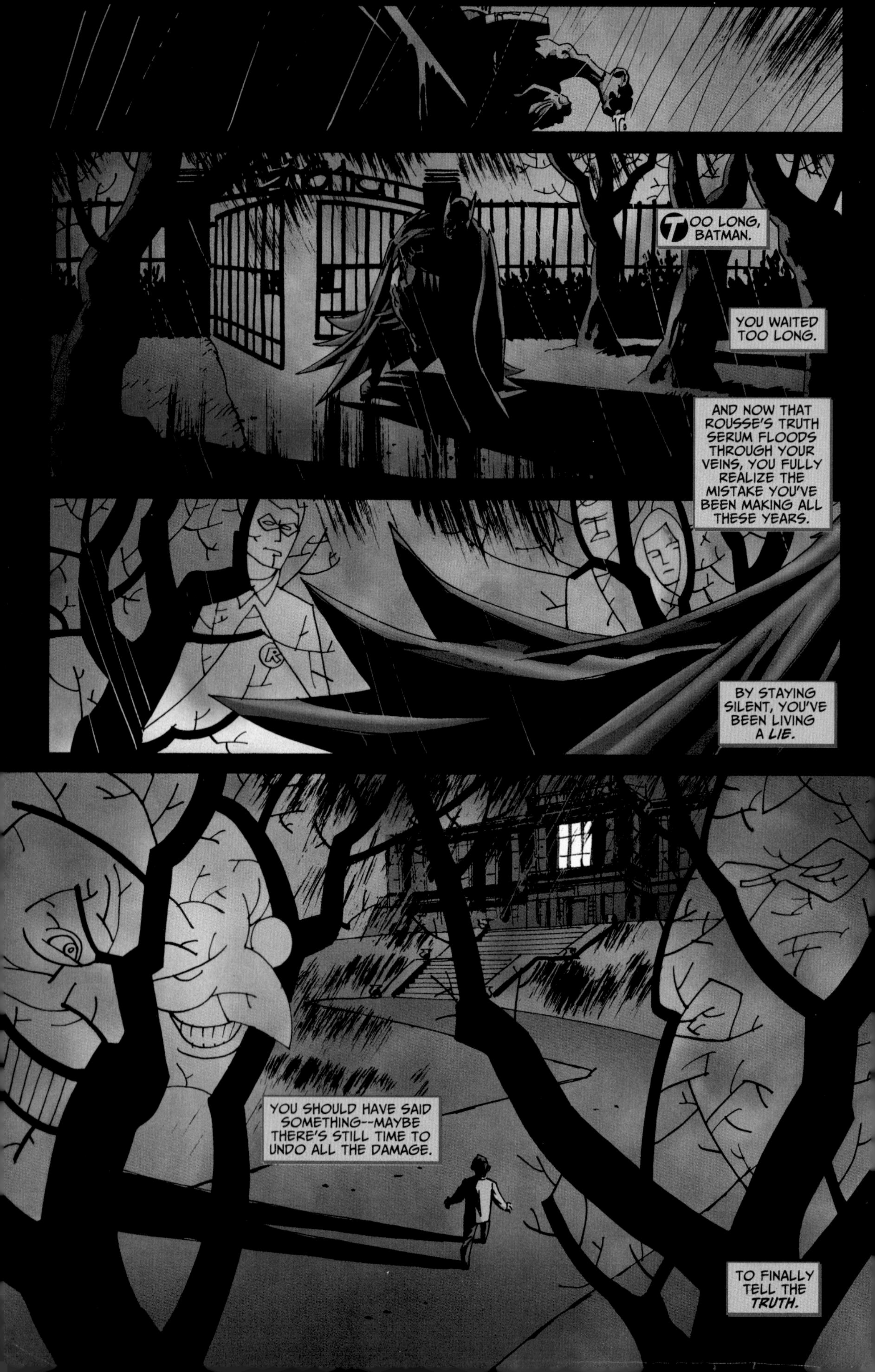
TOO LONG, BATMAN.
YOU WAITED TOO LONG.
AND NOW THAT ROUSSE'S TRUTH SERUM FLOODS THROUGH YOUR VEINS, YOU FULLY REALIZE THE MISTAKE YOU'VE BEEN MAKING ALL THESE YEARS.
BY STAYING SILENT, YOU'VE BEEN LIVING A *LIE*.
YOU SHOULD HAVE SAID SOMETHING--MAYBE THERE'S STILL TIME TO UNDO ALL THE DAMAGE.
TO FINALLY TELL THE *TRUTH*.

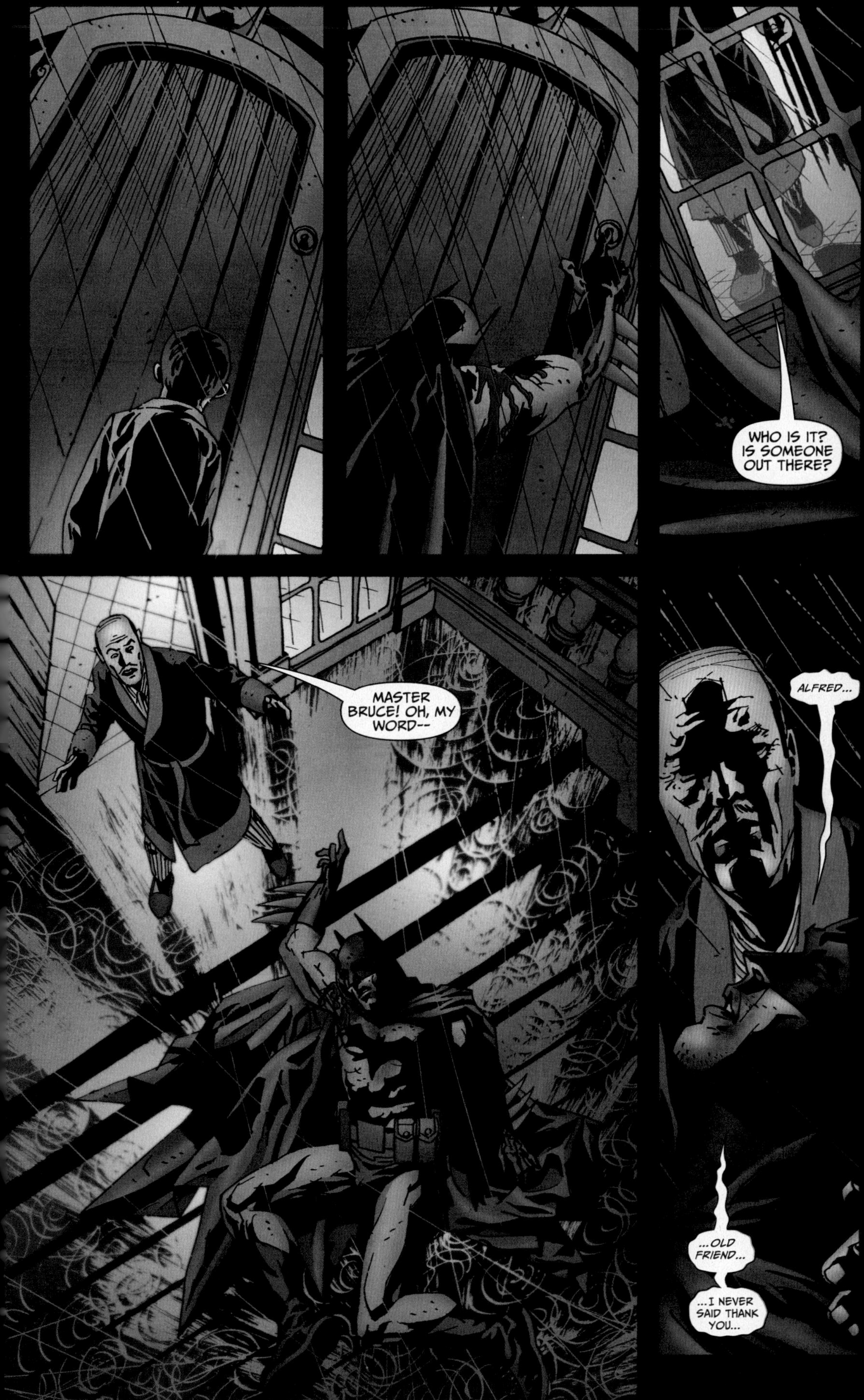
WHO IS IT? IS SOMEONE OUT THERE?
MASTER BRUCE! OH, MY WORD--
ALFRED...
...OLD FRIEND...
...I NEVER SAID THANK YOU...

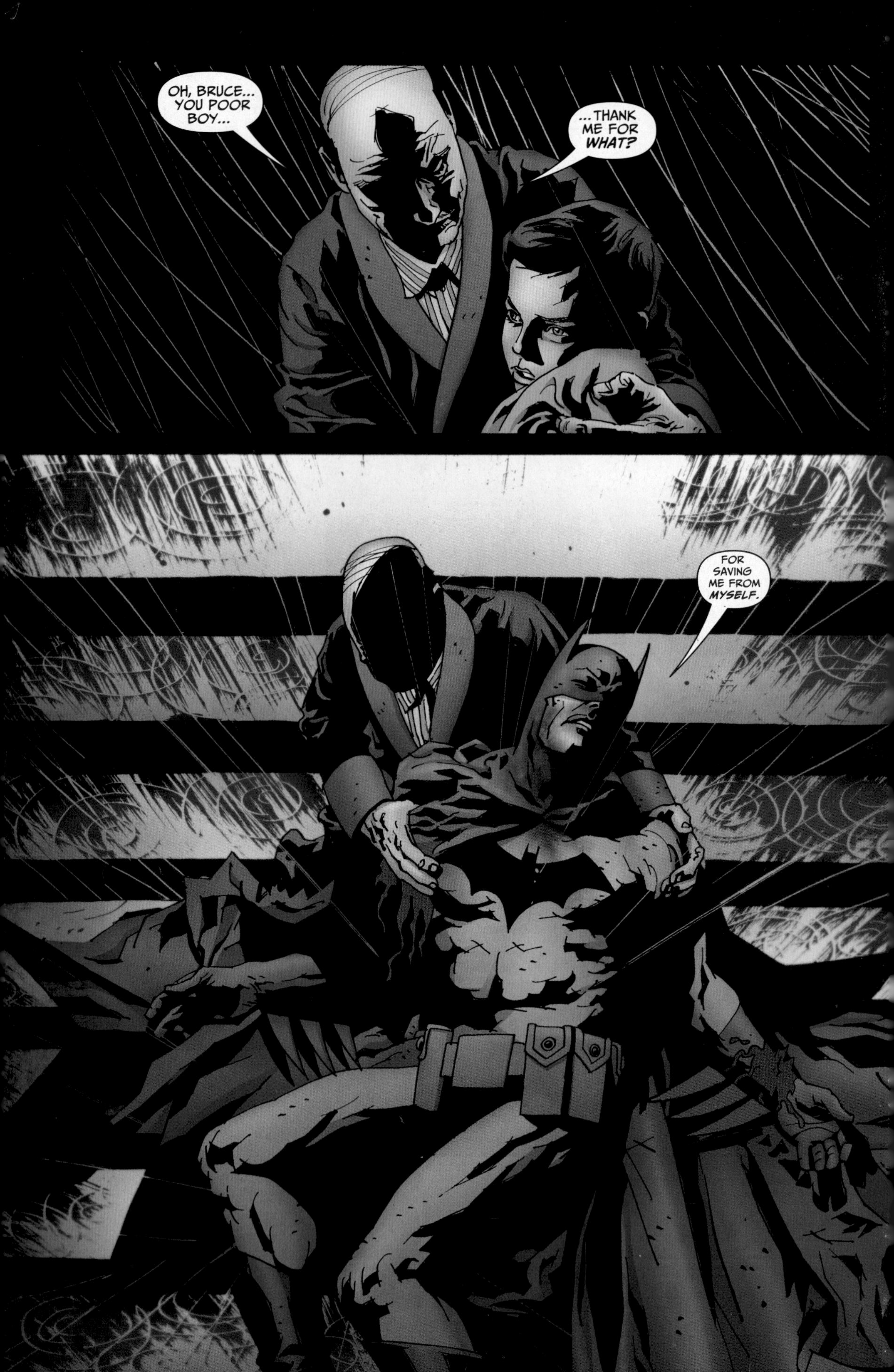
OH, BRUCE... YOU POOR BOY...
...THANK ME FOR *WHAT?*
FOR SAVING ME FROM *MYSELF.*

Chapter five

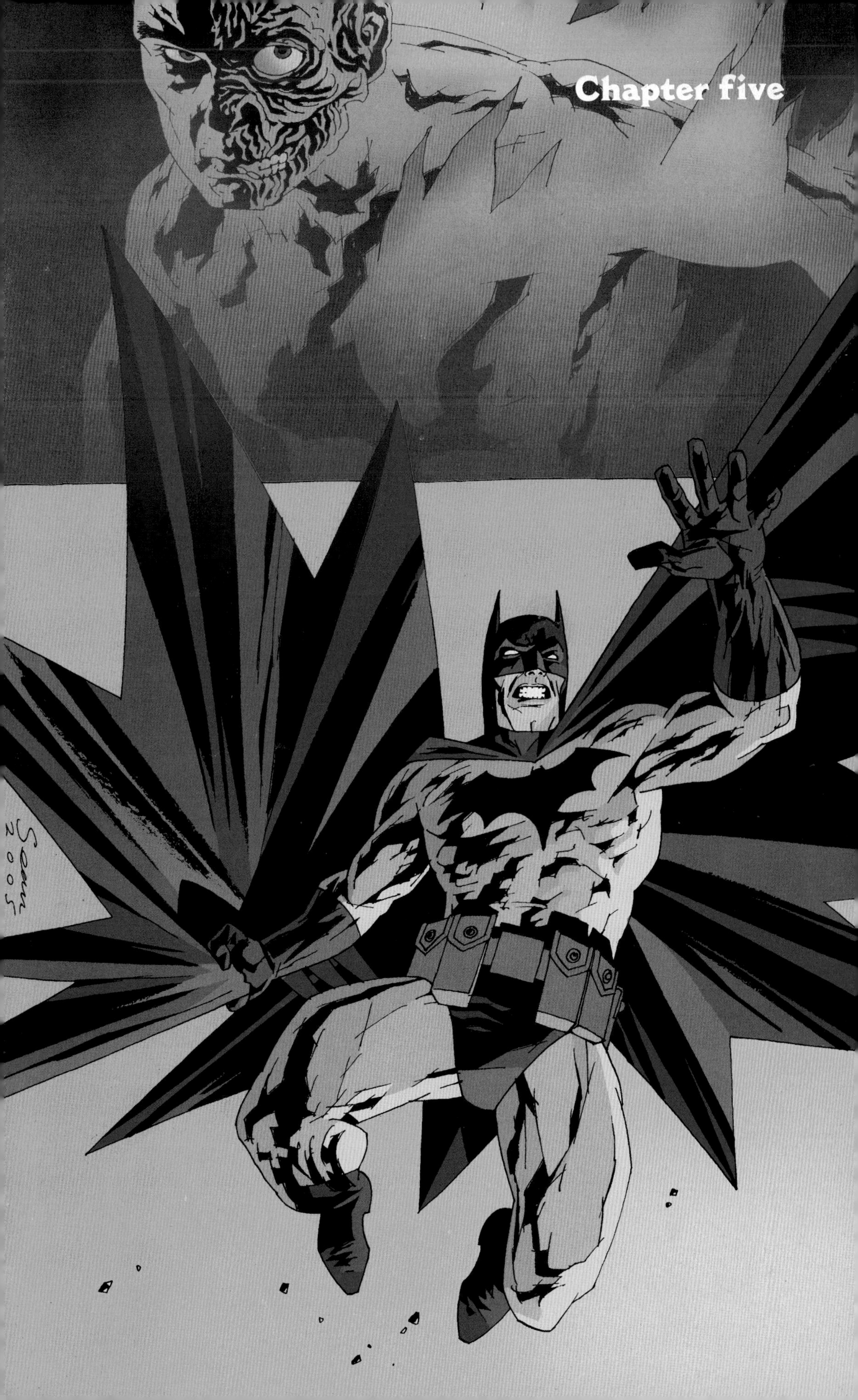
Sean
2005

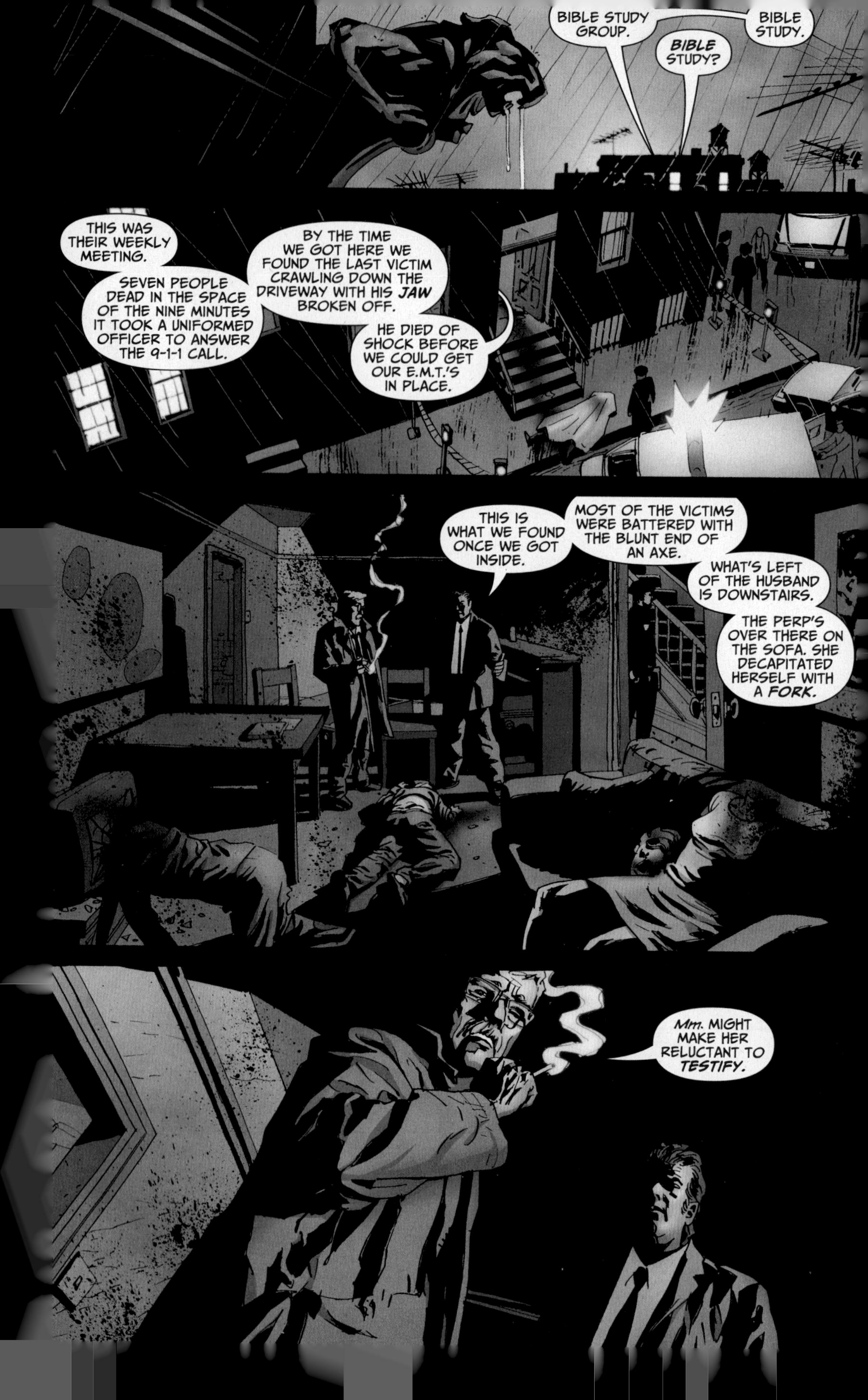
BIBLE STUDY GROUP.
BIBLE STUDY?
BIBLE STUDY.
THIS WAS THEIR WEEKLY MEETING.
SEVEN PEOPLE DEAD IN THE SPACE OF THE NINE MINUTES IT TOOK A UNIFORMED OFFICER TO ANSWER THE 9-1-1 CALL.
BY THE TIME WE GOT HERE WE FOUND THE LAST VICTIM CRAWLING DOWN THE DRIVEWAY WITH HIS *JAW* BROKEN OFF.
HE DIED OF SHOCK BEFORE WE COULD GET OUR E.M.T.'S IN PLACE.
THIS IS WHAT WE FOUND ONCE WE GOT INSIDE.
MOST OF THE VICTIMS WERE BATTERED WITH THE BLUNT END OF AN AXE.
WHAT'S LEFT OF THE HUSBAND IS DOWNSTAIRS.
THE PERP'S OVER THERE ON THE SOFA. SHE DECAPITATED HERSELF WITH A *FORK*.
Mm. MIGHT MAKE HER RELUCTANT TO *TESTIFY*.

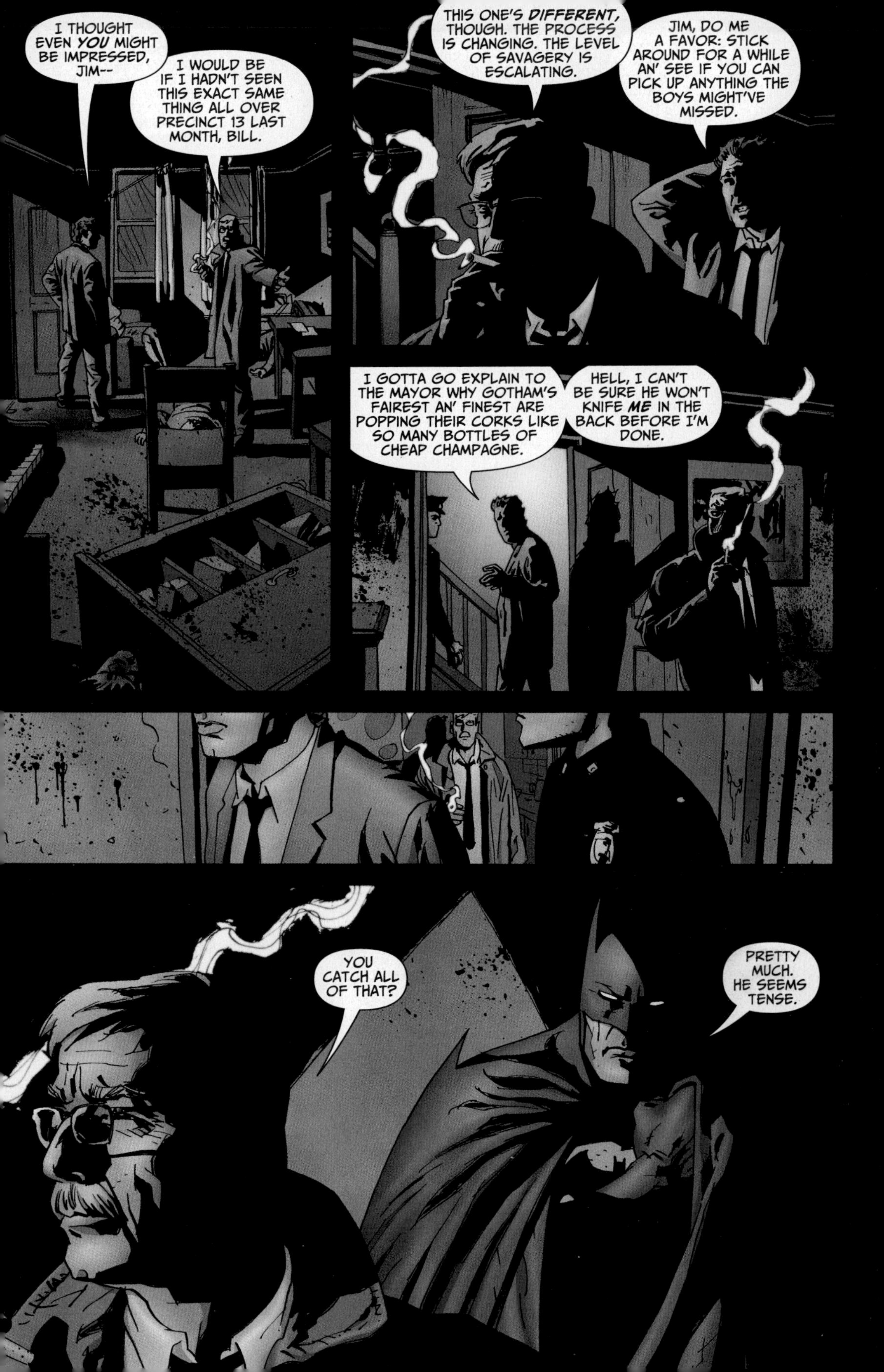
I THOUGHT EVEN YOU MIGHT BE IMPRESSED, JIM--
I WOULD BE IF I HADN'T SEEN THIS EXACT SAME THING ALL OVER PRECINCT 13 LAST MONTH, BILL.
THIS ONE'S DIFFERENT, THOUGH. THE PROCESS IS CHANGING. THE LEVEL OF SAVAGERY IS ESCALATING.
JIM, DO ME A FAVOR: STICK AROUND FOR A WHILE AN' SEE IF YOU CAN PICK UP ANYTHING THE BOYS MIGHT'VE MISSED.
I GOTTA GO EXPLAIN TO THE MAYOR WHY GOTHAM'S FAIREST AN' FINEST ARE POPPING THEIR CORKS LIKE SO MANY BOTTLES OF CHEAP CHAMPAGNE.
HELL, I CAN'T BE SURE HE WON'T KNIFE ME IN THE BACK BEFORE I'M DONE.
YOU CATCH ALL OF THAT?
PRETTY MUCH. HE SEEMS TENSE.

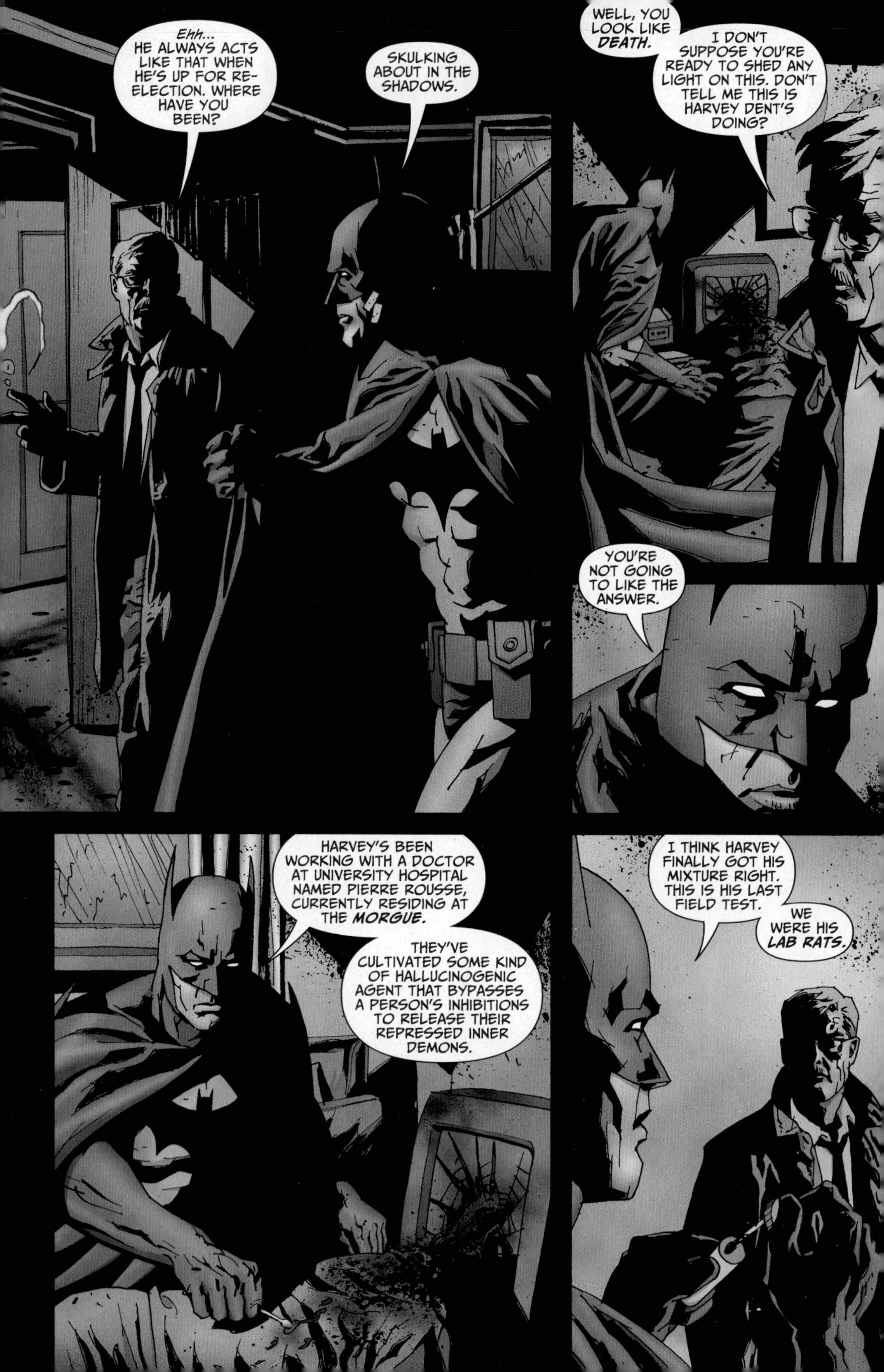

Ehh... HE ALWAYS ACTS LIKE THAT WHEN HE'S UP FOR RE-ELECTION. WHERE HAVE YOU BEEN?
SKULKING ABOUT IN THE SHADOWS.
WELL, YOU LOOK LIKE DEATH.
I DON'T SUPPOSE YOU'RE READY TO SHED ANY LIGHT ON THIS. DON'T TELL ME THIS IS HARVEY DENT'S DOING?
YOU'RE NOT GOING TO LIKE THE ANSWER.
HARVEY'S BEEN WORKING WITH A DOCTOR AT UNIVERSITY HOSPITAL NAMED PIERRE ROUSSE, CURRENTLY RESIDING AT THE MORGUE.
THEY'VE CULTIVATED SOME KIND OF HALLUCINOGENIC AGENT THAT BYPASSES A PERSON'S INHIBITIONS TO RELEASE THEIR REPRESSED INNER DEMONS.
I THINK HARVEY FINALLY GOT HIS MIXTURE RIGHT. THIS IS HIS LAST FIELD TEST.
WE WERE HIS LAB RATS.

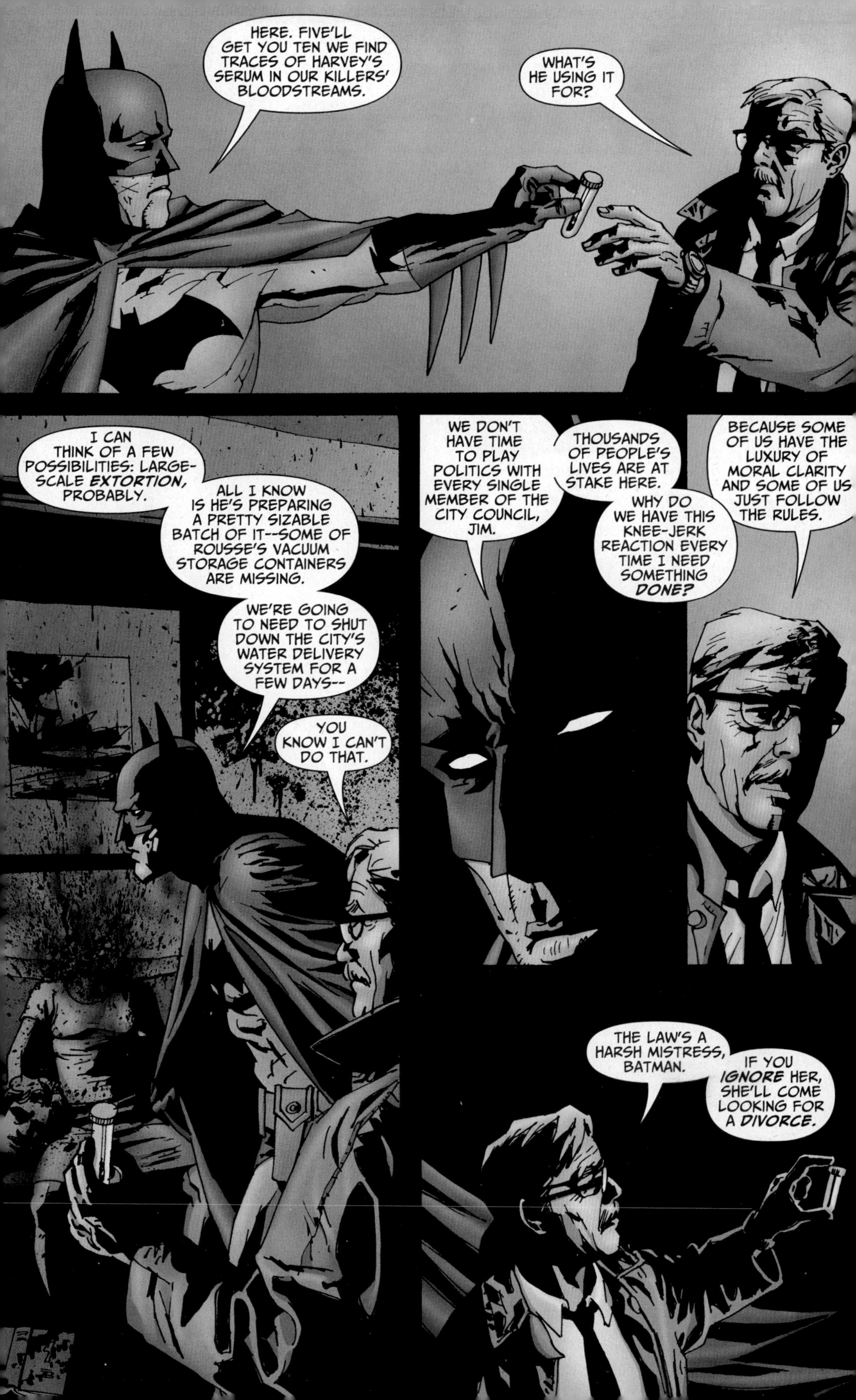
HERE. FIVE'LL GET YOU TEN WE FIND TRACES OF HARVEY'S SERUM IN OUR KILLERS' BLOODSTREAMS.
WHAT'S HE USING IT FOR?
I CAN THINK OF A FEW POSSIBILITIES: LARGE-SCALE EXTORTION, PROBABLY.
ALL I KNOW IS HE'S PREPARING A PRETTY SIZABLE BATCH OF IT--SOME OF ROUSSE'S VACUUM STORAGE CONTAINERS ARE MISSING.
WE'RE GOING TO NEED TO SHUT DOWN THE CITY'S WATER DELIVERY SYSTEM FOR A FEW DAYS--
YOU KNOW I CAN'T DO THAT.
WE DON'T HAVE TIME TO PLAY POLITICS WITH EVERY SINGLE MEMBER OF THE CITY COUNCIL, JIM.
THOUSANDS OF PEOPLE'S LIVES ARE AT STAKE HERE.
WHY DO WE HAVE THIS KNEE-JERK REACTION EVERY TIME I NEED SOMETHING DONE?
BECAUSE SOME OF US HAVE THE LUXURY OF MORAL CLARITY AND SOME OF US JUST FOLLOW THE RULES.
THE LAW'S A HARSH MISTRESS, BATMAN.
IF YOU IGNORE HER, SHE'LL COME LOOKING FOR A DIVORCE.

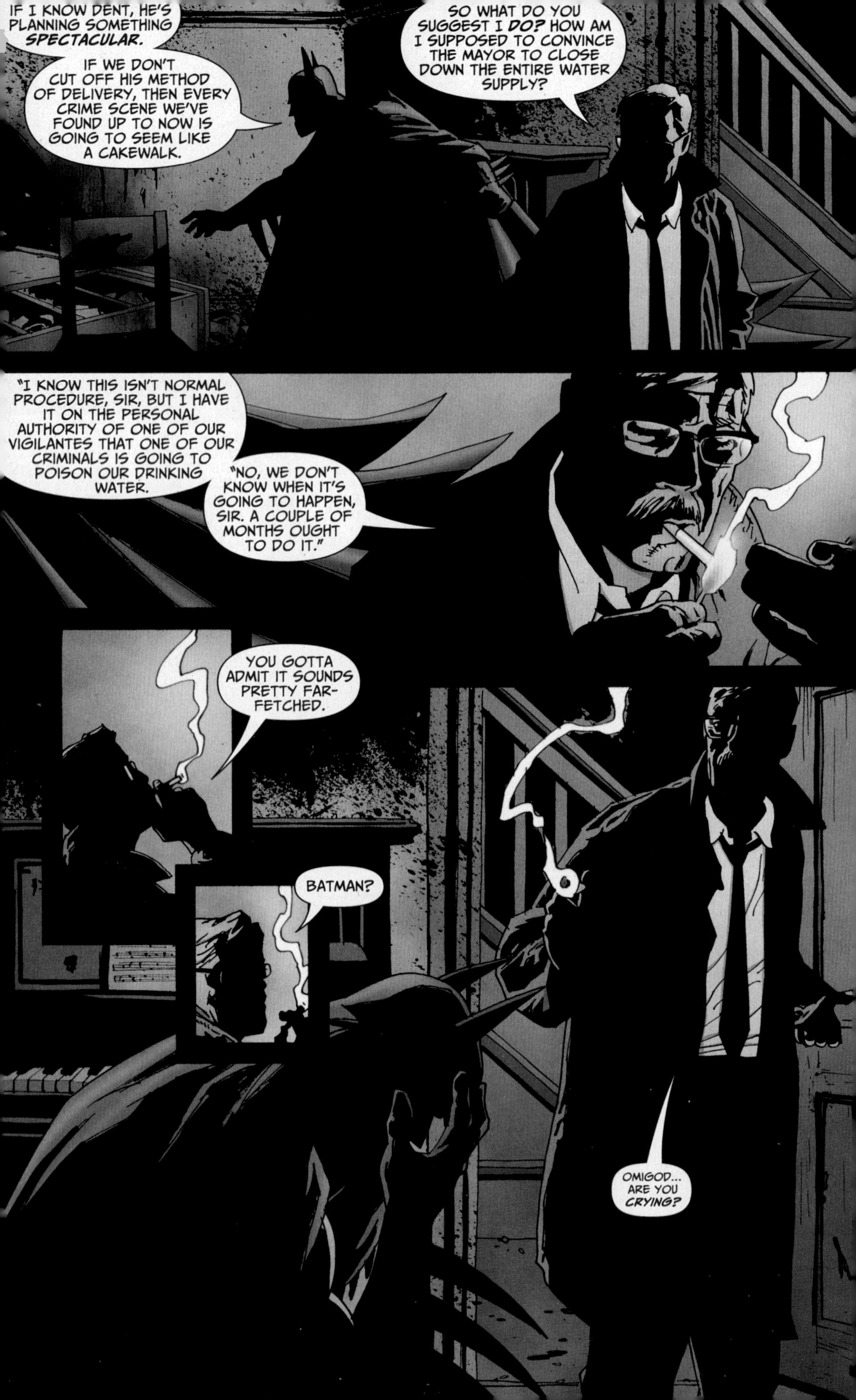
IF I KNOW DENT, HE'S PLANNING SOMETHING SPECTACULAR.
IF WE DON'T CUT OFF HIS METHOD OF DELIVERY, THEN EVERY CRIME SCENE WE'VE FOUND UP TO NOW IS GOING TO SEEM LIKE A CAKEWALK.
SO WHAT DO YOU SUGGEST I DO? HOW AM I SUPPOSED TO CONVINCE THE MAYOR TO CLOSE DOWN THE ENTIRE WATER SUPPLY?
"I KNOW THIS ISN'T NORMAL PROCEDURE, SIR, BUT I HAVE IT ON THE PERSONAL AUTHORITY OF ONE OF OUR VIGILANTES THAT ONE OF OUR CRIMINALS IS GOING TO POISON OUR DRINKING WATER.
"NO, WE DON'T KNOW WHEN IT'S GOING TO HAPPEN, SIR. A COUPLE OF MONTHS OUGHT TO DO IT."
YOU GOTTA ADMIT IT SOUNDS PRETTY FAR-FETCHED.
BATMAN?
OMIGOD... ARE YOU CRYING?

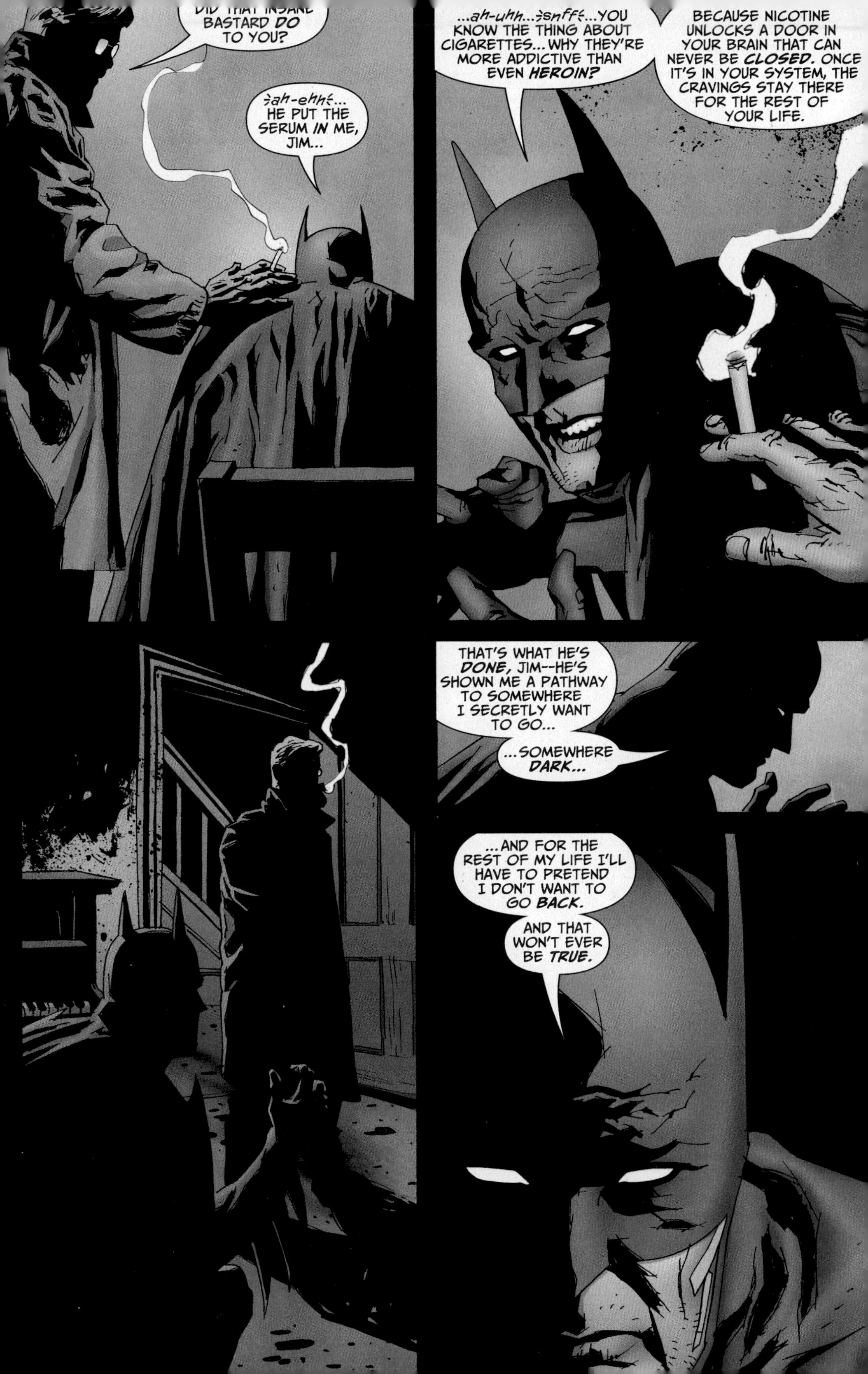
BASTARD DO TO YOU?
ah-ehh... HE PUT THE SERUM IN ME, JIM...
...ah-uhh...snff...YOU KNOW THE THING ABOUT CIGARETTES... WHY THEY'RE MORE ADDICTIVE THAN EVEN HEROIN?
BECAUSE NICOTINE UNLOCKS A DOOR IN YOUR BRAIN THAT CAN NEVER BE CLOSED. ONCE IT'S IN YOUR SYSTEM, THE CRAVINGS STAY THERE FOR THE REST OF YOUR LIFE.
THAT'S WHAT HE'S DONE, JIM--HE'S SHOWN ME A PATHWAY TO SOMEWHERE I SECRETLY WANT TO GO...
...SOMEWHERE DARK...
...AND FOR THE REST OF MY LIFE I'LL HAVE TO PRETEND I DON'T WANT TO GO BACK.
AND THAT WON'T EVER BE TRUE.

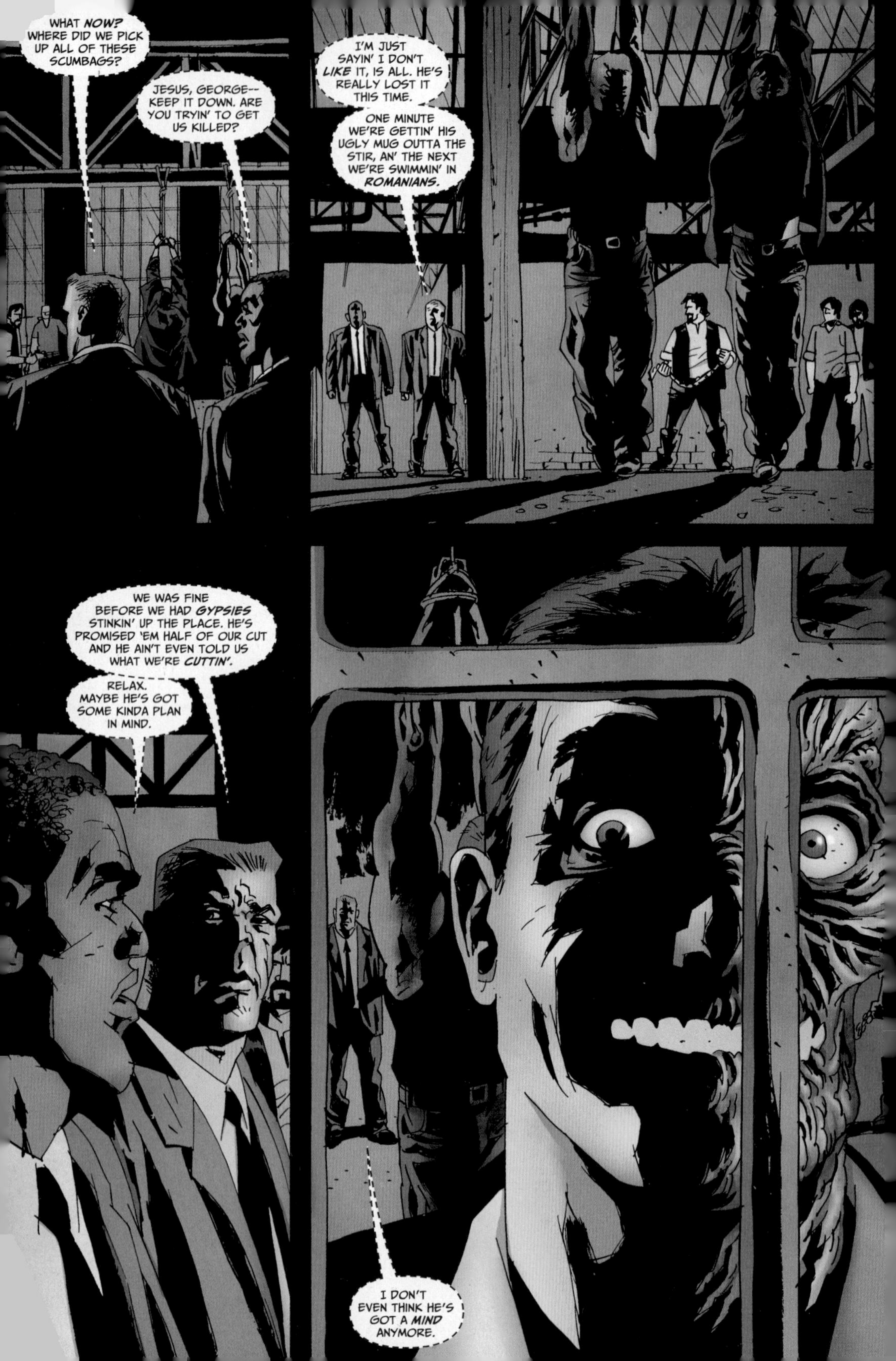
WHAT NOW? WHERE DID WE PICK UP ALL OF THESE SCUMBAGS?
JESUS, GEORGE-- KEEP IT DOWN. ARE YOU TRYIN' TO GET US KILLED?
I'M JUST SAYIN' I DON'T LIKE IT, IS ALL. HE'S REALLY LOST IT THIS TIME.
ONE MINUTE WE'RE GETTIN' HIS UGLY MUG OUTTA THE STIR, AN' THE NEXT WE'RE SWIMMIN' IN ROMANIANS.
WE WAS FINE BEFORE WE HAD GYPSIES STINKIN' UP THE PLACE. HE'S PROMISED 'EM HALF OF OUR CUT AND HE AIN'T EVEN TOLD US WHAT WE'RE CUTTIN'.
RELAX. MAYBE HE'S GOT SOME KINDA PLAN IN MIND.
I DON'T EVEN THINK HE'S GOT A MIND ANYMORE.

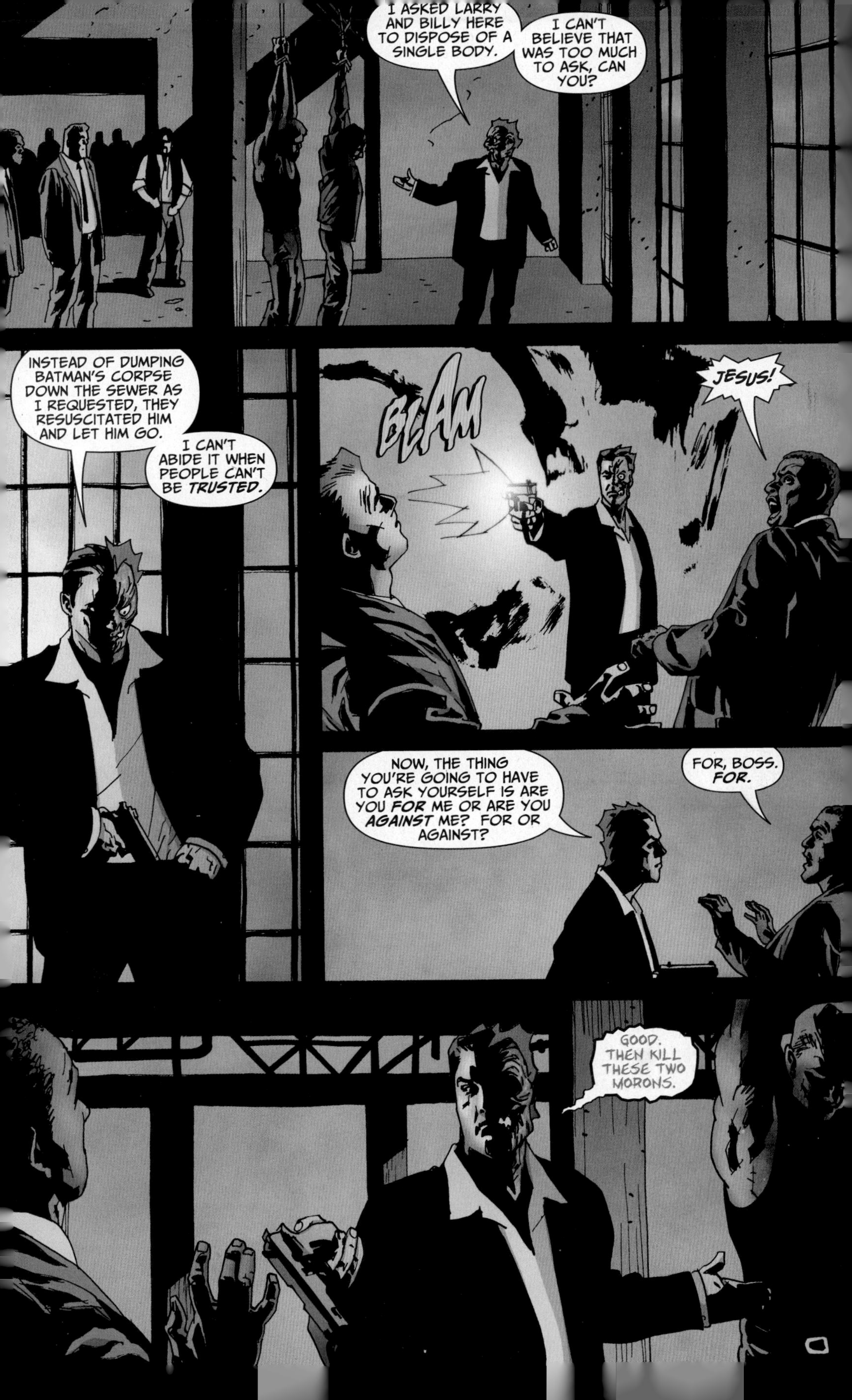
I ASKED LARRY AND BILLY HERE TO DISPOSE OF A SINGLE BODY.
I CAN'T BELIEVE THAT WAS TOO MUCH TO ASK, CAN YOU?
INSTEAD OF DUMPING BATMAN'S CORPSE DOWN THE SEWER AS I REQUESTED, THEY RESUSCITATED HIM AND LET HIM GO.
I CAN'T ABIDE IT WHEN PEOPLE CAN'T BE *TRUSTED.*
BLAM
JESUS!
NOW, THE THING YOU'RE GOING TO HAVE TO ASK YOURSELF IS ARE YOU *FOR* ME OR ARE YOU *AGAINST* ME? FOR OR AGAINST?
FOR, BOSS. *FOR.*
GOOD. THEN KILL THESE TWO MORONS.

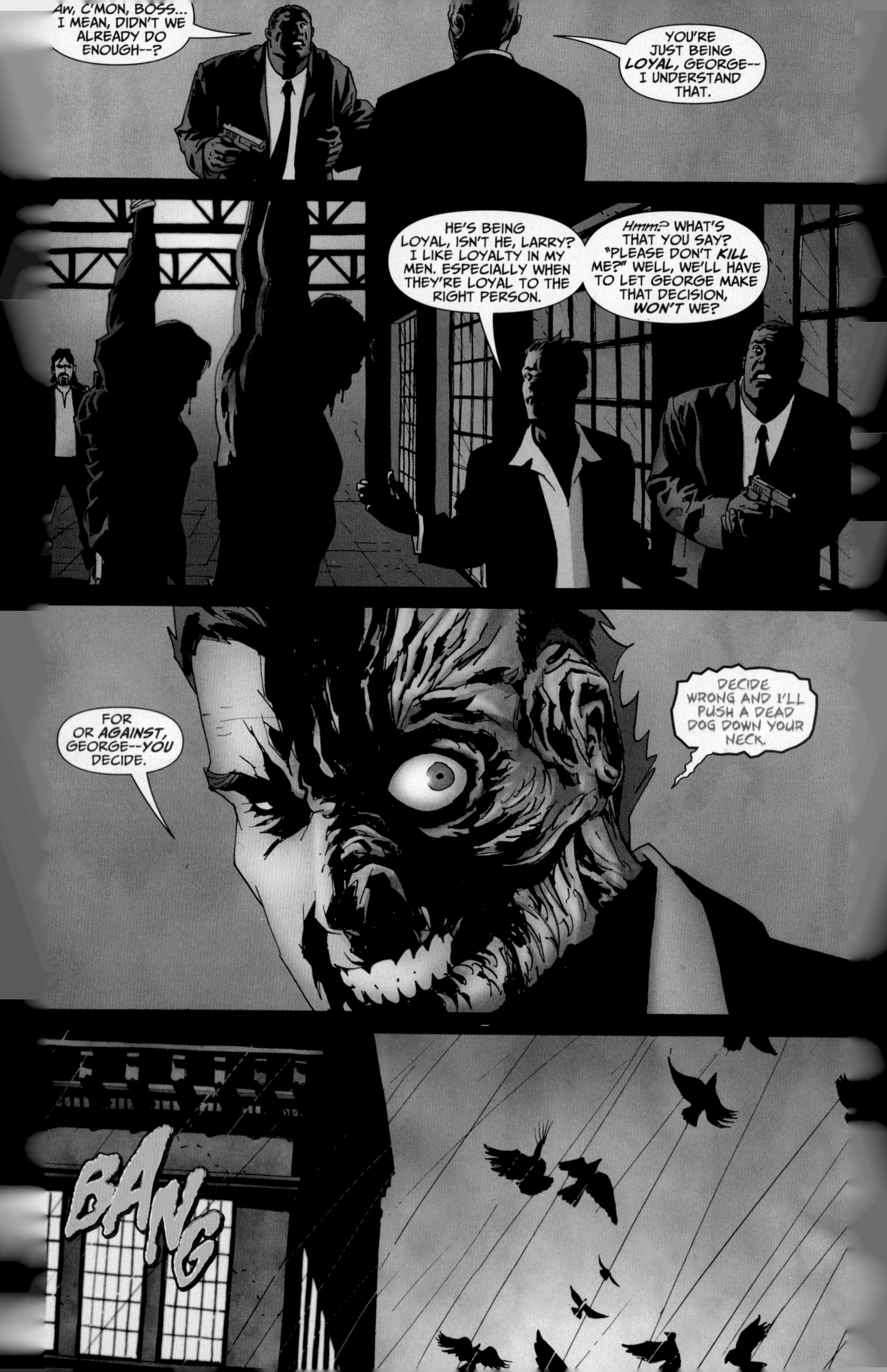
AW, C'MON, BOSS... I MEAN, DIDN'T WE ALREADY DO ENOUGH--?
YOU'RE JUST BEING LOYAL, GEORGE-- I UNDERSTAND THAT.
HE'S BEING LOYAL, ISN'T HE, LARRY? I LIKE LOYALTY IN MY MEN. ESPECIALLY WHEN THEY'RE LOYAL TO THE RIGHT PERSON.
Hmm? WHAT'S THAT YOU SAY? "PLEASE DON'T KILL ME?" WELL, WE'LL HAVE TO LET GEORGE MAKE THAT DECISION, WON'T WE?
FOR OR AGAINST, GEORGE--YOU DECIDE.
DECIDE WRONG AND I'LL PUSH A DEAD DOG DOWN YOUR NECK.
BANG

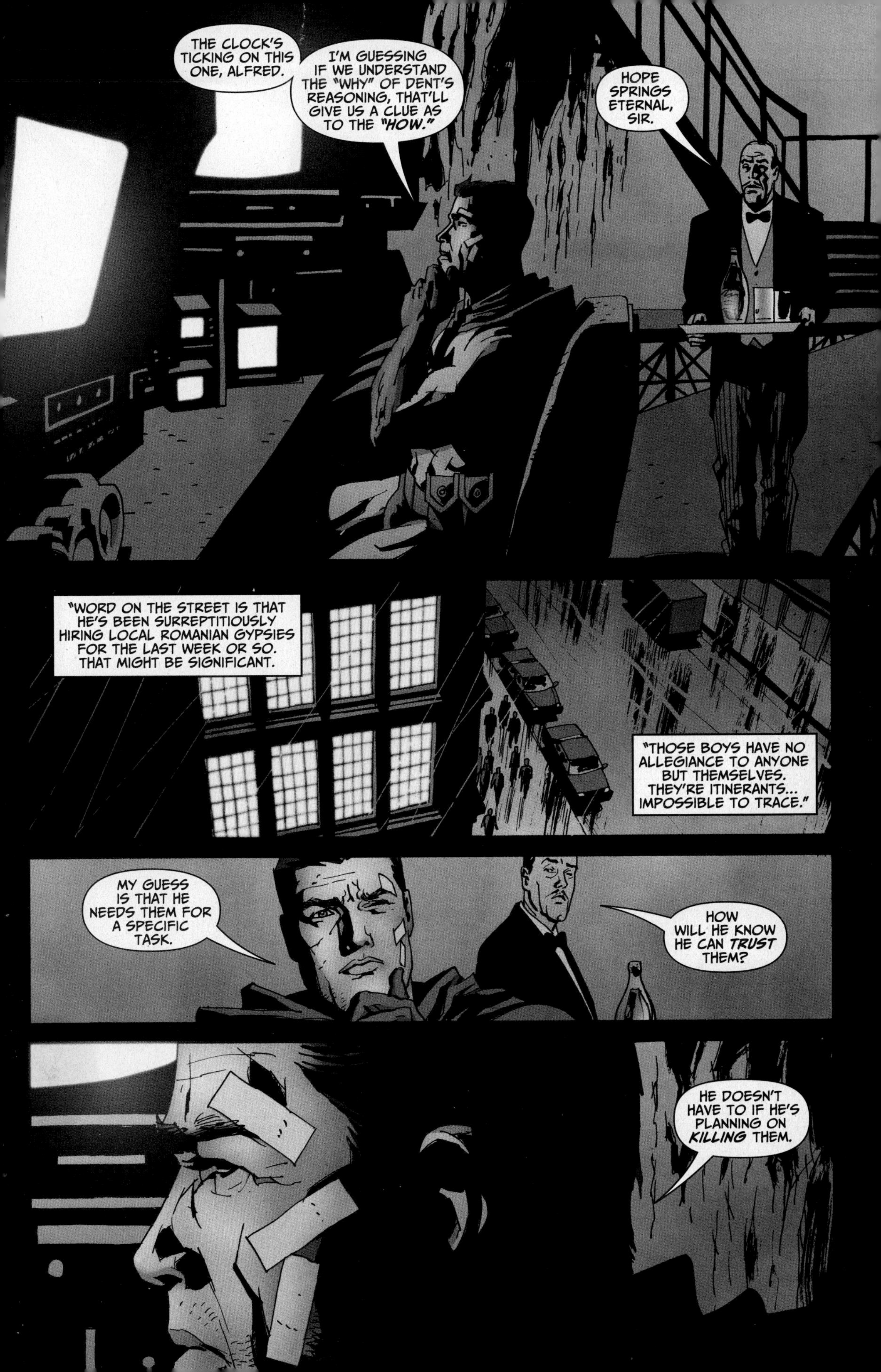
THE CLOCK'S TICKING ON THIS ONE, ALFRED.
I'M GUESSING IF WE UNDERSTAND THE "WHY" OF DENT'S REASONING, THAT'LL GIVE US A CLUE AS TO THE "HOW."
HOPE SPRINGS ETERNAL, SIR.
"WORD ON THE STREET IS THAT HE'S BEEN SURREPTITIOUSLY HIRING LOCAL ROMANIAN GYPSIES FOR THE LAST WEEK OR SO. THAT MIGHT BE SIGNIFICANT.
"THOSE BOYS HAVE NO ALLEGIANCE TO ANYONE BUT THEMSELVES. THEY'RE ITINERANTS... IMPOSSIBLE TO TRACE."
MY GUESS IS THAT HE NEEDS THEM FOR A SPECIFIC TASK.
HOW WILL HE KNOW HE CAN TRUST THEM?
HE DOESN'T HAVE TO IF HE'S PLANNING ON KILLING THEM.

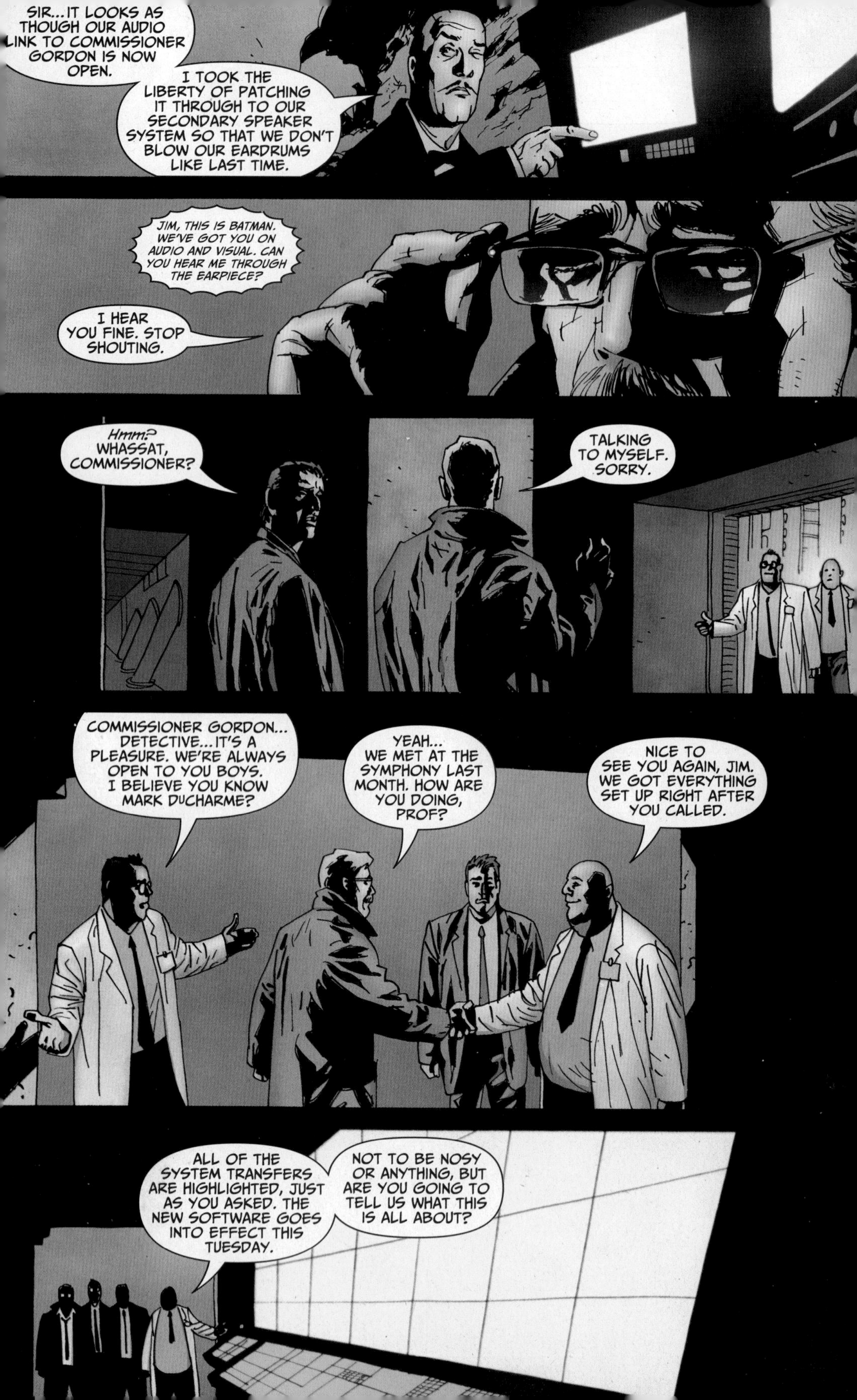
SIR... IT LOOKS AS THOUGH OUR AUDIO LINK TO COMMISSIONER GORDON IS NOW OPEN.
I TOOK THE LIBERTY OF PATCHING IT THROUGH TO OUR SECONDARY SPEAKER SYSTEM SO THAT WE DON'T BLOW OUR EARDRUMS LIKE LAST TIME.
JIM, THIS IS BATMAN. WE'VE GOT YOU ON AUDIO AND VISUAL. CAN YOU HEAR ME THROUGH THE EARPIECE?
I HEAR YOU FINE. STOP SHOUTING.
Hmm? WHASSAT, COMMISSIONER?
TALKING TO MYSELF. SORRY.
COMMISSIONER GORDON... DETECTIVE... IT'S A PLEASURE. WE'RE ALWAYS OPEN TO YOU BOYS. I BELIEVE YOU KNOW MARK DUCHARME?
YEAH... WE MET AT THE SYMPHONY LAST MONTH. HOW ARE YOU DOING, PROF?
NICE TO SEE YOU AGAIN, JIM. WE GOT EVERYTHING SET UP RIGHT AFTER YOU CALLED.
ALL OF THE SYSTEM TRANSFERS ARE HIGHLIGHTED, JUST AS YOU ASKED. THE NEW SOFTWARE GOES INTO EFFECT THIS TUESDAY.
NOT TO BE NOSY OR ANYTHING, BUT ARE YOU GOING TO TELL US WHAT THIS IS ALL ABOUT?

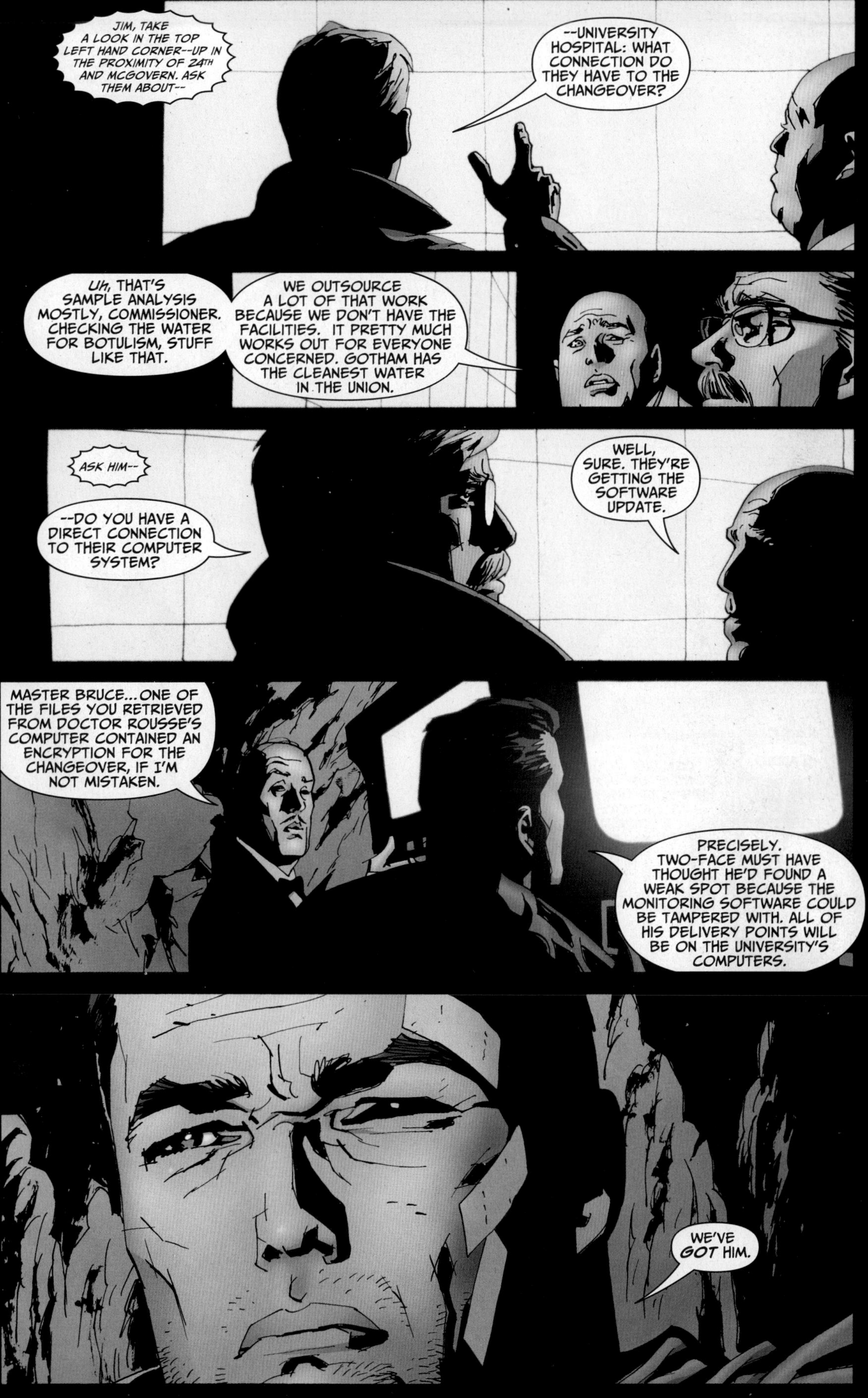
JIM, TAKE A LOOK IN THE TOP LEFT HAND CORNER--UP IN THE PROXIMITY OF 24TH AND MCGOVERN. ASK THEM ABOUT--
--UNIVERSITY HOSPITAL: WHAT CONNECTION DO THEY HAVE TO THE CHANGEOVER?
UH, THAT'S SAMPLE ANALYSIS MOSTLY, COMMISSIONER. CHECKING THE WATER FOR BOTULISM, STUFF LIKE THAT.
WE OUTSOURCE A LOT OF THAT WORK BECAUSE WE DON'T HAVE THE FACILITIES. IT PRETTY MUCH WORKS OUT FOR EVERYONE CONCERNED. GOTHAM HAS THE CLEANEST WATER IN THE UNION.
ASK HIM--
--DO YOU HAVE A DIRECT CONNECTION TO THEIR COMPUTER SYSTEM?
WELL, SURE. THEY'RE GETTING THE SOFTWARE UPDATE.
MASTER BRUCE...ONE OF THE FILES YOU RETRIEVED FROM DOCTOR ROUSSE'S COMPUTER CONTAINED AN ENCRYPTION FOR THE CHANGEOVER, IF I'M NOT MISTAKEN.
PRECISELY. TWO-FACE MUST HAVE THOUGHT HE'D FOUND A WEAK SPOT BECAUSE THE MONITORING SOFTWARE COULD BE TAMPERED WITH. ALL OF HIS DELIVERY POINTS WILL BE ON THE UNIVERSITY'S COMPUTERS.
WE'VE GOT HIM.

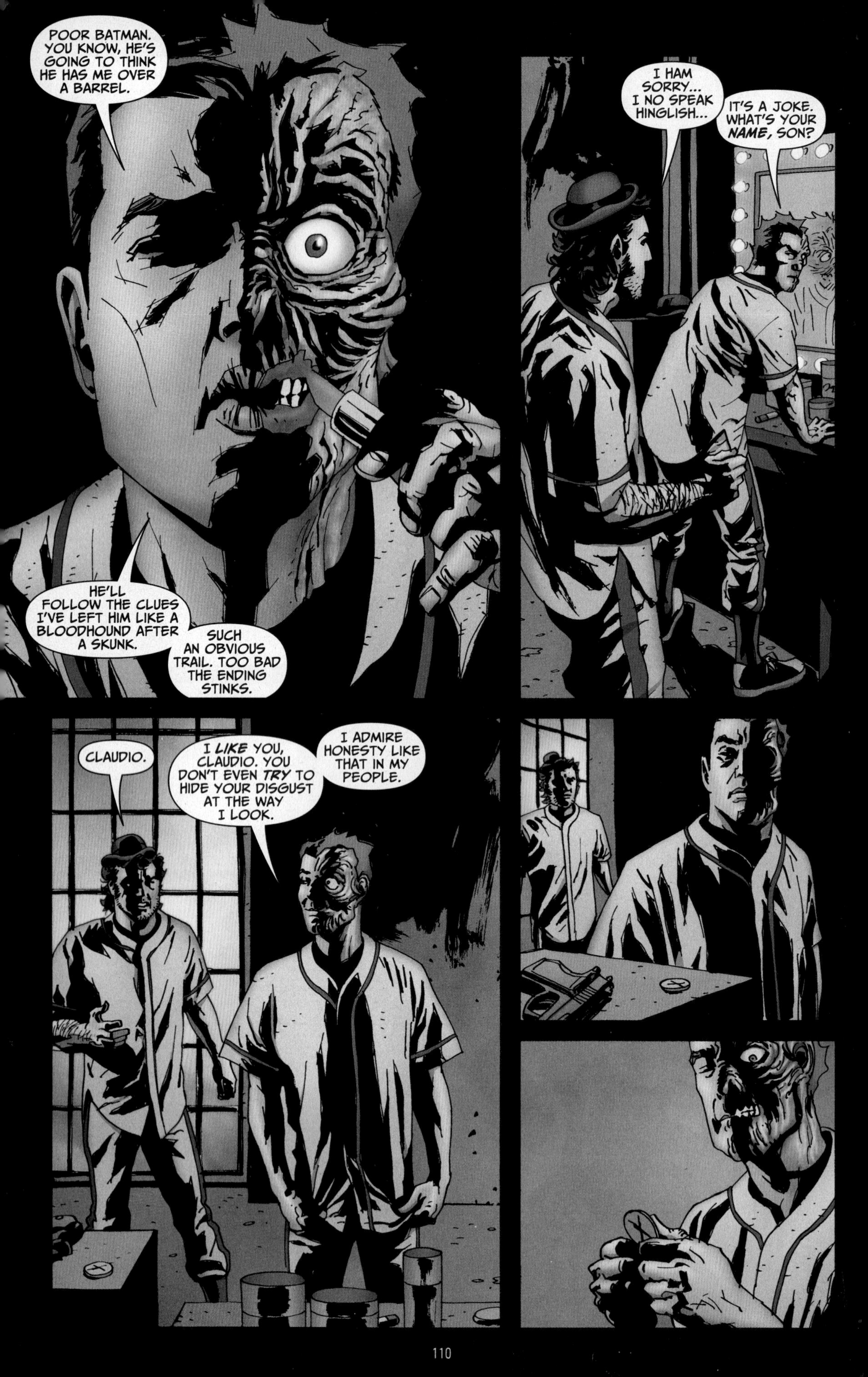
POOR BATMAN. YOU KNOW, HE'S GOING TO THINK HE HAS ME OVER A BARREL.
HE'LL FOLLOW THE CLUES I'VE LEFT HIM LIKE A BLOODHOUND AFTER A SKUNK.
SUCH AN OBVIOUS TRAIL. TOO BAD THE ENDING STINKS.
I HAM SORRY... I NO SPEAK HINGLISH...
IT'S A JOKE. WHAT'S YOUR NAME, SON?
CLAUDIO.
I LIKE YOU, CLAUDIO. YOU DON'T EVEN TRY TO HIDE YOUR DISGUST AT THE WAY I LOOK.
I ADMIRE HONESTY LIKE THAT IN MY PEOPLE.

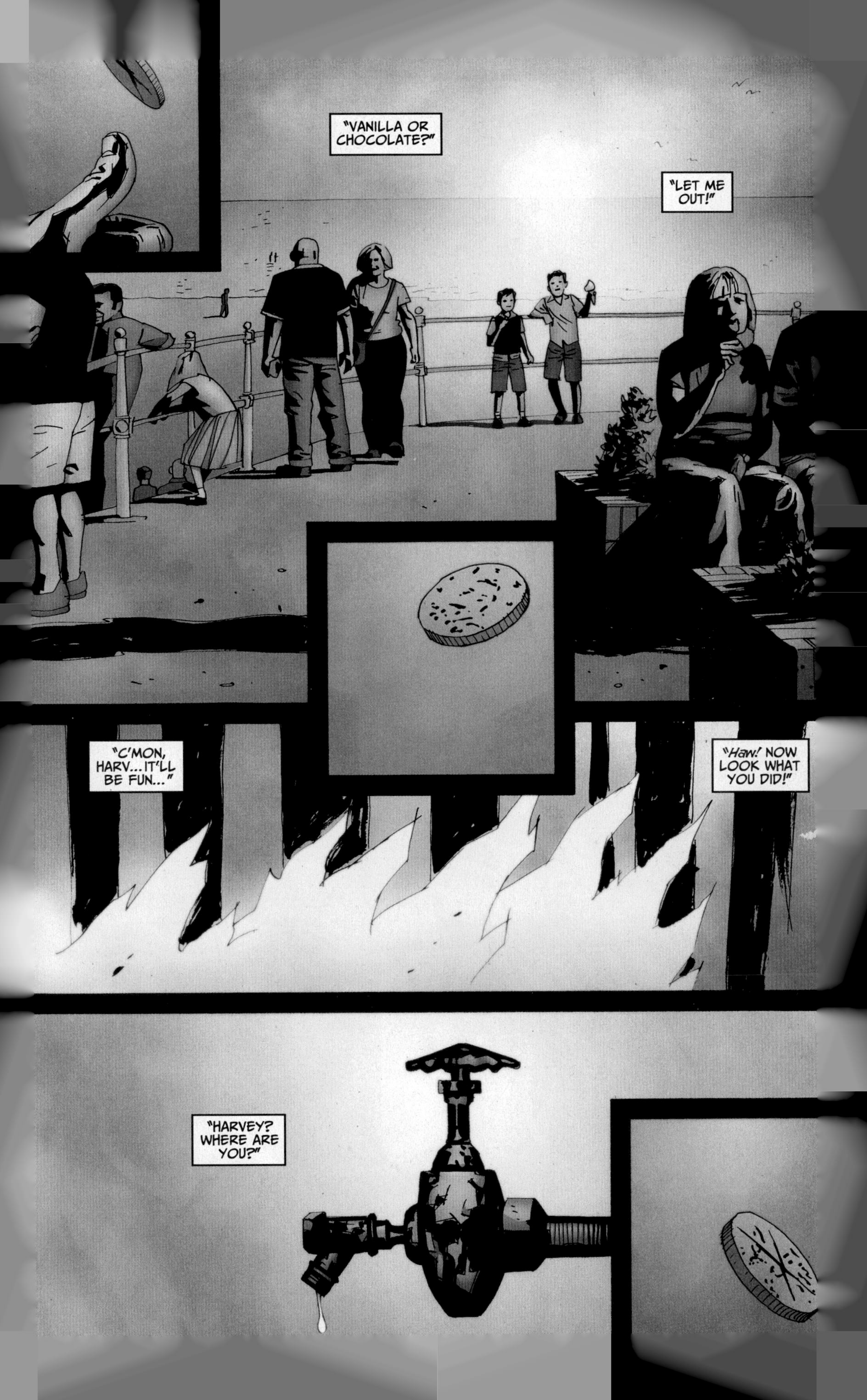
"VANILLA OR CHOCOLATE?"
"LET ME OUT!"
"C'MON, HARV... IT'LL BE FUN..."
"*Haw!* NOW LOOK WHAT YOU DID!"
"HARVEY? WHERE ARE YOU?"

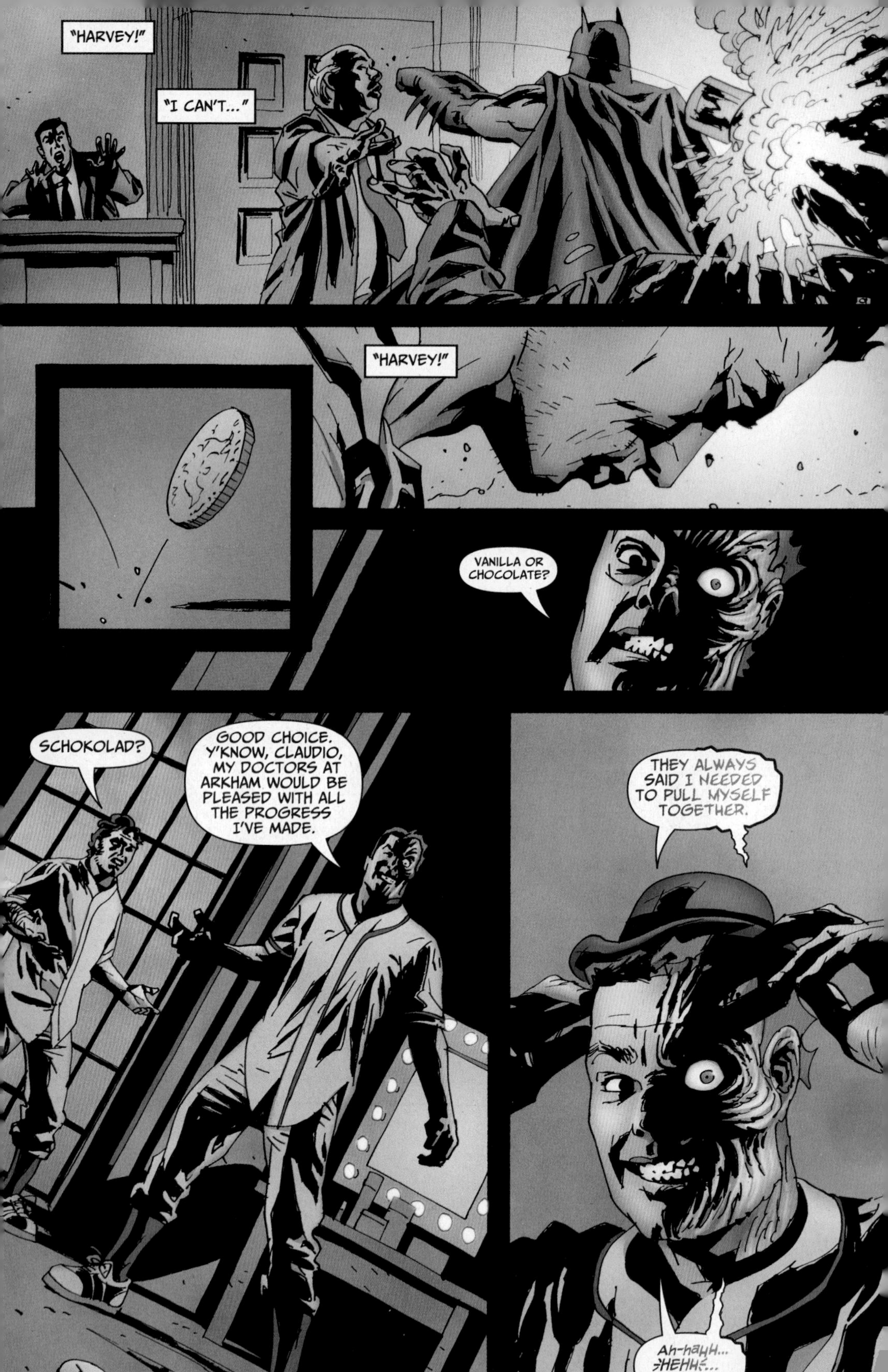
"HARVEY!"
"I CAN'T..."
"HARVEY!"
VANILLA OR CHOCOLATE?
SCHOKOLAD?
GOOD CHOICE. Y'KNOW, CLAUDIO, MY DOCTORS AT ARKHAM WOULD BE PLEASED WITH ALL THE PROGRESS I'VE MADE.
THEY ALWAYS SAID I NEEDED TO PULL MYSELF TOGETHER.
Ah-haHH... HEHH... HA HA HA!

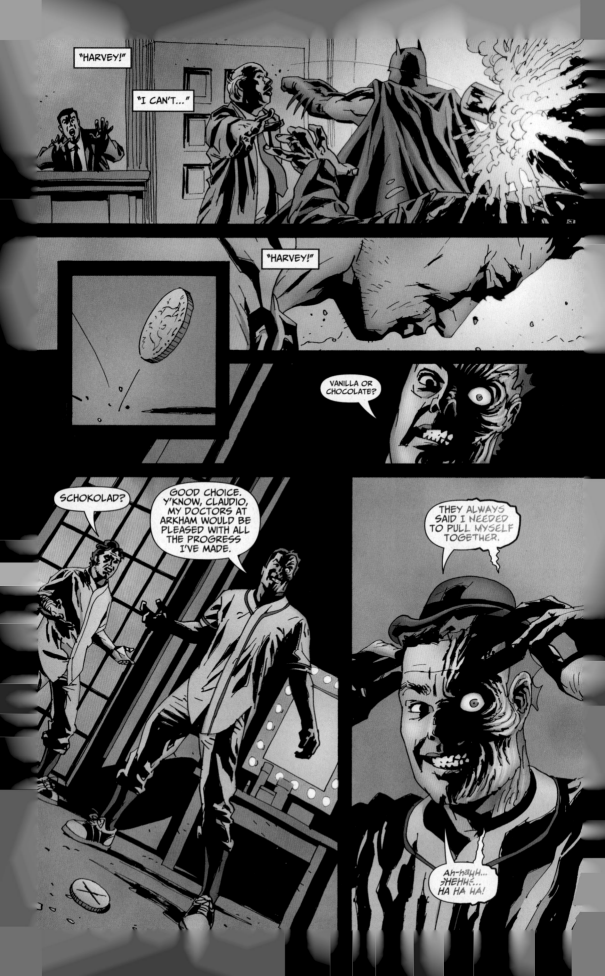

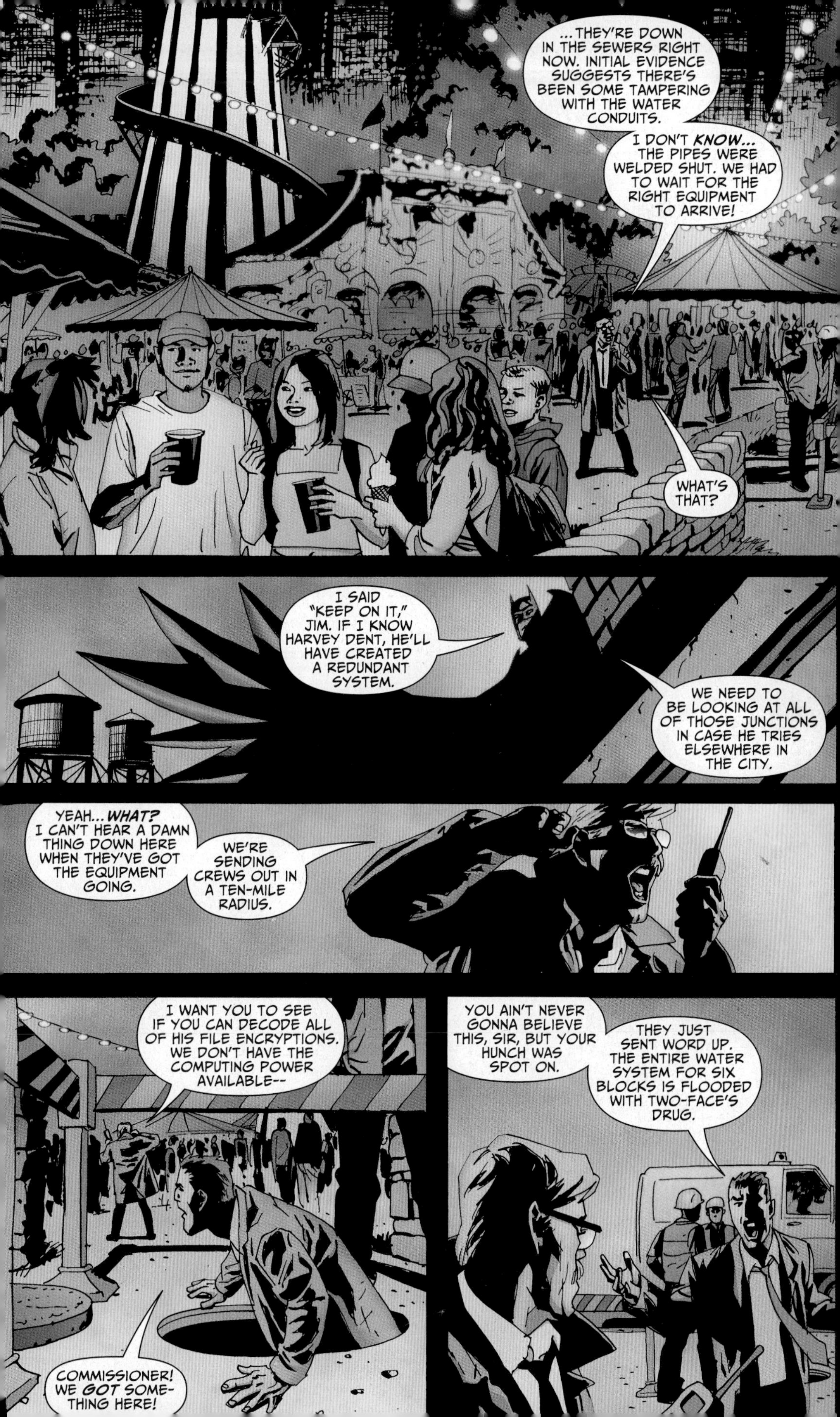
...THEY'RE DOWN IN THE SEWERS RIGHT NOW. INITIAL EVIDENCE SUGGESTS THERE'S BEEN SOME TAMPERING WITH THE WATER CONDUITS.
I DON'T KNOW... THE PIPES WERE WELDED SHUT. WE HAD TO WAIT FOR THE RIGHT EQUIPMENT TO ARRIVE!
WHAT'S THAT?
I SAID "KEEP ON IT," JIM. IF I KNOW HARVEY DENT, HE'LL HAVE CREATED A REDUNDANT SYSTEM.
WE NEED TO BE LOOKING AT ALL OF THOSE JUNCTIONS IN CASE HE TRIES ELSEWHERE IN THE CITY.
YEAH... WHAT? I CAN'T HEAR A DAMN THING DOWN HERE WHEN THEY'VE GOT THE EQUIPMENT GOING.
WE'RE SENDING CREWS OUT IN A TEN-MILE RADIUS.
I WANT YOU TO SEE IF YOU CAN DECODE ALL OF HIS FILE ENCRYPTIONS. WE DON'T HAVE THE COMPUTING POWER AVAILABLE--
COMMISSIONER! WE GOT SOME-THING HERE!
YOU AIN'T NEVER GONNA BELIEVE THIS, SIR, BUT YOUR HUNCH WAS SPOT ON.
THEY JUST SENT WORD UP. THE ENTIRE WATER SYSTEM FOR SIX BLOCKS IS FLOODED WITH TWO-FACE'S DRUG.

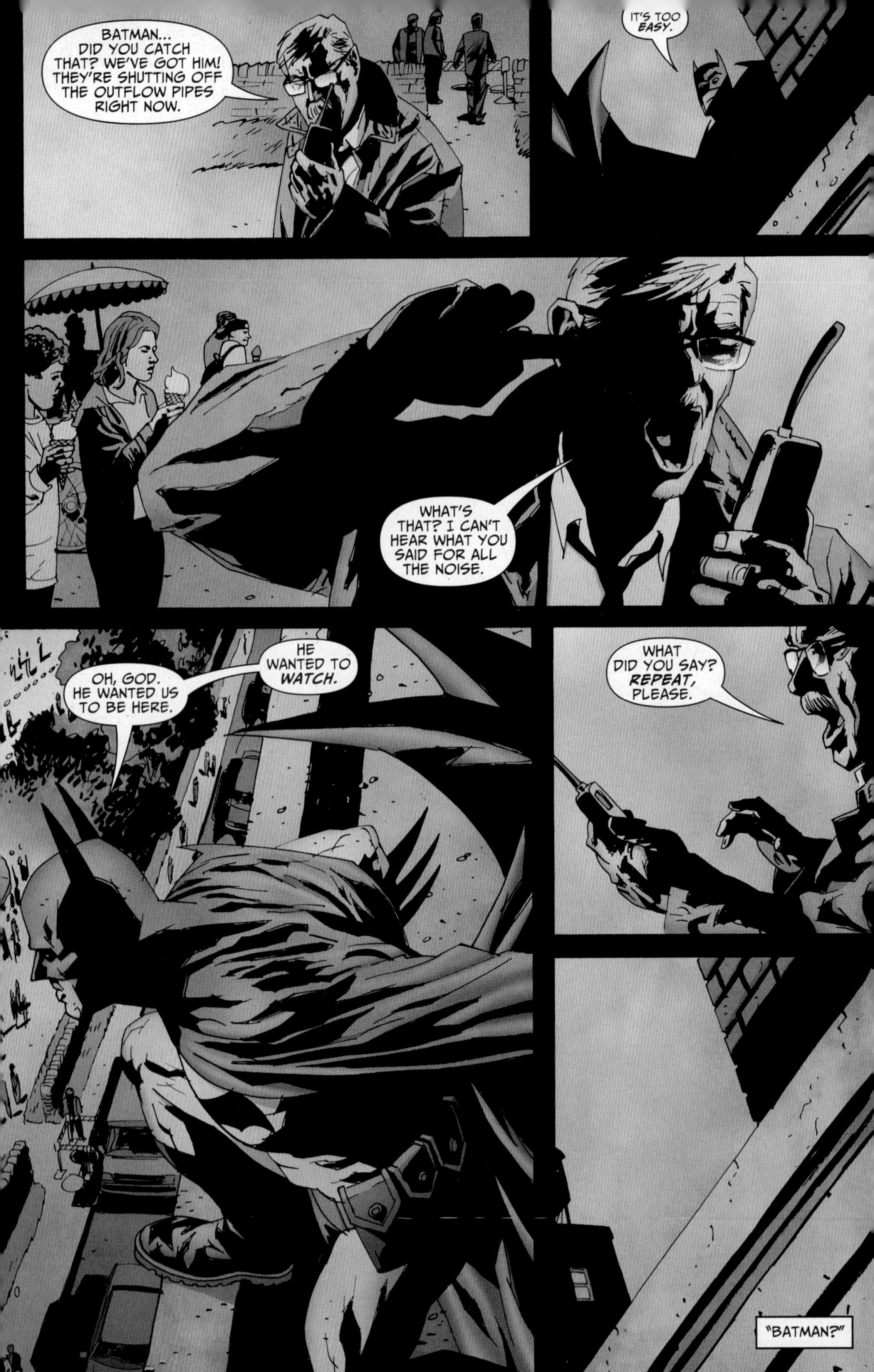
BATMAN... DID YOU CATCH THAT? WE'VE GOT HIM! THEY'RE SHUTTING OFF THE OUTFLOW PIPES RIGHT NOW.
IT'S TOO *EASY.*
WHAT'S THAT? I CAN'T HEAR WHAT YOU SAID FOR ALL THE NOISE.
OH, GOD. HE WANTED US TO BE HERE.
HE WANTED TO *WATCH.*
WHAT DID YOU SAY? ***REPEAT,*** PLEASE.
"BATMAN?"

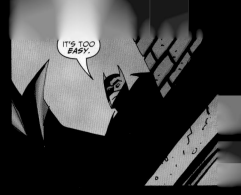

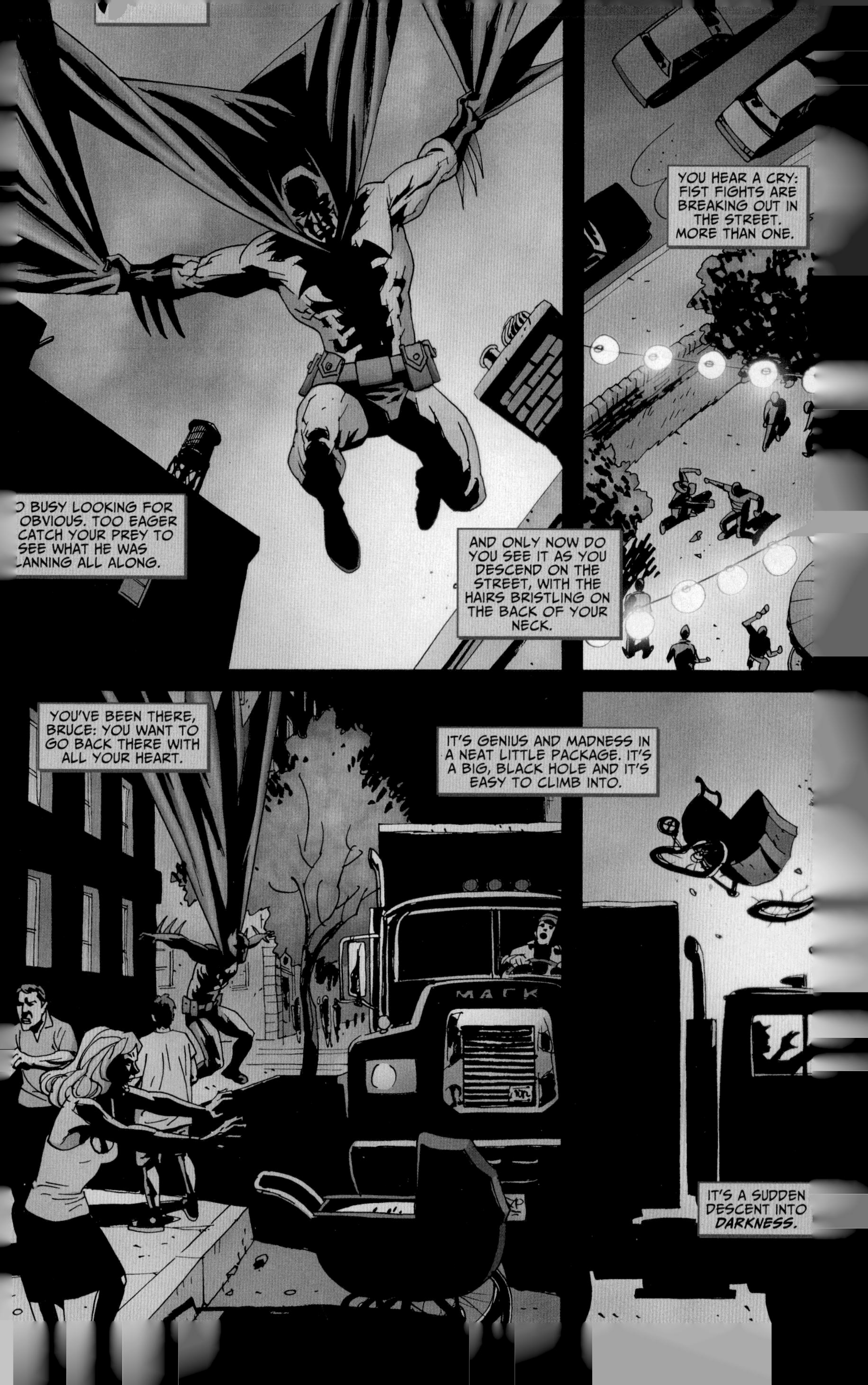
O BUSY LOOKING FOR
OBVIOUS. TOO EAGER
CATCH YOUR PREY TO
SEE WHAT HE WAS
LANNING ALL ALONG.
AND ONLY NOW DO YOU SEE IT AS YOU DESCEND ON THE STREET, WITH THE HAIRS BRISTLING ON THE BACK OF YOUR NECK.
YOU HEAR A CRY: FIST FIGHTS ARE BREAKING OUT IN THE STREET. MORE THAN ONE.
YOU'VE BEEN THERE, BRUCE: YOU WANT TO GO BACK THERE WITH ALL YOUR HEART.
IT'S GENIUS AND MADNESS IN A NEAT LITTLE PACKAGE. IT'S A BIG, BLACK HOLE AND IT'S EASY TO CLIMB INTO.
MACK
IT'S A SUDDEN DESCENT INTO *DARKNESS*.

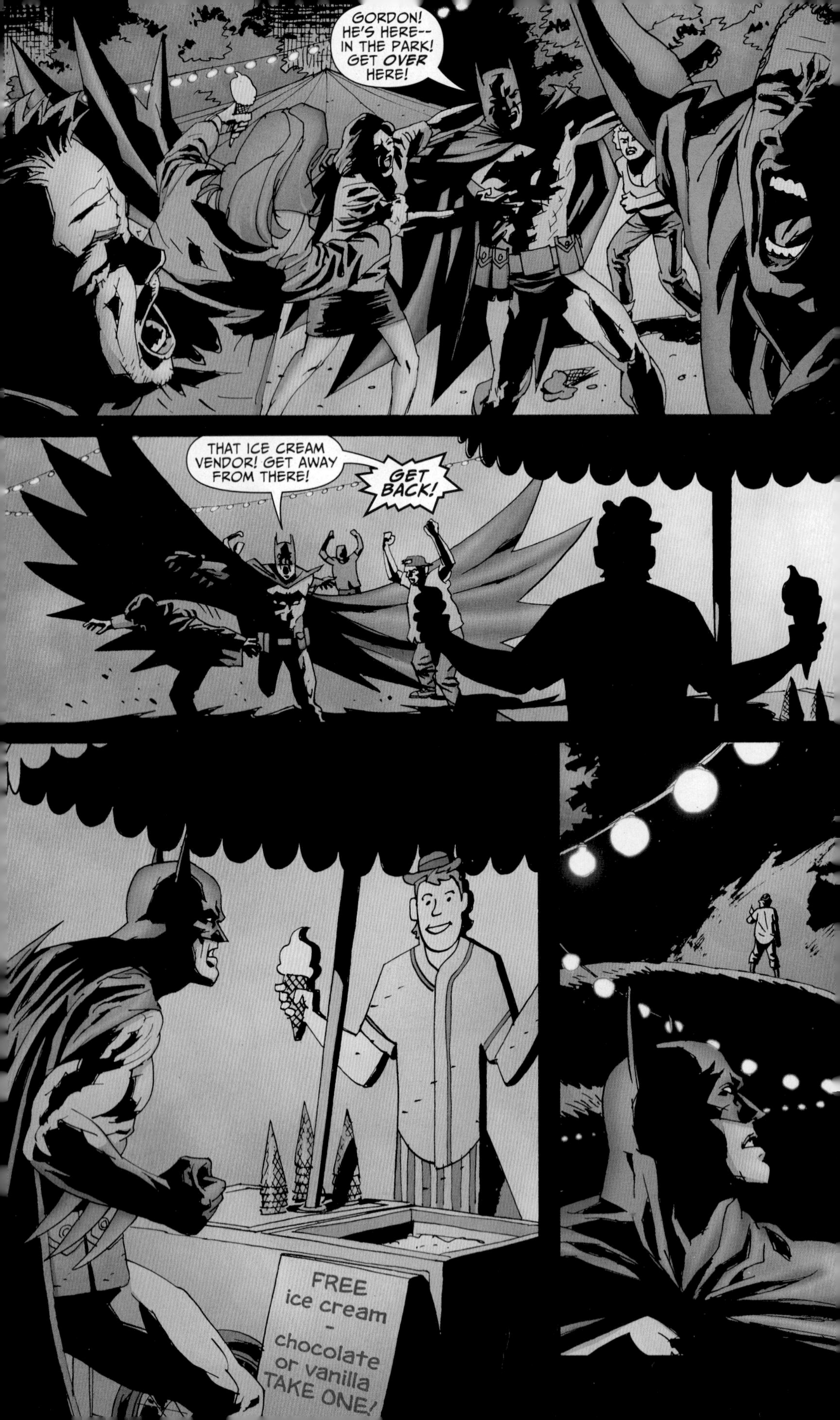
GORDON! HE'S HERE-- IN THE PARK! GET OVER HERE!
THAT ICE CREAM VENDOR! GET AWAY FROM THERE!
GET BACK!
FREE ice cream - chocolate or vanilla TAKE ONE!

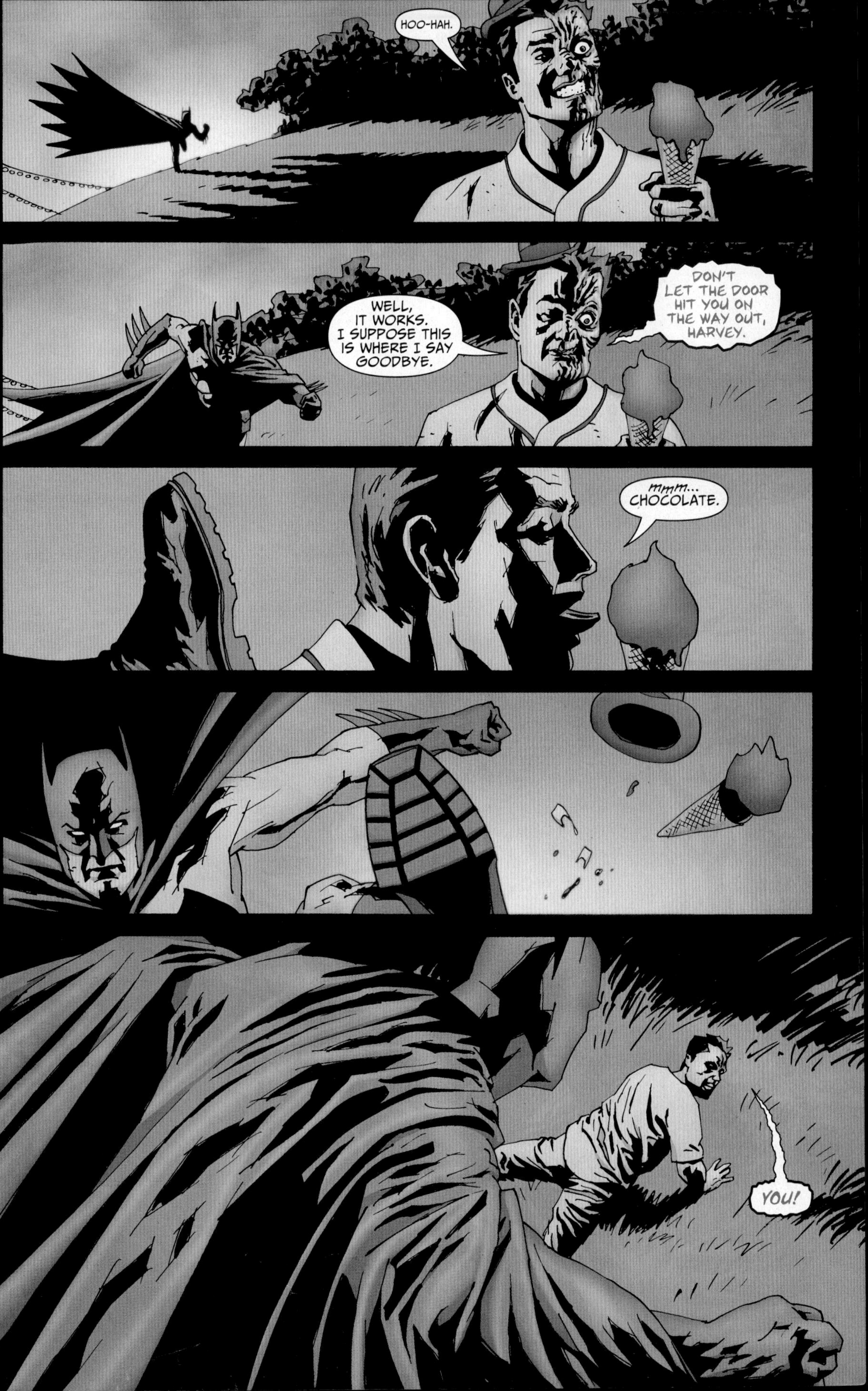
HOO-HAH.
WELL, IT WORKS. I SUPPOSE THIS IS WHERE I SAY GOODBYE.
DON'T LET THE DOOR HIT YOU ON THE WAY OUT, HARVEY.
mmm... CHOCOLATE.
YOU!

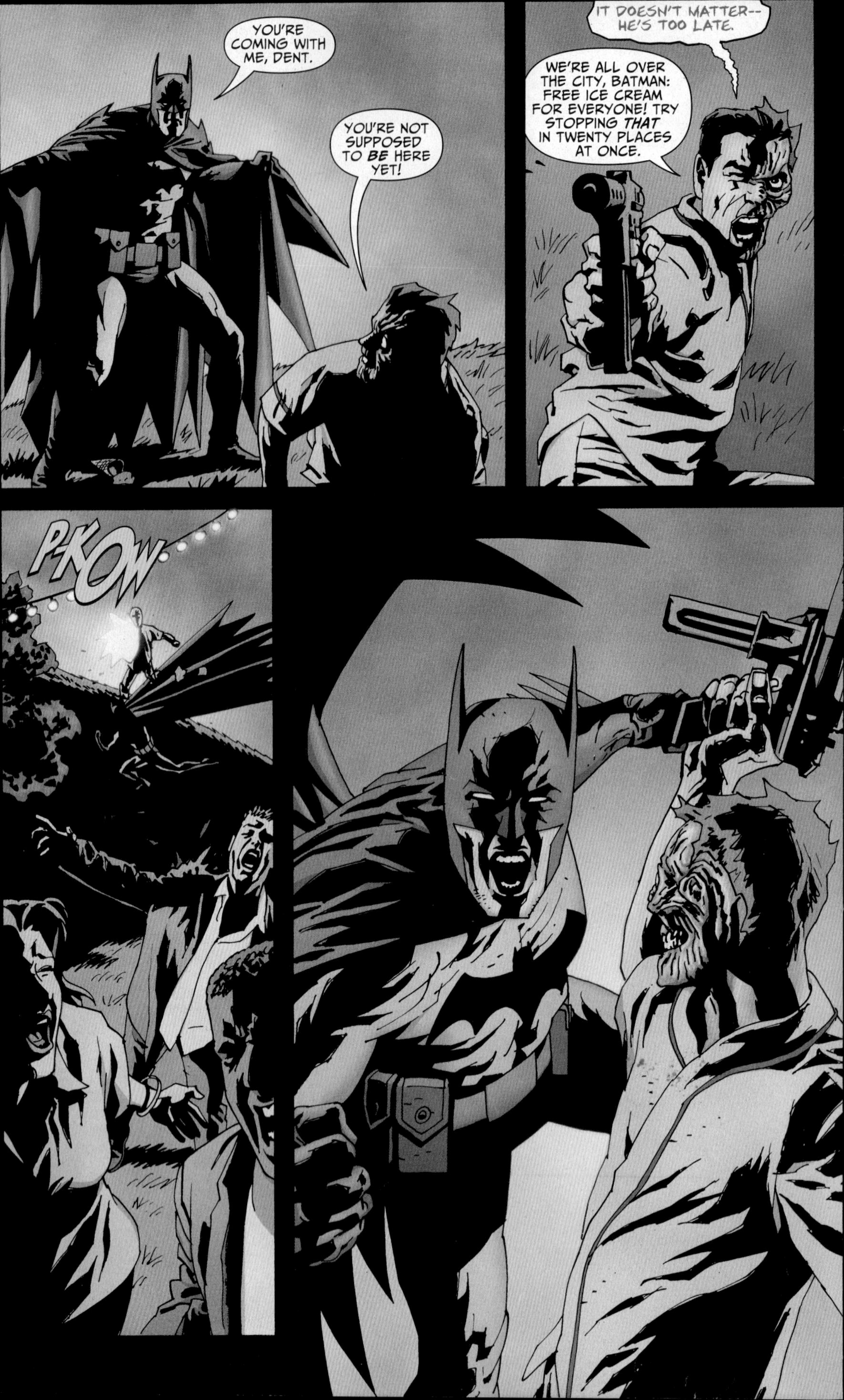
YOU'RE COMING WITH ME, DENT.
YOU'RE NOT SUPPOSED TO *BE* HERE YET!
IT DOESN'T MATTER-- HE'S TOO LATE.
WE'RE ALL OVER THE CITY, BATMAN: FREE ICE CREAM FOR EVERYONE! TRY STOPPING *THAT* IN TWENTY PLACES AT ONCE.
P-KOW

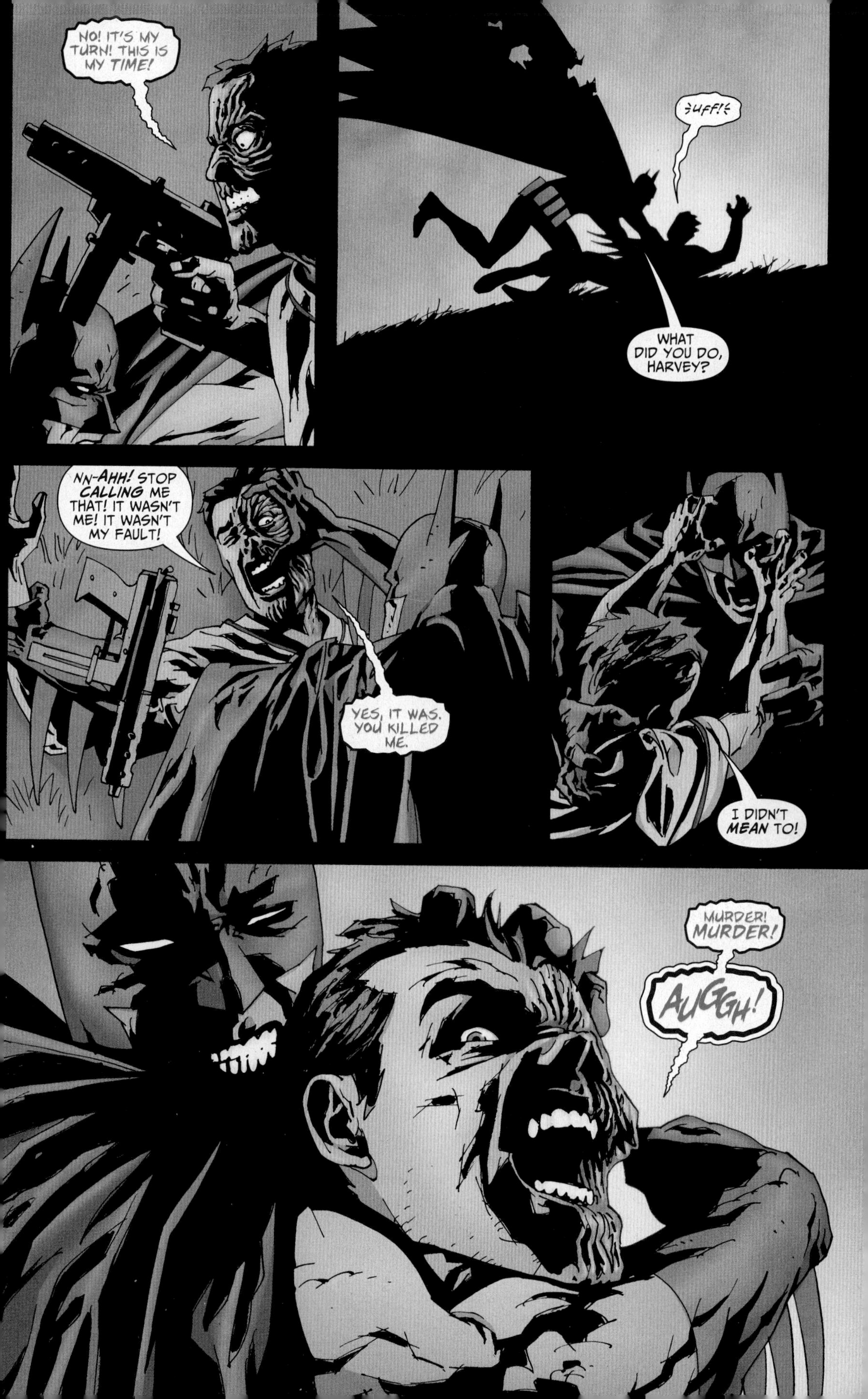
NO! IT'S MY TURN! THIS IS MY TIME!
UFF!
WHAT DID YOU DO, HARVEY?
NN-AHH! STOP CALLING ME THAT! IT WASN'T ME! IT WASN'T MY FAULT!
YES, IT WAS. YOU KILLED ME.
I DIDN'T MEAN TO!
MURDER! MURDER!
AUGGH!

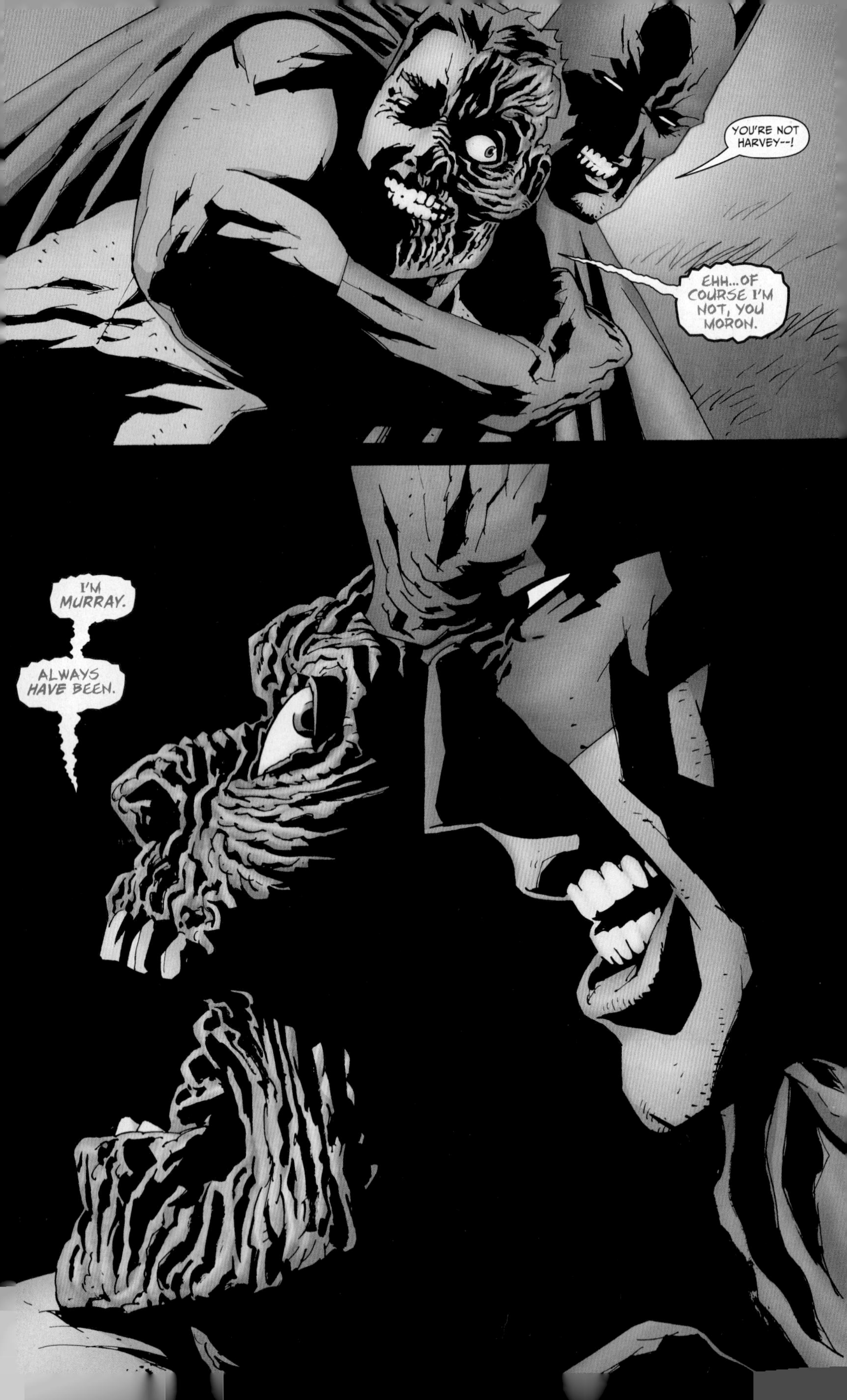
YOU'RE NOT HARVEY--!
EHH...OF COURSE I'M NOT, YOU MORON.
I'M MURRAY.
ALWAYS HAVE BEEN.

Chapter six

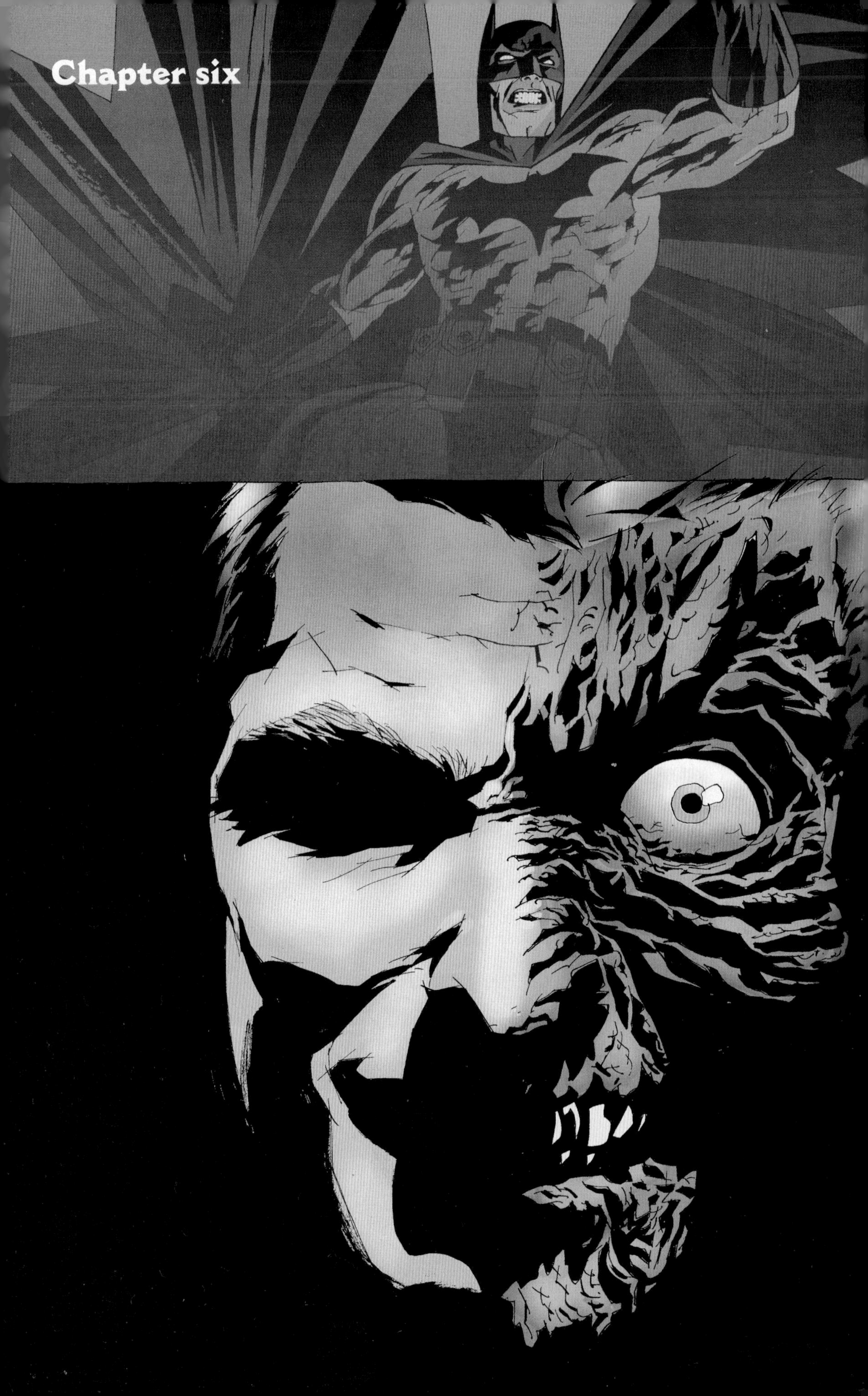

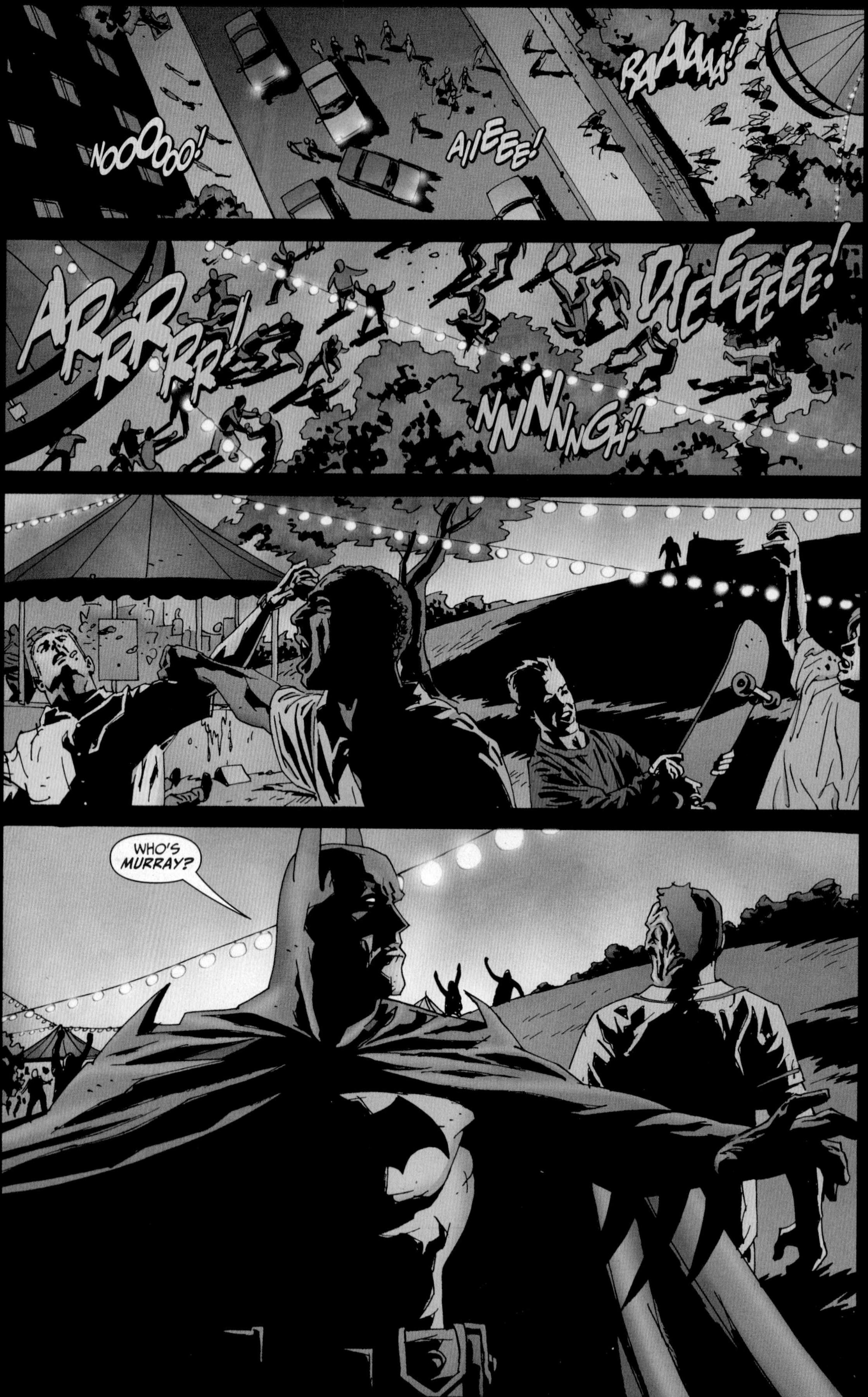
RAAAAA!
NOOOOOO!
AIIEEE!
ARRRRRR!
DIEEEEEE!
NNNNNGH!
WHO'S MURRAY?

I AM, YOU LITTLE PUNK. HARVEY'S BROTHER. ALWAYS *HAVE* BEEN, MORE'S THE PITY.

HE DIDN'T TELL YOU BECAUSE HE'S ASHAMED. BUT NOT OF ME. OF *HIMSELF.*

MHH...I *LOVE* THIS. REMINDS ME OF WHEN ME AN' HARV WERE KIDS.

I DON'T UNDERSTAND... MURRAY? DID HARVEY *DO* SOMETHING HE *SHOULDN'T* HAVE?

NO!

≶*HUFF!*≷

NOTHING! I DIDN'T DO *NOTHING!* HE'S A *LIAR!*

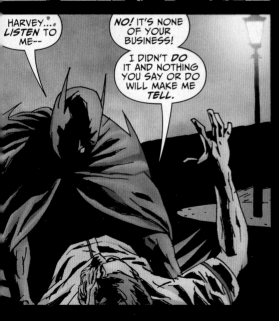

HARVEY... *LISTEN* TO ME--

NO! IT'S NONE OF YOUR BUSINESS!

I DIDN'T *DO* IT AND NOTHING YOU SAY OR DO WILL MAKE ME *TELL.*

TELL HIM, HARVEY, YOU LITTLE *TOOL!* TELL HIM THE TRUTH!

Nnah... I *CAN'T!* THEY'LL PUT ME IN JAIL!

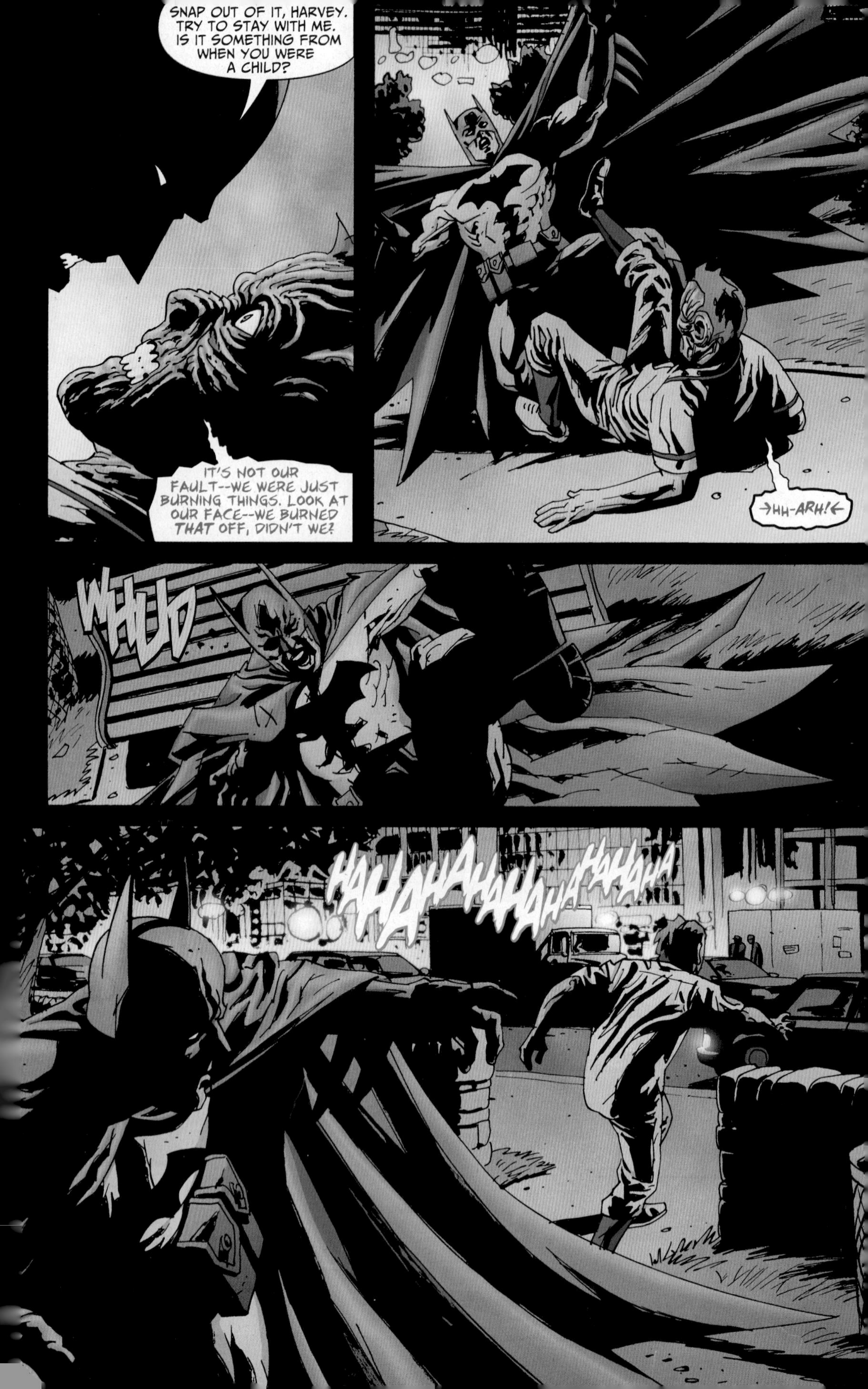
SNAP OUT OF IT, HARVEY. TRY TO STAY WITH ME. IS IT SOMETHING FROM WHEN YOU WERE A CHILD?
IT'S NOT OUR FAULT--WE WERE JUST BURNING THINGS. LOOK AT OUR FACE--WE BURNED THAT OFF, DIDN'T WE?
HH-ARH!
WHUD
HAHAHAHAHAHAHAHAHAHAHA

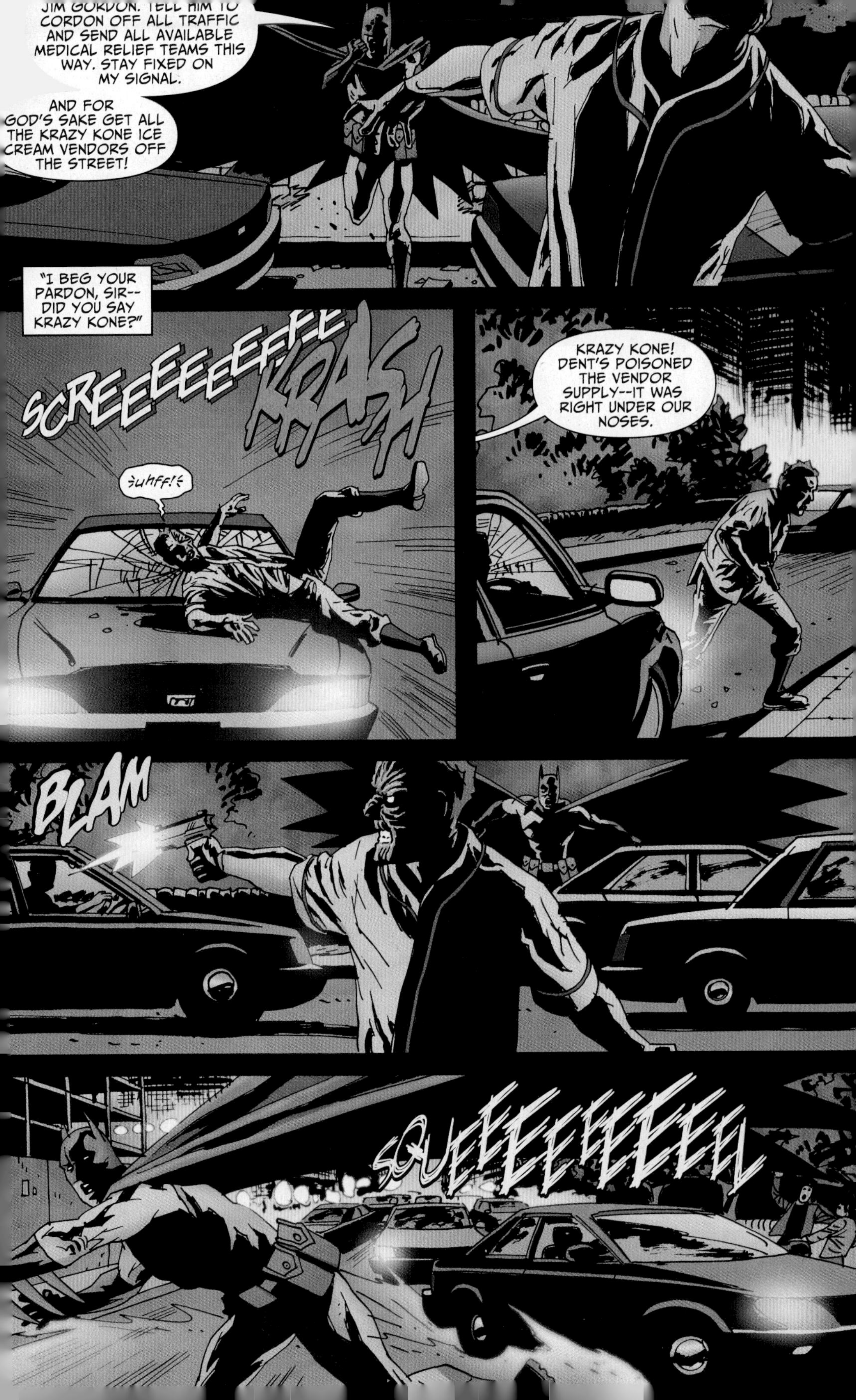
JIM GORDON. TELL HIM TO CORDON OFF ALL TRAFFIC AND SEND ALL AVAILABLE MEDICAL RELIEF TEAMS THIS WAY. STAY FIXED ON MY SIGNAL.
AND FOR GOD'S SAKE GET ALL THE KRAZY KONE ICE CREAM VENDORS OFF THE STREET!
"I BEG YOUR PARDON, SIR--DID YOU SAY KRAZY KONE?"
SCREEEEEEEEEE
KRASH
UHFF!
KRAZY KONE! DENT'S POISONED THE VENDOR SUPPLY--IT WAS RIGHT UNDER OUR NOSES.
BLAM
SQUEEEEEEEEEEL

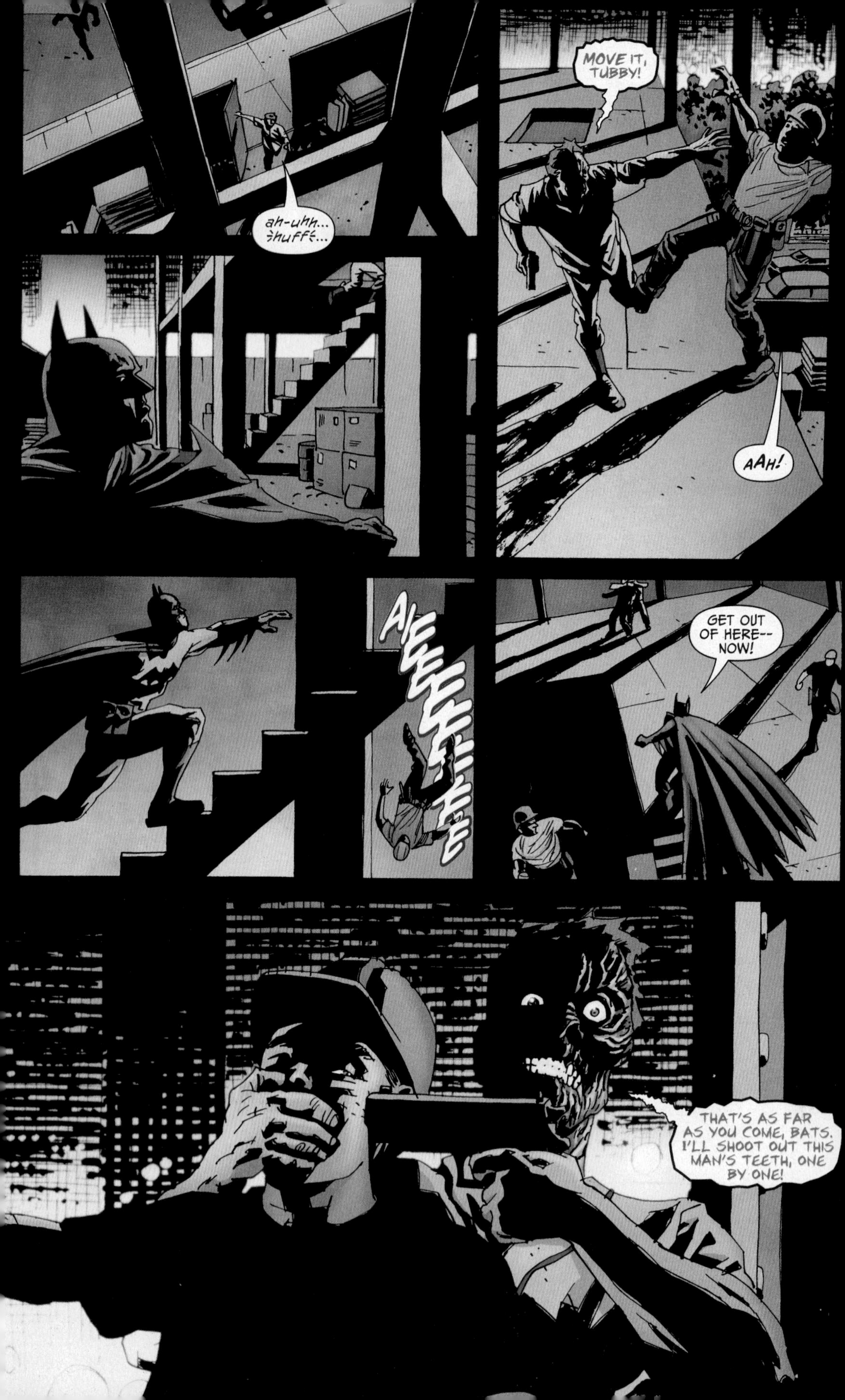
ah-uhh...
shuff...
MOVE IT, TUBBY!
AAH!
AIEEEEEEEE
GET OUT OF HERE-- NOW!
THAT'S AS FAR AS YOU COME, BATS. I'LL SHOOT OUT THIS MAN'S TEETH, ONE BY ONE!

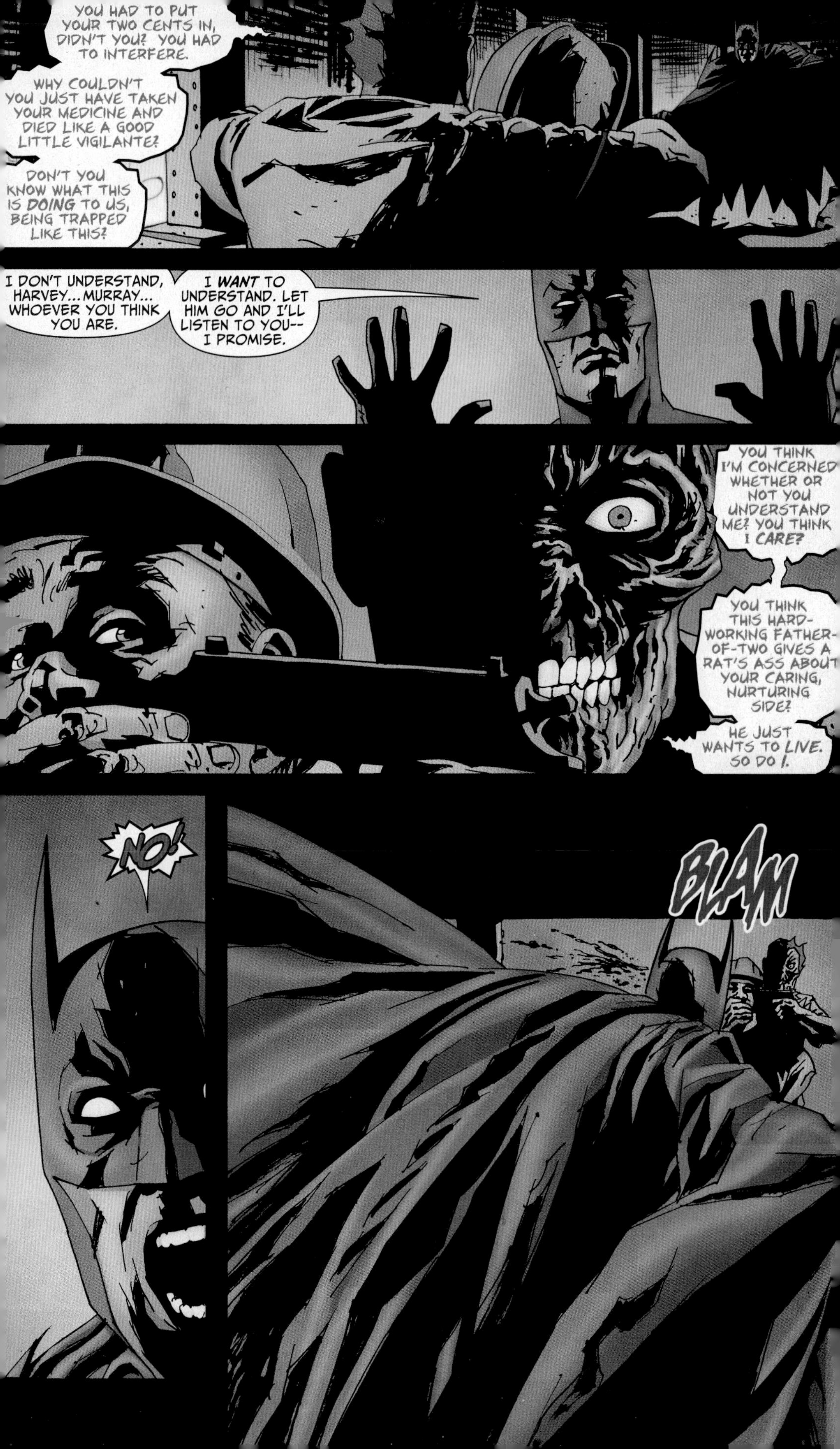
YOU HAD TO PUT YOUR TWO CENTS IN, DIDN'T YOU? YOU HAD TO INTERFERE.
WHY COULDN'T YOU JUST HAVE TAKEN YOUR MEDICINE AND DIED LIKE A GOOD LITTLE VIGILANTE?
DON'T YOU KNOW WHAT THIS IS DOING TO US, BEING TRAPPED LIKE THIS?
I DON'T UNDERSTAND, HARVEY...MURRAY... WHOEVER YOU THINK YOU ARE.
I WANT TO UNDERSTAND. LET HIM GO AND I'LL LISTEN TO YOU-- I PROMISE.
YOU THINK I'M CONCERNED WHETHER OR NOT YOU UNDERSTAND ME? YOU THINK I CARE?
YOU THINK THIS HARD-WORKING FATHER-OF-TWO GIVES A RAT'S ASS ABOUT YOUR CARING, NURTURING SIDE?
HE JUST WANTS TO LIVE. SO DO I.
NO!
BLAM

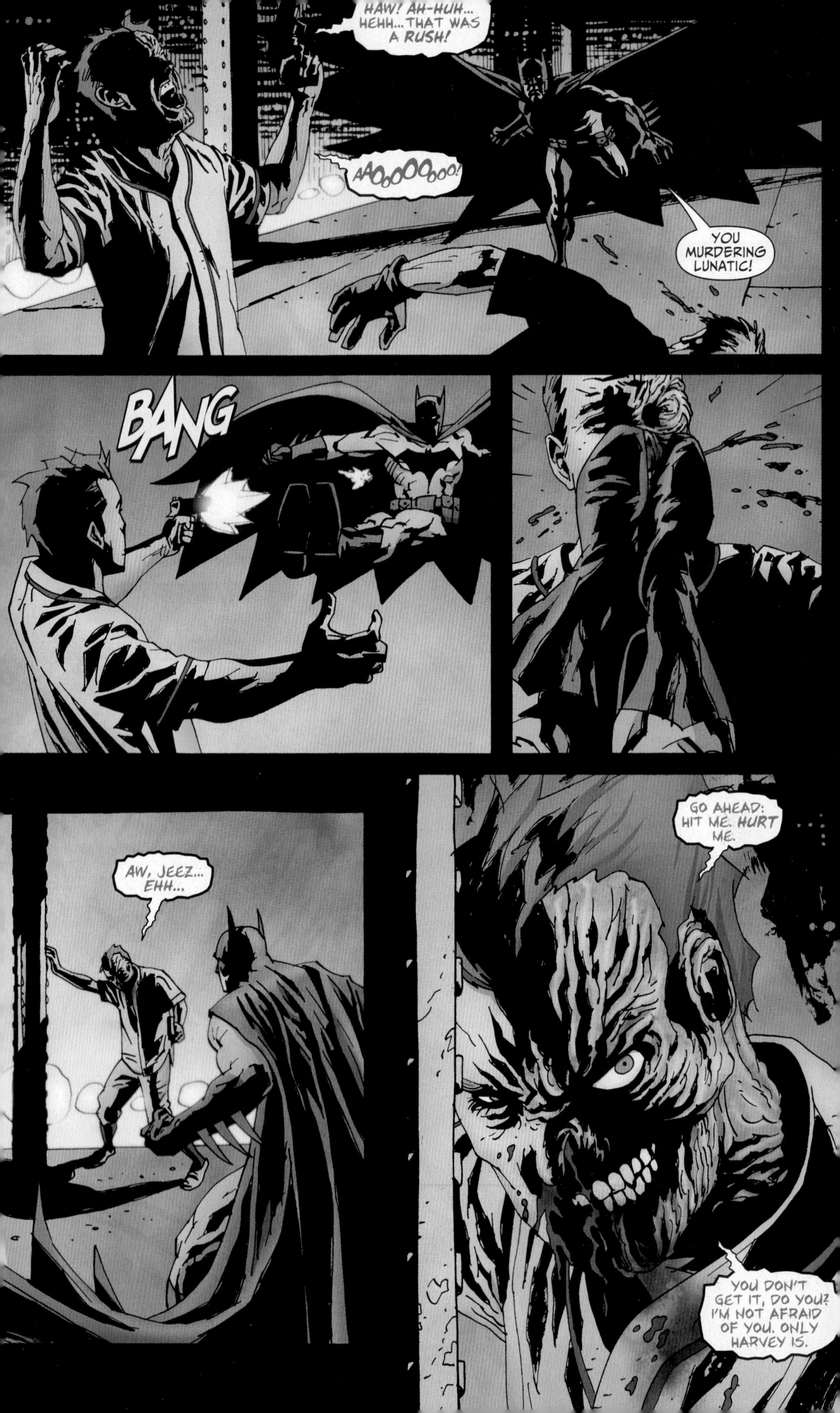
HAW! AH-HUH... HEHH... THAT WAS A RUSH!
AAOoOOOooo!
YOU MURDERING LUNATIC!
BANG
AW, JEEZ... EHH...
GO AHEAD: HIT ME. HURT ME.
YOU DON'T GET IT, DO YOU? I'M NOT AFRAID OF YOU. ONLY HARVEY IS.

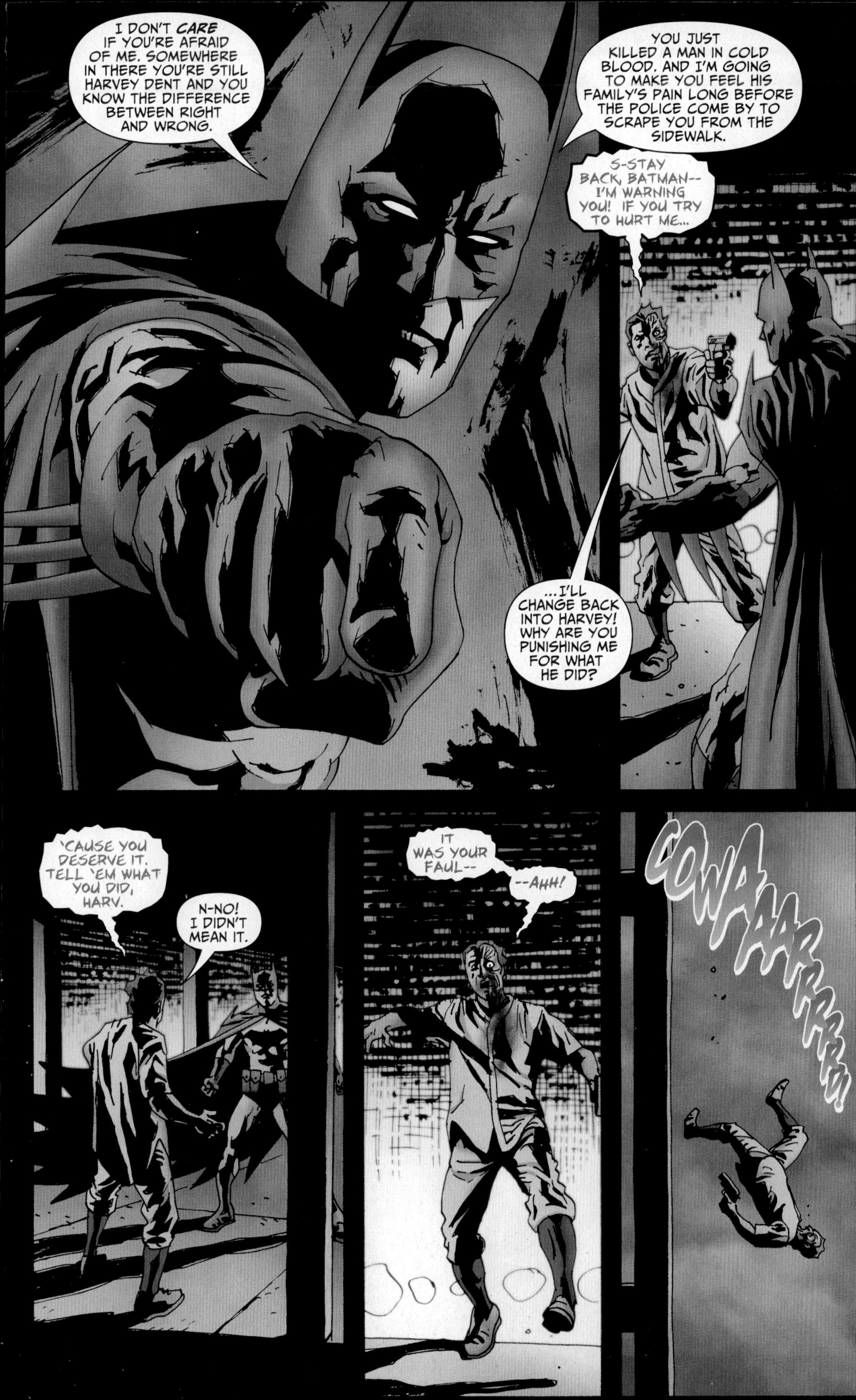
I DON'T *CARE* IF YOU'RE AFRAID OF ME. SOMEWHERE IN THERE YOU'RE STILL HARVEY DENT AND YOU KNOW THE DIFFERENCE BETWEEN RIGHT AND WRONG.
YOU JUST KILLED A MAN IN COLD BLOOD. AND I'M GOING TO MAKE YOU FEEL HIS FAMILY'S PAIN LONG BEFORE THE POLICE COME BY TO SCRAPE YOU FROM THE SIDEWALK.
S-STAY BACK, BATMAN-- I'M WARNING YOU! IF YOU TRY TO HURT ME...
...I'LL CHANGE BACK INTO HARVEY! WHY ARE YOU PUNISHING ME FOR WHAT HE DID?
'CAUSE YOU DESERVE IT. TELL 'EM WHAT YOU DID, HARV.
N-NO! I DIDN'T MEAN IT.
IT WAS YOUR FAUL--
--AHH!
COWAAARRRRRR!

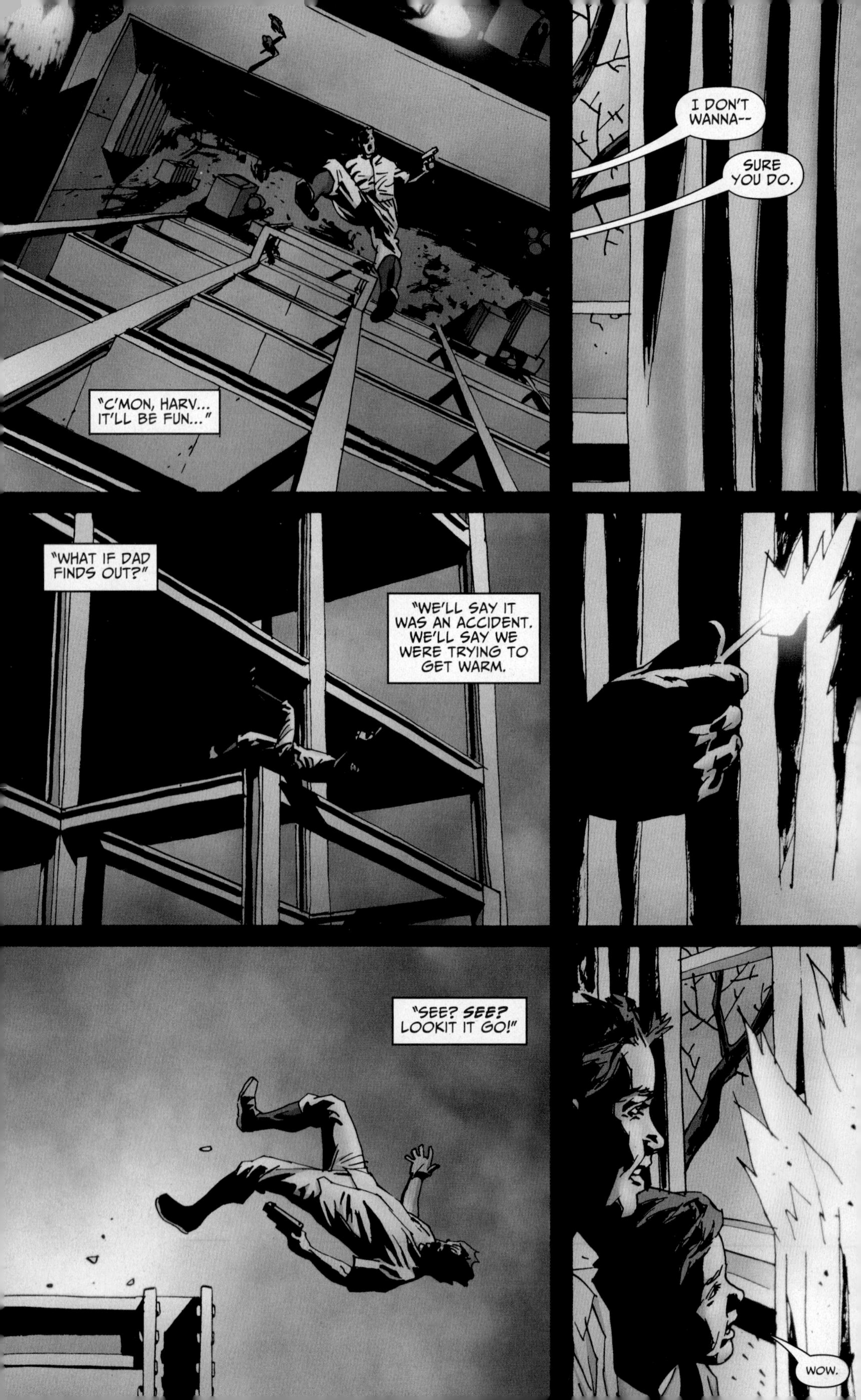
"C'MON, HARV...
IT'LL BE FUN..."
I DON'T WANNA--
SURE YOU DO.
"WHAT IF DAD FINDS OUT?"
"WE'LL SAY IT WAS AN ACCIDENT. WE'LL SAY WE WERE TRYING TO GET WARM.
"SEE? ***SEE?*** LOOKIT IT GO!"
WOW.

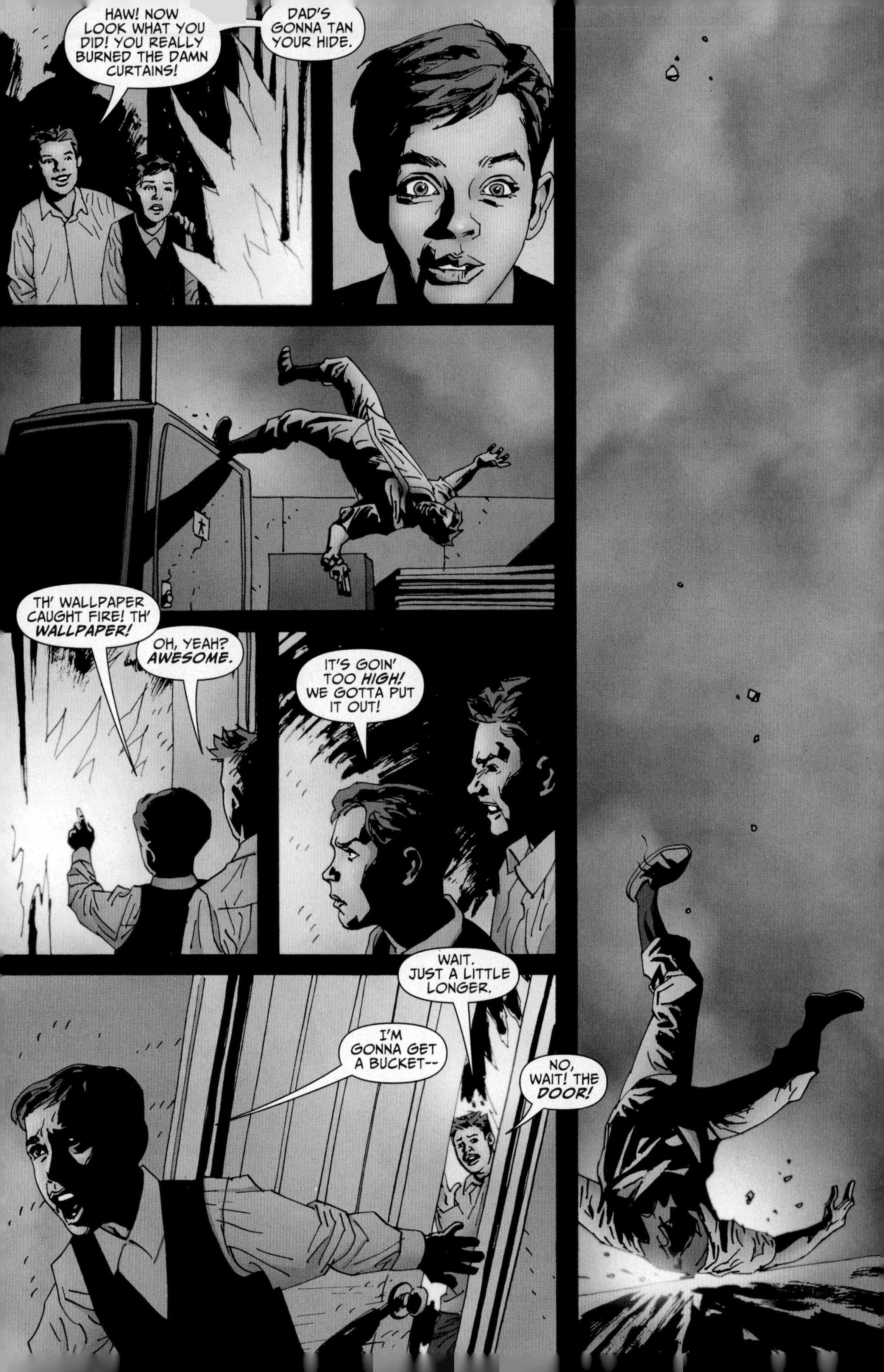
HAW! NOW LOOK WHAT YOU DID! YOU REALLY BURNED THE DAMN CURTAINS!
DAD'S GONNA TAN YOUR HIDE.
TH' WALLPAPER CAUGHT FIRE! TH' WALLPAPER!
OH, YEAH? AWESOME.
IT'S GOIN' TOO HIGH! WE GOTTA PUT IT OUT!
WAIT. JUST A LITTLE LONGER.
I'M GONNA GET A BUCKET--
NO, WAIT! THE DOOR!

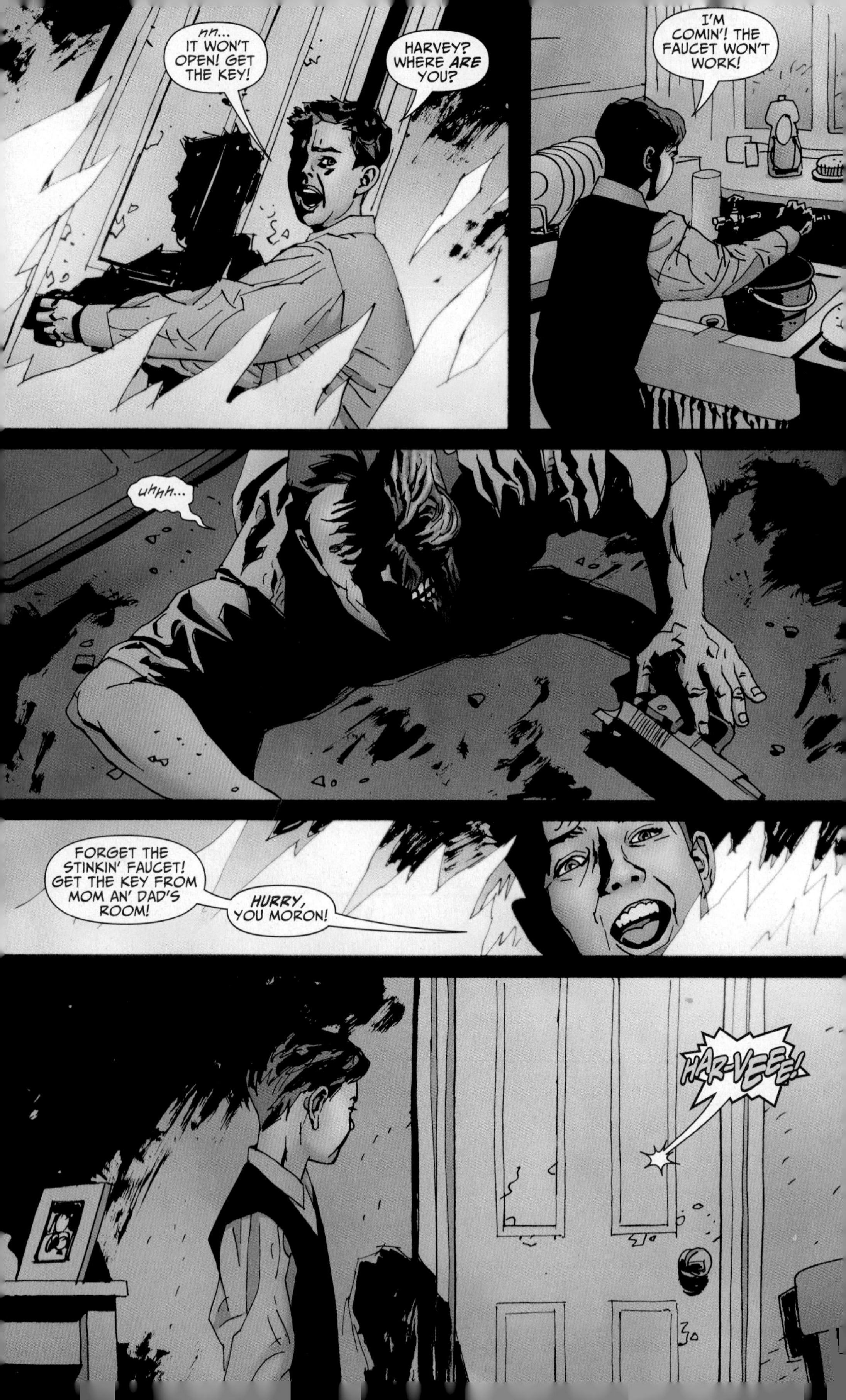

nn... IT WON'T OPEN! GET THE KEY!
HARVEY? WHERE ARE YOU?
I'M COMIN'! THE FAUCET WON'T WORK!
uhhh...
FORGET THE STINKIN' FAUCET! GET THE KEY FROM MOM AN' DAD'S ROOM!
HURRY, YOU MORON!
HAR-VEEE!

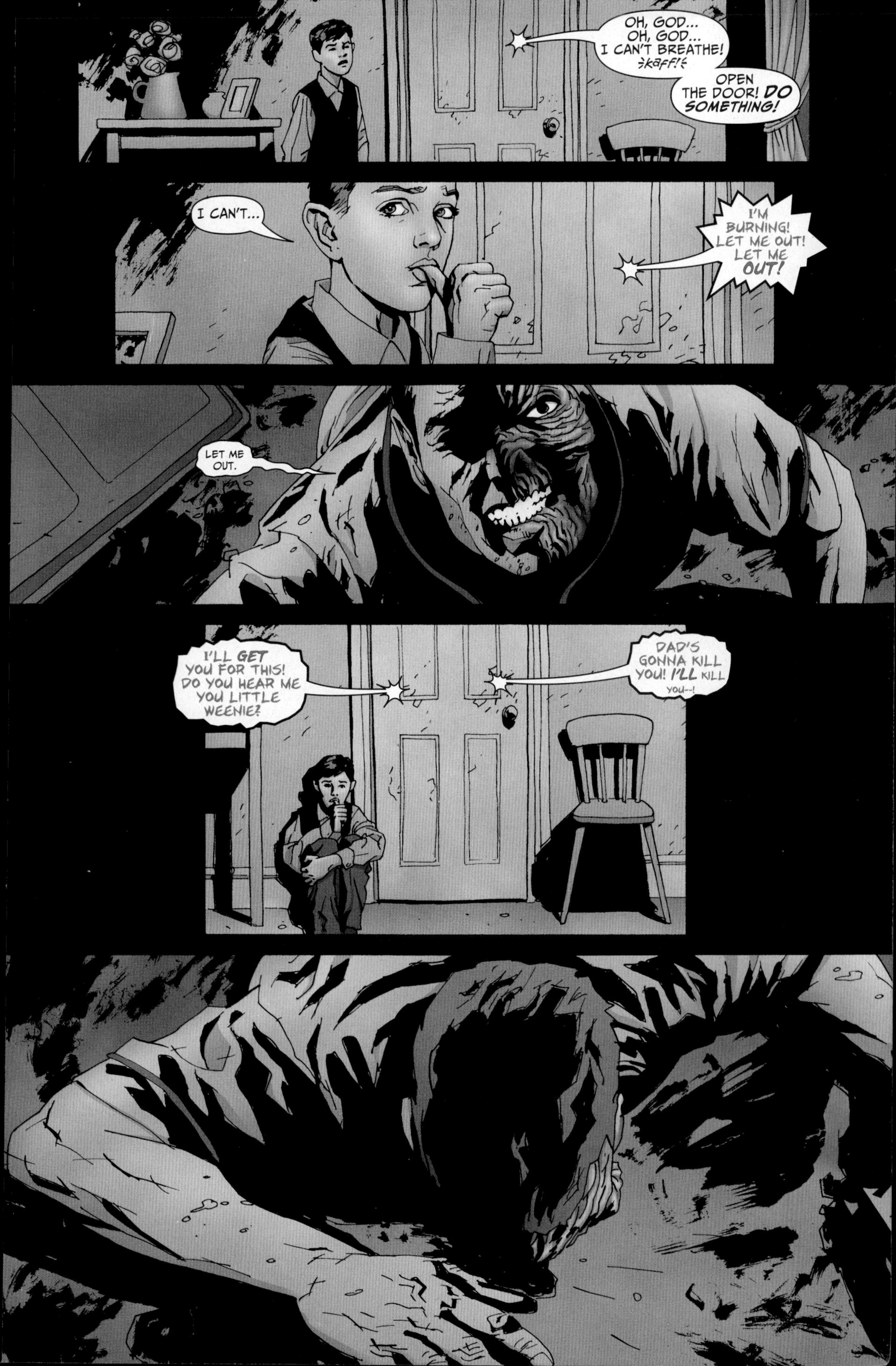
OH, GOD... OH, GOD... I CAN'T BREATHE! kaff!
OPEN THE DOOR! DO SOMETHING!
I CAN'T...
I'M BURNING! LET ME OUT! LET ME OUT!
LET ME OUT.
I'LL GET YOU FOR THIS! DO YOU HEAR ME YOU LITTLE WEENIE?
DAD'S GONNA KILL YOU! I'LL KILL YOU--!

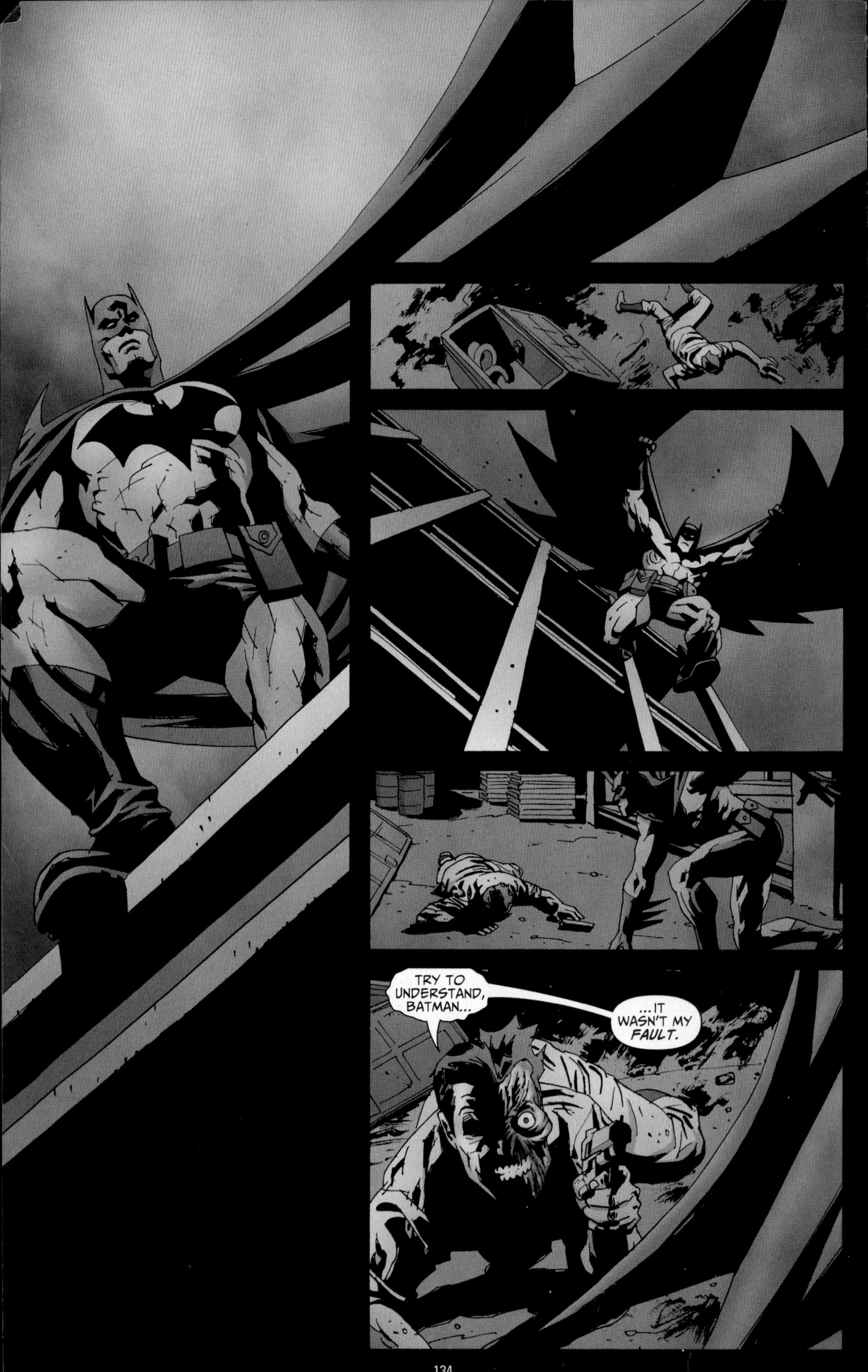
TRY TO UNDERSTAND, BATMAN...
...IT WASN'T MY *FAULT*.

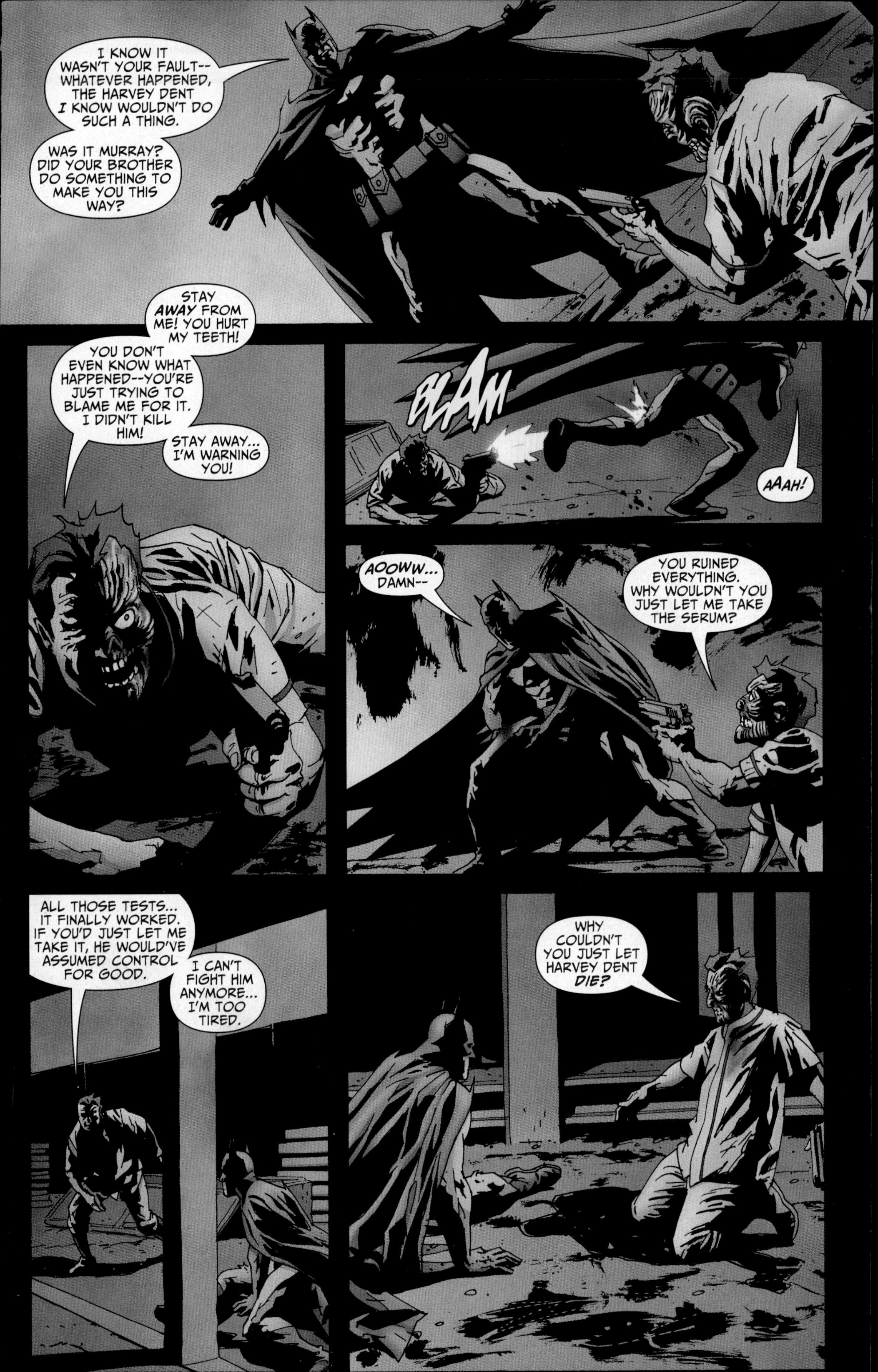
I KNOW IT WASN'T YOUR FAULT-- WHATEVER HAPPENED, THE HARVEY DENT I KNOW WOULDN'T DO SUCH A THING.
WAS IT MURRAY? DID YOUR BROTHER DO SOMETHING TO MAKE YOU THIS WAY?
STAY AWAY FROM ME! YOU HURT MY TEETH!
YOU DON'T EVEN KNOW WHAT HAPPENED--YOU'RE JUST TRYING TO BLAME ME FOR IT. I DIDN'T KILL HIM!
STAY AWAY... I'M WARNING YOU!
BLAM
AAAH!
AOOWW... DAMN--
YOU RUINED EVERYTHING. WHY WOULDN'T YOU JUST LET ME TAKE THE SERUM?
ALL THOSE TESTS... IT FINALLY WORKED. IF YOU'D JUST LET ME TAKE IT, HE WOULD'VE ASSUMED CONTROL FOR GOOD.
I CAN'T FIGHT HIM ANYMORE... I'M TOO TIRED.
WHY COULDN'T YOU JUST LET HARVEY DENT DIE?

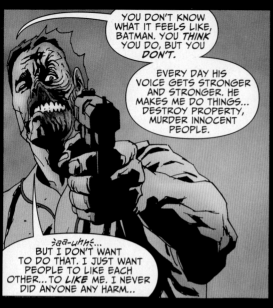

YOU DON'T KNOW WHAT IT FEELS LIKE, BATMAN. YOU *THINK* YOU DO, BUT YOU *DON'T.*

EVERY DAY HIS VOICE GETS STRONGER AND STRONGER. HE MAKES ME DO THINGS... DESTROY PROPERTY, MURDER INNOCENT PEOPLE.

ₐₐₐ-ₐₕₕₕ... BUT I DON'T WANT TO DO THAT. I JUST WANT PEOPLE TO LIKE EACH OTHER...TO *LIKE* ME. I NEVER DID ANYONE ANY HARM...

HE DOESN'T HAVE TO WIN. YOU'RE TOO GOOD A MAN INSIDE TO LET THAT HAPPEN.

MURRAY'S THE WEAK ONE-- HE'S THE BULLY YOU HIDE BEHIND WHEN THE GOING GETS ROUGH.

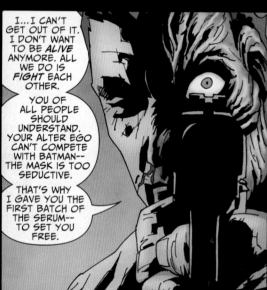

I...I CAN'T GET OUT OF IT. I DON'T WANT TO BE *ALIVE* ANYMORE. ALL WE DO IS *FIGHT* EACH OTHER.

YOU OF ALL PEOPLE SHOULD UNDERSTAND. YOUR ALTER EGO CAN'T COMPETE WITH BATMAN-- THE MASK IS TOO SEDUCTIVE.

THAT'S WHY I GAVE YOU THE FIRST BATCH OF THE SERUM-- TO SET YOU FREE.

BUT IT DIDN'T WORK.

ALL MEN ARE TWO MEN, HARVEY, WHETHER YOU LIKE IT OR NOT.

MAYBE YOU DON'T LIKE YOUR PARENTS...MAYBE YOU DON'T LIKE YOUR NOSE OR YOUR CROOKED TEETH BUT THAT'S WHAT YOU'VE GOT.

TEETH CAN BE FIXED.

SO CAN BRAINS.

DON'T LISTEN TO HIM, WEENIE. BLOW HIS SMUG LOUSY HEAD OFF. FOR ONCE IN YOUR LIFE, BE A MAN.

NNNOOO... QUIT IT, MURRAY! *QUIT* IT!

GET OUT OF MY *HEAD!*

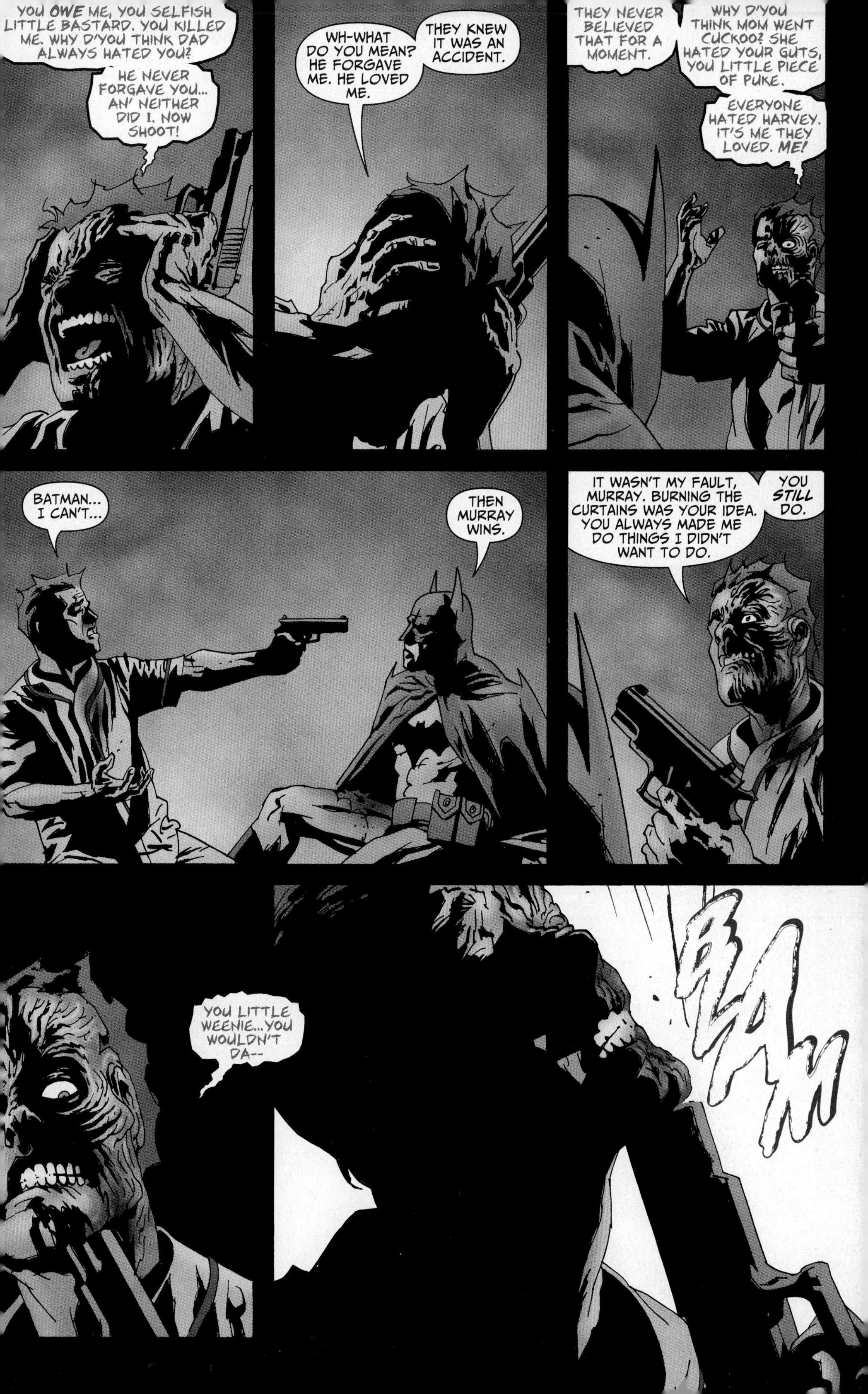

YOU OWE ME, YOU SELFISH LITTLE BASTARD. YOU KILLED ME. WHY D'YOU THINK DAD ALWAYS HATED YOU?
HE NEVER FORGAVE YOU... AN' NEITHER DID I. NOW SHOOT!
WH-WHAT DO YOU MEAN? HE FORGAVE ME. HE LOVED ME.
THEY KNEW IT WAS AN ACCIDENT.
THEY NEVER BELIEVED THAT FOR A MOMENT.
WHY D'YOU THINK MOM WENT CUCKOO? SHE HATED YOUR GUTS, YOU LITTLE PIECE OF PUKE.
EVERYONE HATED HARVEY. IT'S ME THEY LOVED. ME!
BATMAN... I CAN'T...
THEN MURRAY WINS.
IT WASN'T MY FAULT, MURRAY. BURNING THE CURTAINS WAS YOUR IDEA. YOU ALWAYS MADE ME DO THINGS I DIDN'T WANT TO DO.
YOU STILL DO.
YOU LITTLE WEENIE...YOU WOULDN'T DA--
BLAM

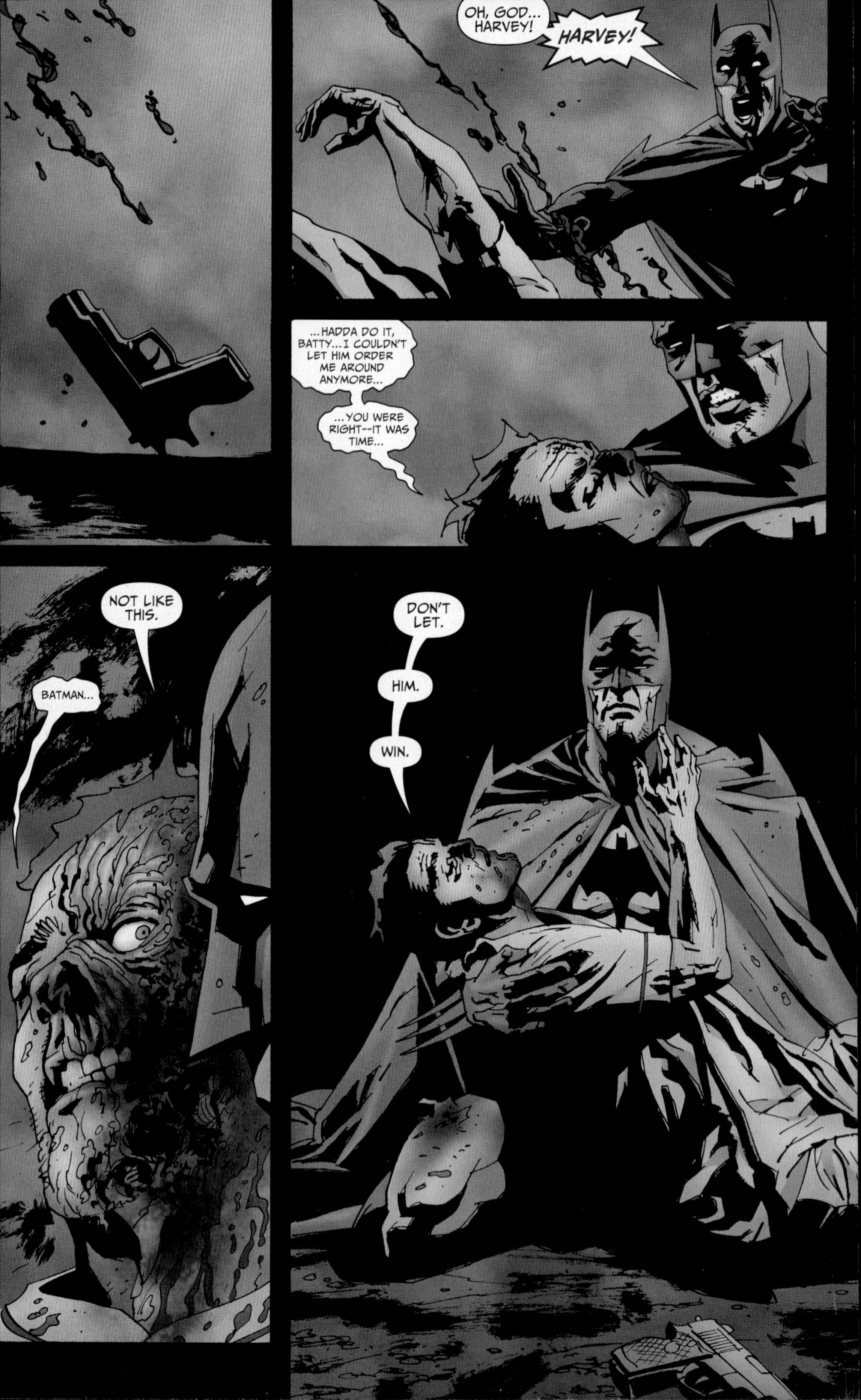
OH, GOD... HARVEY!
HARVEY!
...HADDA DO IT, BATTY...I COULDN'T LET HIM ORDER ME AROUND ANYMORE...
...YOU WERE RIGHT--IT WAS TIME...
NOT LIKE THIS.
BATMAN...
DON'T LET.
HIM.
WIN.

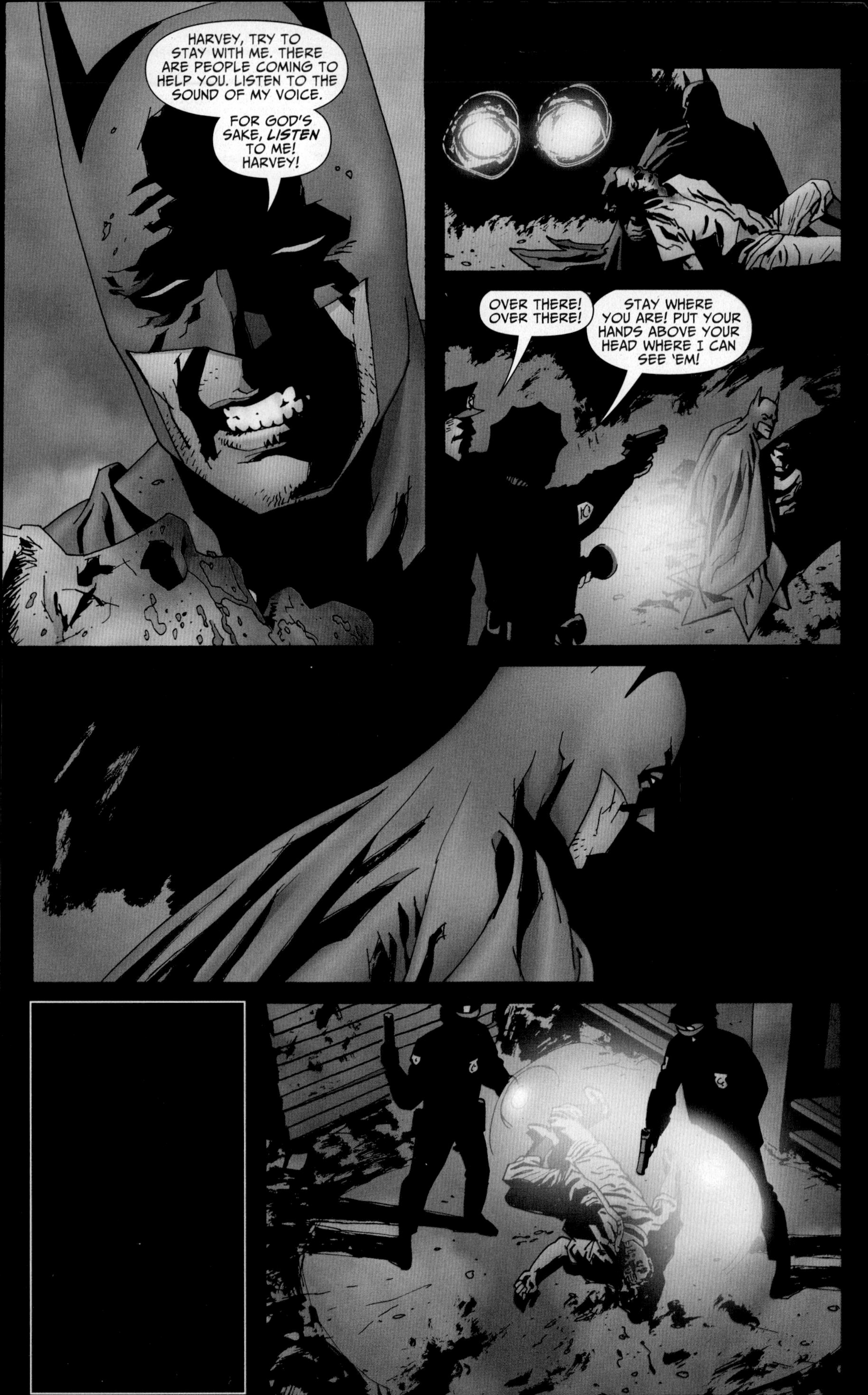
HARVEY, TRY TO STAY WITH ME. THERE ARE PEOPLE COMING TO HELP YOU. LISTEN TO THE SOUND OF MY VOICE.
FOR GOD'S SAKE, LISTEN TO ME! HARVEY!
OVER THERE! OVER THERE!
STAY WHERE YOU ARE! PUT YOUR HANDS ABOVE YOUR HEAD WHERE I CAN SEE 'EM!

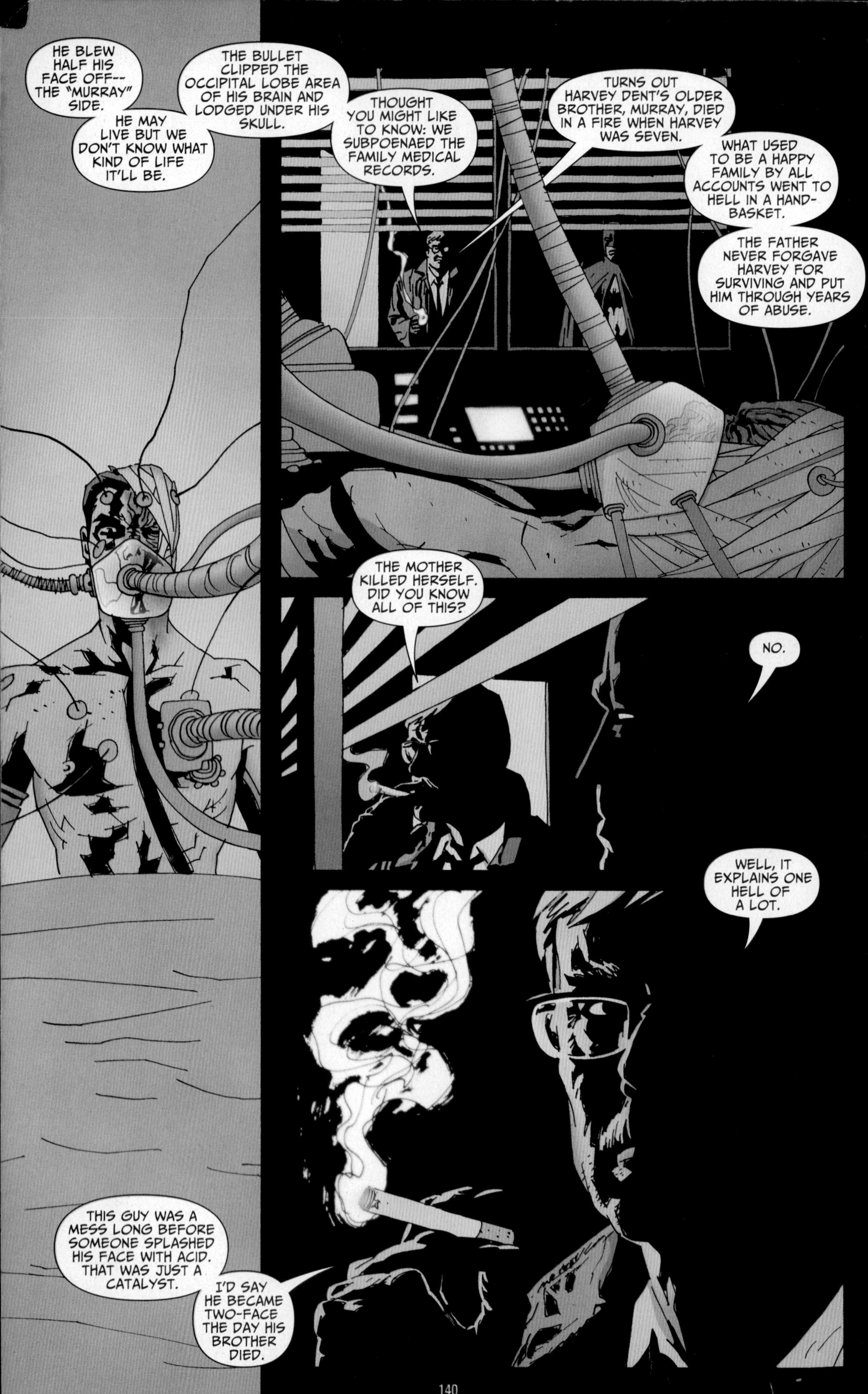
HE BLEW HALF HIS FACE OFF-- THE "MURRAY" SIDE.
HE MAY LIVE BUT WE DON'T KNOW WHAT KIND OF LIFE IT'LL BE.
THE BULLET CLIPPED THE OCCIPITAL LOBE AREA OF HIS BRAIN AND LODGED UNDER HIS SKULL.
THOUGHT YOU MIGHT LIKE TO KNOW: WE SUBPOENAED THE FAMILY MEDICAL RECORDS.
TURNS OUT HARVEY DENT'S OLDER BROTHER, MURRAY, DIED IN A FIRE WHEN HARVEY WAS SEVEN.
WHAT USED TO BE A HAPPY FAMILY BY ALL ACCOUNTS WENT TO HELL IN A HAND-BASKET.
THE FATHER NEVER FORGAVE HARVEY FOR SURVIVING AND PUT HIM THROUGH YEARS OF ABUSE.
THE MOTHER KILLED HERSELF. DID YOU KNOW ALL OF THIS?
NO.
WELL, IT EXPLAINS ONE HELL OF A LOT.
THIS GUY WAS A MESS LONG BEFORE SOMEONE SPLASHED HIS FACE WITH ACID. THAT WAS JUST A CATALYST.
I'D SAY HE BECAME TWO-FACE THE DAY HIS BROTHER DIED.

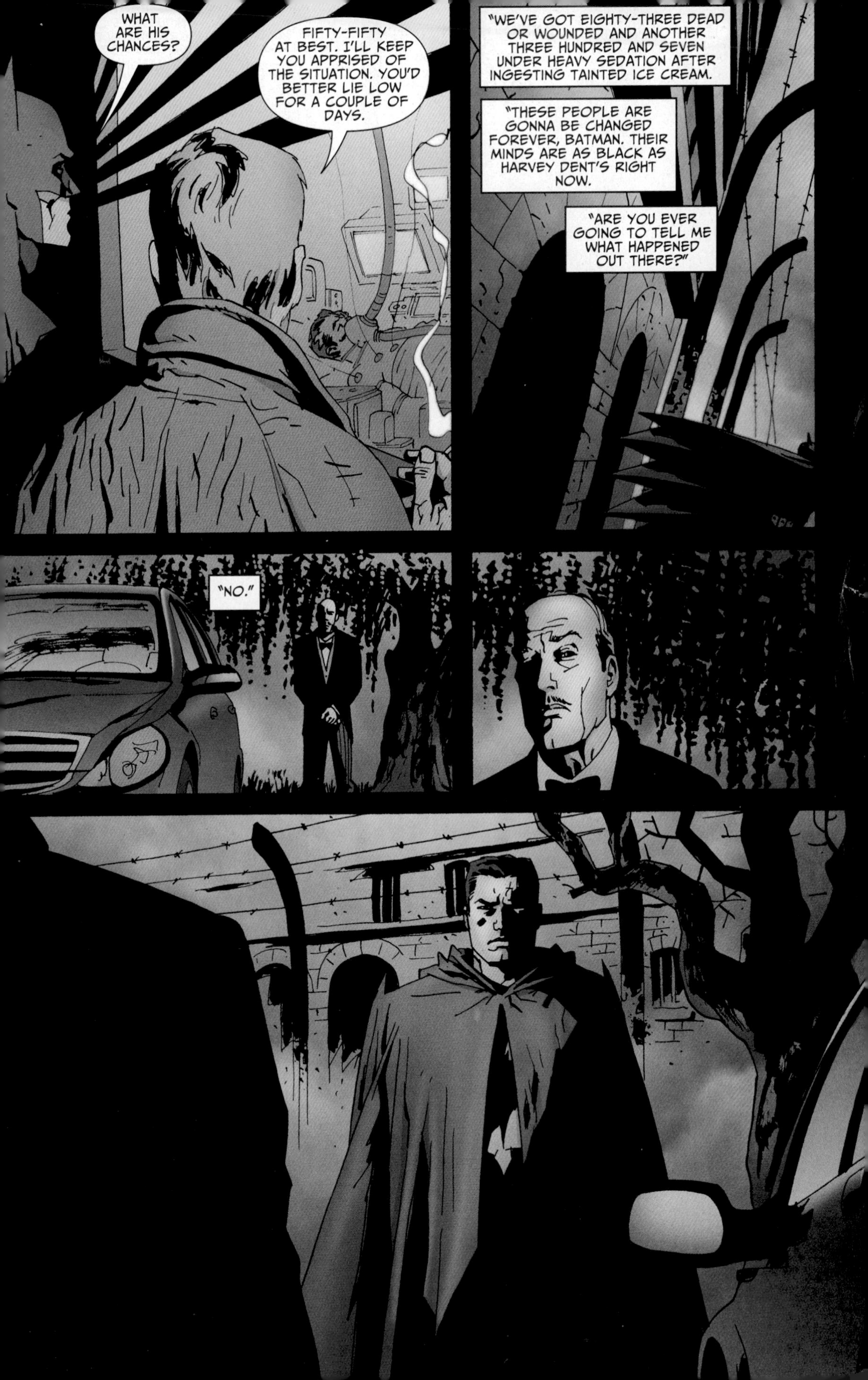
WHAT ARE HIS CHANCES?
FIFTY-FIFTY AT BEST. I'LL KEEP YOU APPRISED OF THE SITUATION. YOU'D BETTER LIE LOW FOR A COUPLE OF DAYS.
"WE'VE GOT EIGHTY-THREE DEAD OR WOUNDED AND ANOTHER THREE HUNDRED AND SEVEN UNDER HEAVY SEDATION AFTER INGESTING TAINTED ICE CREAM.
"THESE PEOPLE ARE GONNA BE CHANGED FOREVER, BATMAN. THEIR MINDS ARE AS BLACK AS HARVEY DENT'S RIGHT NOW.
"ARE YOU EVER GOING TO TELL ME WHAT HAPPENED OUT THERE?"
"NO."

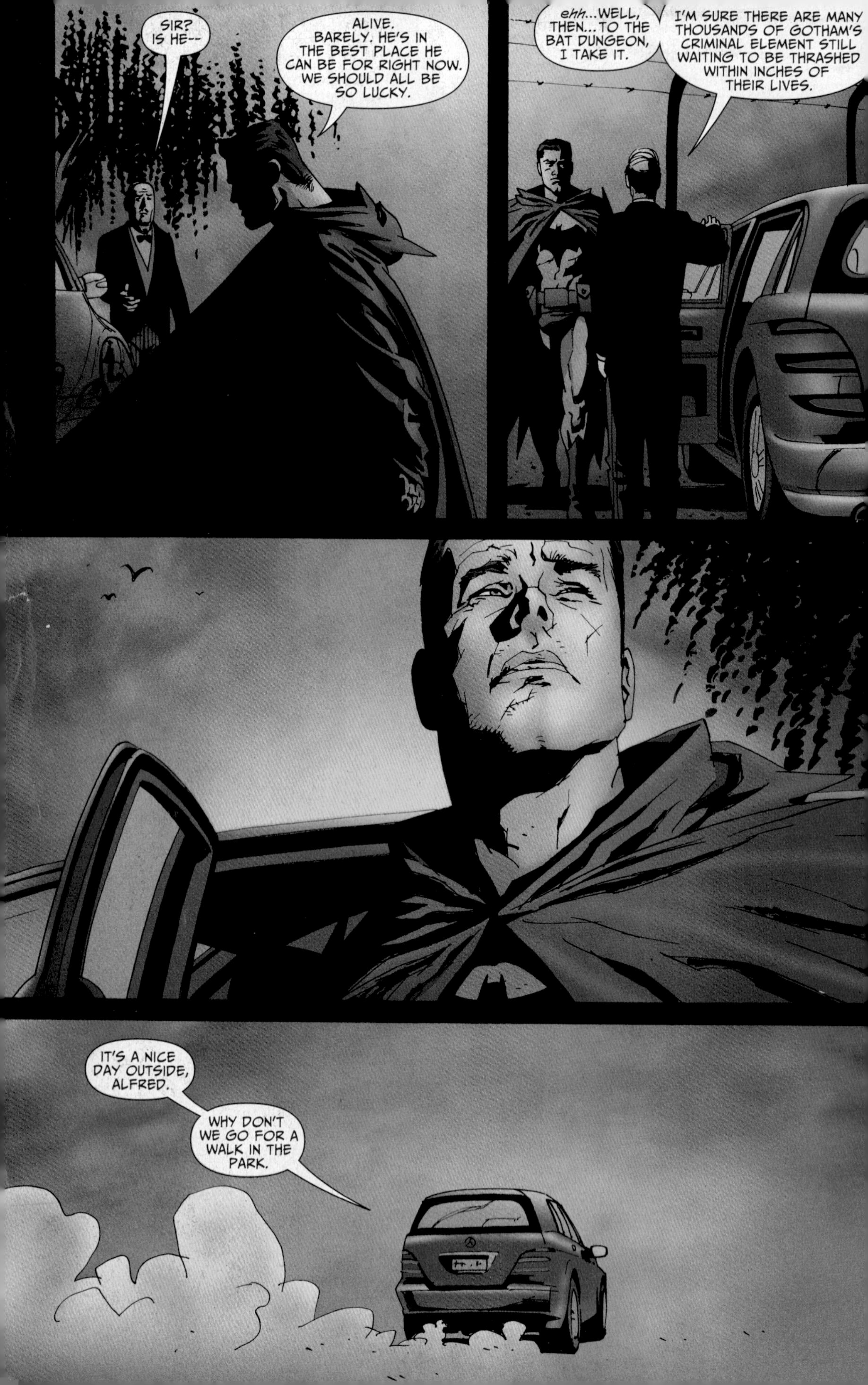
SIR? IS HE--
ALIVE. BARELY. HE'S IN THE BEST PLACE HE CAN BE FOR RIGHT NOW. WE SHOULD ALL BE SO LUCKY.
ehh...WELL, THEN...TO THE BAT DUNGEON, I TAKE IT.
I'M SURE THERE ARE MANY THOUSANDS OF GOTHAM'S CRIMINAL ELEMENT STILL WAITING TO BE THRASHED WITHIN INCHES OF THEIR LIVES.
IT'S A NICE DAY OUTSIDE, ALFRED.
WHY DON'T WE GO FOR A WALK IN THE PARK.